Britain's
Best
PUBS

AA

This product includes mapping data licensed from Ordnance Survey® with the permission of the Controller of Her Majesty's Stationery Office. © Crown copyright 2010. All rights reserved. Licence number 100021153.

Maps prepared by the Mapping Services Department of The Automobile Association.

Maps © AA Media Limited 2010.

Advertising Sales:
advertisementsales@theAA.com

Editorial:
lifestyleguides@theAA.com

Typeset by AA Lifestyle Guides

Printed in E.U by G. Canale & C

Editorial contributors: Philip Bryant

Cover credits:
Front Cover: The Durham Ox, North Yorkshire
Back Cover: (t) Pear Tree Inn, Wiltshire, (c) Jack in the Green Inn, Devon, (b) AA/C Sawyer

A CIP catalogue record for this book is available from the British Library

ISBN: 978-0-7495-6466-7

Published by AA Publishing, which is a trading name of AA Media Limited, whose registered office is:
Fanum House, Basing View, Basingstoke, Hampshire RG21 4EA
Registered number 06112600

theAA.com/shop

A04113

Britain's Best
PUBS

Contents

Welcome

Britain's Best Pubs is for anyone who enjoys eating and drinking well in formal or informal surroundings. Where stars have been awarded, you can relax in the knowledge that the rooms have been inspected and rated by the AA.

Britain's Best

In this fully updated and revised guide to Britain's Best Pubs you'll find a selection of pubs and hostelries from cosy inns on old coach routes to smart gastro-pubs in towns and cities. Though very different in conception and setting, they all share a commitment to providing refreshment and serving good food based on fresh (and local where possible) produce cooked to order. Hospitality is warm and welcoming, and real ales and well-known brands are offered alongside decent wines. The index and map sections at the back of this guide will help you to find a wide range of towns and villages to visit in search of an authentic pub experience. To help you make the most of your visit we've included recommended places to see in the area of your choice.

A Place to Stay

Room prices for single and double occupation are shown where the accommodation has been inspected and rated by the AA under our Hotel and Guest Accommodation Schemes. Many places will also offer variable rates and special offer breaks so it's worth asking when you book.

Accommodation varies from pubs with two or three rooms, to much grander inns and hotels with all the extras (although most of the places included in this guide have fewer than 20 rooms). Whatever their size or style, all the places selected for inclusion in Britain's Best Pubs have the same best qualities in common: good food, beer served in relaxed and inviting surroundings and great value for money.

Using the Guide

Britain's Best Pubs has been designed to enable you to find both establishments and locations quickly and efficiently. Each entry provides clear information about the opening hours, food, facilities, and nearby recommended places to visit.

See page 3 to browse the main gazetteer section by county. If you want to find a pub in a specific location use the Location Index (page 349). Alternatively, use the Pub Index (page 358) to find an establishment by name.

Finding your way

The main section of the guide is divided into three main parts covering England, Scotland and

Wales. The counties within each of these sections are ordered alphabetically as are the town or village locations (shown in capital letters as part of the address) within each county. Finally, the establishments are listed alphabetically under each location name. Towns names featured in the guide are shown in the map section at the back of the guide.

The Old Inn

★★★ ◉ ⬚ INN

Address: Ash Lane, WHITCHURCH, Salisbury,
            SA38 2PP
Tel: 01963 300123
Email: oldinn@pubgroup.co.uk
Website: www.pubgroup.co.uk/oldrectory
Map ref: 3 TQ32
Directions: Next to church at S end of Whitchurch
Open: 11.30–3 5.30–11 (Sun 12-3) ㅛ L 11–2 D 7–9
◉ L 12–2 D 6–9 Rooms: 8 S £35–40 D £75–100 Facilities: Gardens Parking
Notes: ⊁ ⊕ Free House ♟ 7

Tucked away down a leafy lane, The Old Inn is the perfect place for a relaxing drink and a good meal. This old inn has been beautifully restored and extended, with its character carefully preserved. The perfect place for walkers hiking the nearby Ridgeway, the garden offers a shady retreat for lunch and in colder weather log fires and leather sofas provide a warm and welcome resting place. There are two bars, where meals can also be enjoyed, as well as a comfortable and spacious oak-beamed restaurant providing a more formal environment. The menu makes good use of local organic produce with well-cooked dishes that will satisfy the heartiest appetite. The en suite bedrooms are simply furnished and decorated with many of the thoughtful extras usually associated with superior hotels.

Recommended in the area

Salisbury Cathedral; New Forest National Park; Stonehenge and Salisbury Plain

❶ Stars and Symbols

A star rating denotes where an entry has been inspected under one of two separate schemes; either the AA Guest Accommodation Scheme or the AA Hotel Scheme.

Pubs rated under the Guest Accommodation Scheme have been given a descriptive category designator: B&B, Guest House,

Farmhouse, Inn, Restaurant with Rooms or Guest Accommodation.

Pubs in the Hotel Scheme also have their own descriptive designator: Town House Hotel, Country House Hotel, Small Hotel. See pages 8–10 for more information on the AA ratings and awards scheme.

continued

Egg cups 🥚 and Pies 🥧 – These symbols denote where the breakfast or dinner are really special, and have an emphasis on freshly prepared ingredients.

Rosette awards ⊛ – This is the AA's food award (see page 9 for further details).

❷ Contact Details

The pub address includes a locator or place name in capitals (e.g. NORWICH). Within each county, entries are ordered alphabetically first by this place name and then by the name of the establishment.

Telephone and fax numbers, and e-mail and website addresses are given where available and are believed correct at the time of going to press but changes may occur. The latest establishment details can be found at theAA.com.

Website addresses have been supplied by the establishments and lead you to websites that are not under the control of AA Media Limited (AAML). AAML has no control over and accepts no responsibility or liability in respect of the material on any such websites. By including the addresses of third-party websites AAML does not intend to solicit business.

❸ Map Reference

Each establishment in this guide is given a map reference for a location which can be found in the atlas section at the back of the guide. It is composed of the map page number (1–13) and two-figure map reference based on the National Grid.

For example: **Map 05 SU48**

05 refers to the page number of the map section at the back of the guide

SU is the National Grid lettered square (representing 100,000sq metres) in which the location will be found

4 is the figure reading across the top and bottom of the map page

8 is the figure reading down each side of the map page

❹ Directions

Where possible, directions have been given from the nearest motorway or A road.

❺ Open

Indicates the opening hours of the establishment and, if appropriate, any dates when it may be closed for business.

🍴 Bar Meals

Indicates the times and days when the proprietors have told us that bar food can be ordered.

🍽 Restaurant

Indicates the times and days when proprietors have told us that food can be ordered from the restaurant. Please be aware that last orders could vary by up to 30 minutes.

❻ Room Information

Room information is only shown where accommodation has been inspected by the AA. The number of letting bedrooms with a bath or shower en suite are indicated. Bedrooms that have a private bathroom adjacent may be included as en suite. Further details on private bathroom and en suite provision may also be included in the description text (see ❾).

Always phone in advance to ensure that the establishment has the room facilities that you require.

Prices: Charges shown are per night except where specified. S denotes bed and breakfast per person (single). D denotes bed and breakfast for two people sharing a room (double).

In some cases prices are also given for family rooms, also on a per night basis. Prices are indications only, so check what is included before booking.

❼ Facilities

This section lists a selection of facilities offered by the pub such as garden details or children's play area. If you have young children it may be worth checking what facilities are available.

Additional facilities, such as access for the disabled, or notes about other services (e.g. if credit card details are not accepted) may be listed here.

Parking is listed if available. Other types of parking (on road or Park and Ride) may also be possible; check the descriptions for further information. Phone the establishment in advance of your arrival if unsure.

❽ Notes

This section provides specific details relating to:

Smoking policy: Smoking in public areas is now banned in England, Scotland and Wales.

The proprietor can designate one or more bedrooms with ventilation systems where the occupants can smoke, but communal areas must be smoke-free.

Dogs: Establishments that state 'no dogs' should accept assist/guide dogs. (Under the Discrimination Disability Act 1995 access should be allowed for guide dogs and assistance dogs). Some places that do accept dogs may restrict the size and breed and the rooms into which they can be taken. Please check the policy when booking.

⊕ This symbol is followed by text that indicates the name of the brewery to which the pub is tied or the company which owns it, or where the pub is a free house and independently owned and run.

♟ Indicates the number of wines available by the glass.

❾ Description

The description of the pub includes amongst other information, a background to the establishment, the type of eating options available and, where relevant, information about the accommodation.

❿ Recommended in the area

This indicates local places of interest, and potential day trips and activities.

Key to symbols

★	Black stars (see page 8)
☆	Yellow Stars (see page 8)
★	Red Stars (see page 8)
🆄	Unconfirmed rating
◎	AA Rosette (see page 9)
⚱	Breakfast Award in Guest Accommodation scheme
⬷	Dinner Award in Guest Accommodation scheme
3 TQ28	Map reference
S	Single room
D	Double room
ᴪ	Children allowed
ᴪ	No children under age specified
⊗	No dogs allowed in area indicated
ᴙ	Dogs allowed in area indicated
Wi-fi	Wireless network connection
▤	Bar meals
◥◎◤	Restaurant meals
L	Lunch
D	Dinner
⊕	Pub status (Chain or Free House)
♟ 30	Number of wines available by the glass

AA Ratings and Awards

Star ratings shown in Britain's Best Pub guide indicate where the accommodation available has been inspected by the AA under either its Guest Accommodation or Hotel Schemes.

Guest Accommodation and Hotel Schemes

The AA inspects and rates establishments under two different accommodation schemes. Guest houses, B&Bs, farmhouses, inns and Restaurants with Rooms are rated under the Guest Accommodation Scheme and hotels are rated under the Hotel Scheme. Establishments recognised by the AA pay an annual fee according to the rating and the number of bedrooms. This rating is not transferable if an establishment changes hands.

Common Standards

A few years ago, the accommodation inspection organisations (The AA, VisitBritain, VisitScotland and VisitWales) undertook extensive consultation with consumers and the hospitality industry which resulted in new quality standards for rating establishments. Guests can now be confident that a star-rated B&B or a hotel anywhere in the UK and Ireland will offer consistent quality and facilities.

The system of ratings also uses descriptive designators to classify the establishment – see pages 9 and 10 for a fuller explanation.

★ Stars

AA Stars classify guest accommodation at five levels of quality, from one at the simplest, to five at the highest level of quality in the scheme.

★ Yellow stars indicate that the accommodation is in the top ten per cent of its star rating. Yellow stars only apply to 3, 4 and 5 star establishments.

★ Red stars highlight the best hotels in each star rating category within the AA Hotel Scheme.

Check theAA.com for up-to-date information and current ratings.

The Inspection Process

Establishments applying for AA recognition are visited by a qualified AA accommodation inspectors as a mystery guest. Inspectors stay overnight to make a thorough test of the accommodation, food and hospitality. After paying the bill the following morning, they identify themselves and ask to be shown around the premises. The inspector completes a full report,

resulting in a recommendation for the appropriate star rating. After this first visit, the establishment will receive an annual visit to check that standards are maintained. If it changes hands, the new owners must re-apply for a rating.

Guests can expect to find the following minimum standards at all levels:
- Pleasant and helpful welcome and service, and sound standards of housekeeping and maintenance
- Comfortable accommodation equipped to modern standards
- Bedding and towels changed for each new guest, and at least weekly if the room is taken for a long stay
- Adequate storage, heating, lighting and comfortable seating
- A sufficient hot water supply at reasonable times
- A full cooked breakfast. (If this is not provided, the fact must be advertised and a substantial continental breakfast must be offered.)

Designators (Guest Accommodation)

All AA rated guest accommodation is given one of six descriptive designators to help potential guests understand the different types of accommodation available in Britain. The following are included in this guide.

B&B: Accommodation is provided in a private house run by the owner and with no more than six guests. There may be restricted access to the establishment particularly in the late morning and the afternoon.

GUEST HOUSE: Provides for more than six paying guests and usually offers more services than a B&B, for example dinner, which may be served by staff as well as the owner. London prices tend to be higher than outside the capital, and normally only bed and breakfast is provided, although some establishments do provide a full meal service. Check on the service and facilities offered before booked as details may change during the currency of this guide.

FARMHOUSE: A farmhouse usually provides good value B&B or guesthouse accommodation and excellent home cooking on a working farm or smallholding. Sometimes the land has been sold and only the house remains, but many are working farms and some farmers are happy to allow visitors to look around, or even to help feed the animals. However, you should always exercise care and never leave children unsupervised. The farmhouses are listed under towns or villages, but do ask for directions when booking.

continued

AA Rosette Awards

Out of the many thousands of restaurants in the UK, the AA identifies some 2,000 as the best. The following is an outline of what to expect from restaurants with AA Rosette Awards. For a more detailed explanation of Rosette criteria please see theAA.com

◉ Excellent local restaurants serving food prepared with care, understanding and skill, using good quality ingredients.

◉◉ The best local restaurants, which aim for and achieve higher standards, better consistency and where a greater precision is apparent in the cooking. There will be obvious attention to the selection of quality ingredients.

◉◉◉ Outstanding restaurants that demand recognition well beyond their local area.

◉◉◉◉ Amongst the very best restaurants in the British Isles, where the cooking demands national recognition.

◉◉◉◉◉ The finest restaurants in the British Isles, where the cooking stands comparison with the best in the world.

INN: Traditional inns often have a cosy bar, convivial atmosphere, good beer and pub food. Those listed in the guide will provide breakfast in a suitable room, and should also serve light meals during licensing hours. The character of the properties vary according to whether they are country inns or town establishments. Check arrival times as these may be restricted to opening hours.

RESTAURANT WITH ROOMS: These restaurants offer overnight accommodation with the restaurant being the main business and open to non-residents. The restaurant usually offers a high standard of food and service.

GUEST ACCOMMODATION: Establishments that meet the minimum entry requirements are eligible for this designator.

Designators (Hotels)
All AA rated hotels are given a descriptive designator to identify the different types of hotel available. Included in this guide are the following:

HOTEL: The majority of establishments in this guide come under the category of Hotel.

TOWN HOUSE HOTEL: A small, individual city or town centre property, which provides a high degree or personal service and privacy

COUNTRY HOUSE HOTEL: These may vary in size and are located in a rural area.

SMALL HOTEL: Has less than 20 bedrooms and is managed by its owner.

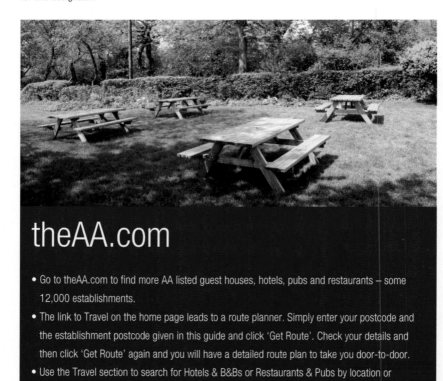

theAA.com

- Go to theAA.com to find more AA listed guest houses, hotels, pubs and restaurants – some 12,000 establishments.
- The link to Travel on the home page leads to a route planner. Simply enter your postcode and the establishment postcode given in this guide and click 'Get Route'. Check your details and then click 'Get Route' again and you will have a detailed route plan to take you door-to-door.
- Use the Travel section to search for Hotels & B&Bs or Restaurants & Pubs by location or establishment name. Scroll down the list of finds for the interactive map and local routes.
- Postcode searches can also be made on www.ordnancesurvey.co.uk and www.multimap.com which will also provide useful aerial views of your destination.

Useful Information

If you're unsure about any of the facilities offered, always check with the establishment before you visit or book accommodation. Up-to-date information on all pubs in this guide can be found at the travel section of theAA.com

Fire Precautions and Safety
Many of the establishments listed in the guide are subject to the requirements of the Fire Precautions Act of 1971. All establishments should display details of how to summon assistance in the event of an emergency at night.

Dogs
Some establishments that accept dogs may restrict the size and breed of dogs permitted. Under the Discrimination Disability Act 1995 access should be allowed for guide dogs and assistance dogs.

Children
Restrictions for children are given at the end of entries. When booking a meal you would be advised to check that children are welcome.

Smoking Regulations
Please see page 7.

Facilities for Disabled Guests
The final stage (Part III) of the Disability Discrimination Act (access to Goods and Services) came into force in October 2004. This means that service providers may have to consider making permanent physical adjustments to their premises. For further information, see the government website www.disability.gov.uk. The establishments in this guide should all be aware of their responsibilities under the Act. We recommend that you always telephone in advance to ensure that the establishment you have chosen has appropriate facilities.

Complaints

Readers who have any cause to complain about accommodation, food and drink or service are urged to do so on the spot. This should provide an opportunity for the proprietor to correct matters. If a personal approach fails in connection with accommodation, readers can write to the editor of the guide at Lifestyle Guides, Fanum House, Basingstoke, Hants RG21 4EA.

The AA may at its sole discretion investigate any complaints received from guide users for the purpose of making any necessary amendments to the guide. The AA will not in any circumstances act as a representative or negotiator or undertake to obtain compensation or enter into any correspondence or deal with the matter in any other way whatsoever. The AA will not guarantee to take any specific action.

Bank and Public Holidays 2010

New Year's Day	1st January
New Year's Holiday	2nd January (Scotland)
Good Friday	2nd April
Easter Monday	5th April
May Day Bank Holiday	3rd May
Spring Bank Holiday	31st May
August Holiday	2nd August (Scotland)
Late Summer Holiday	30th August
St Andrew's Day	30th November (Scotland)
Christmas Day	25th December
Boxing Day	26th December

Online booking with **theAA.com/travel**

Book online...

Check in...

and Relax...

Take the hassle out of booking accommodation online with our new and improved site

Visit

theAA.com/travel

to search by availability and book hundreds of AA inspected and rated hotels and B&Bs in real time

Plus, find more information on:

Restaurants & Pubs • Caravan & Camping • Self Catering • Holidays • Ferries • Airport Parking • Car Hire

Travel

For the road ahead

ENGLAND

Scorhill Stone circle, Dartmoor National Park

BEDFORDSHIRE

View towards Ampthill from Laurel Wood

The Muntjac

Address: 71 High Street, HARROLD, MK43 7BJ
Tel: 01234 721500
Email: muntjacharrold@hotmail.co.uk
Map ref: 3 SP95
Directions: Telephone for directions
Open: all week
Facilities: Parking Garden
Notes: ⊕ FREE HOUSE ☻ 7

The Muntjac, a 17th century former coaching inn,
is a freehouse situated in the picturesque North Bedfordshire village of Harrold. Within easy reach of
Bedford, Northampton and Milton Keynes, the location is perfect for those who need the amenities
provided by these towns but also enjoy the beauty of the English countryside. Alan and Collette Cooper
took on the pub in March 2008 and quickly built up a reputation for excellent real ales, lagers, ciders,
wines, spirits and soft drinks. Local micro-breweries, including Frog Island (Northampton), White Park
(Cranfield) and Harrold Calvados Society are supported, allowing for some unusual 'one-off' real ales
and ciders. In the winter months you will not only be welcomed by friendly staff but by the warmth of a
real fire. The restaurant at the rear of the property is independently run by Harrolds Indian Cuisine who
offer excellent, cooked to order, dishes both to eat in and to take away. The extensive menu includes
fish, chicken, lamb or vegetarian dishes. A home delivery service is also offered within the local area.
En suite accommodation is available.

Recommended in the area

Shuttleworth Collection; Grafham Water Centre; Woburn Abbey

Hare and Hounds

Address: OLD WARDEN, Biggleswade, SG18 9HQ
Tel: 01767 627225
Fax: 01767 627209
Website: www.charleswells.co.uk
Map ref: 3 TL14
Directions: From Bedford turn right off A603 (or left from A600) to Old Warden. Also accessed from Biggleswade rdbt on A1
Closed: Mon (ex BH) **Facilities:** Parking Garden
Notes: ⊕ CHARLES WELLS ☤ 8

You'll see the 200-year-old Hare & Hounds as you reach the heart of this prosperous, leafy Shuttleworth estate village. Your first impression – a good one for sure - will be quickly endorsed, assuming it's a cold day, by the sight of two blazing log fires as you head for the bar and, irrespective of the weather, the three, warm red- and cream-painted country dining rooms with timbered walls, contemporary furnishings and fresh flowers. Food is clearly taken seriously by the chef/proprietor, judging by the bar and restaurant menus that list well-balanced choices of traditional and modern dishes. Every effort is made to use local, organic produce, including game and poultry from a nearby farm, 40-day certificated Scottish beef, fish from sustainable stocks, and vegetables, fruits and herbs from the pub's own allotment. Typically, start with smoked chicken and avocado salad or Portland dressed crab. Then, try pan-fried fillets of Cornish mackerel or braised local rabbit with smoked bacon, button mushrooms, shallots and wholegrain mustard and tarragon sauce. Finish with rhubarb crumble and vanilla ice cream, or a selection of British and Irish cheeses from Neal's Yard. There is a good choice of real ales and some of the wide choice of wines comes from the local Warden Abbey vineyard.

Recommended in the area

Shuttleworth Collection; Swiss Garden; Knebworth

BERKSHIRE

Windsor Marina

The Queen's Arms Country Inn

Address: EAST GARSTON, RG17 7ET
Tel: 01488 648757
Fax: 01488 648642
Email: info@queensarmshotel.co.uk
Map ref: 3 SU37
Directions: M4 junct 14, 4m onto A338 to Great
Shefford, then East Garston
Open: all week ⓑ **L** all wk 12-2 **D** all wk 7-9
◥◎◣ **L** all wk 12-2 **D** all wk 7-9 **Facilities:** Parking
Garden **Notes:** ⊕ MILLERS COLLECTION ◄♦ ◄┩

Hunting enthusiast and head chef Matt Green-Armytage has partnered with Lucy Townsend to show customers of this Lambourn Valley inn what good taste means – in every respect. The food, for example, is made from the freshest seasonal produce available, with regularly changing menus offering Maldon oysters with sweet and sour red wine onions; braised pig's cheeks with white pudding mash and scrumpy sauce: steamed Cornish sea bass with fennel and tomato dressing; and game and poultry from local shoots and farms. Horses almost outnumber people in this area, so why not spend a day riding.
Recommended in the area
Uffington White Horse; Ashdown House (NT); Ridgeway National Trail

The Crown & Garter

★★★★ ⇔ INN
Address: Inkpen Common, HUNGERFORD, RG17 9QR
Tel: 01488 668325
Email: gill.hern@btopenworld.com
Website: www.crownandgarter.com
Map ref: 3 SU36 **Directions:** From A4 to Kintbury
& Inkpen. At village store left into Inkpen Rd, Inkpen
Common 2m **Open:** 12-3 5.30-11 (Sun 12-5
7-10.30, closed Mon & Tue lunch) ⓑ ◥◎◣ **L** Wed-Sat
12-2, Sun 12-2.30 **D** Mon-Sat 6.30-9.30 **Rooms:** 8
en suite (8 GF) **S** £69.50 **D** £99 **Facilities:** Parking Garden **Notes:** ⊕ FREE HOUSE ♥ 9

A family-owned, personally run 17th-century inn in a really pretty part of Berkshire, its ancient charm can best be seen in the bar area, where there's a huge inglenook fireplace and beams. You can eat in the bar, the restaurant, or in the enclosed beer garden, choosing from a variety of dishes all freshly prepared on the premises from local produce. There are daily fish and seafood specials available. Eight separate, spacious en suite bedrooms are situated around a pretty cottage garden.
Recommended in the area
Newbury Racecourse; Combe Gibbet; Highclere Castle

Henry VIII gate at Windsor Castle

The Swan Inn

★★★★ 🏨 🍷 INN

Address: Craven Road, Lower Green, Inkpen,
HUNGERFORD, RG17 9DX
Tel: 01488 668326
Fax: 01488 668306
Email: enquiries@theswaninn-organics.co.uk
Website: www.theswaninn-organics.co.uk
Map ref: 3 SU36
Directions: S down High St (A338), under rail bridge,
left to Hungerford Common. Right to Inkpen **Open:**

11-11 (Sun 12-10.30) **Closed:** 25-26 Dec 🍽 **L** 12-2 **D** 7-9.30 🍽 **L** Wed-Sun 12-2.30 **D** Wed-Sat
7-9.30 **Rooms:** 10 en suite **S** £60-70 **D** £80-95 **Facilities:** Parking Garden **Notes:** ⊕ FREE HOUSE 👥

Retaining much of its character, this 17th-century inn is owned by local organic beef farmers (there's a
farm shop too) and menus feature their own and local organic produce. Vegetarian, fish and children's
menus are available. The beamed inn is set below Walbury Iron Age hill fort, and enjoys spectacular
views. Four real ales from Butts Brewery are offered, plus an organic wine list.

Recommended in the area

Kennet and Avon Canal; Newbury Racecourse; Avebury Stone Circle

Bird In Hand Country Inn

Address: Bath Road, KNOWL HILL,
Twyford, RG10 9UP
Tel: 01628 826622 & 822781
Fax: 01628 826748
Email: sthebirdinhand@aol.com
Website: www.birdinhand.co.uk
Map ref: 3 SU87
Directions: On A4, 5m W of Maidenhead,
7m E of Reading
Open: all week Mon-Sat 11am-11pm (Sun noon-
10.30pm) **Rooms:** 15 en suite (6 GF) **S** £50-£100
D £70-£120 **Facilities:** Parking Garden **Notes:** ⏣ FREE HOUSE ⁑ ⌁ ♟ 12

Dating back to the 14th century, this charming country inn has been owned by the same family for three generations. Legend has it that George III granted it a royal charter in the 18th century for the hospitality he was shown, and a royal welcome is still the order of the day. Today the inn serves a host of real ales and a large selection of wines by the glass in the oak-panelled bar, which in winter boasts a huge open fire. In summer months, a pretty beer garden and fountain patio provide the backdrop for the brick-built barbecue and spit roast. Inside, an extensive menu is available from both the bar and the attractive restaurant, which overlooks the courtyard and fountain. Diners can choose from a range of traditional dishes, such as hearty steak and kidney pudding with Guinness, pork belly in Calvados or whole roast stuffed quail with apricot and thyme, through to European-based options such as tapas, mezze and paella. There are also a number of daily specials and a cold buffet is available at lunchtime. The inn's en suite bedrooms have all been refurbished and include many modern facilities such as Wi-fi and direct-dial telephones.

Recommended in the area

Legoland; Odds Park Farm; Wellington Country Park

The Yew Tree Inn

◎◎

Address: Hollington Cross, Andover Road, Highclere, NEWBURY, RG20 9SE
Tel: 01635 253360
Fax: 01635 255035
Email: info@theyewtree.net
Website: www.theyewtree.net
Map ref: 3 SU46
Directions: A34 toward Southampton, 2nd exit bypass Highclere, onto A343 at rdbt, through village, pub on right
Open: all week ఈ **L** Mon-Sat 12-2.30, Sun 12-3 **D** all wk 6-9
♥ **L** Mon-Sat 12-2.30, Sun 12-3 **D** all wk 6-9
Facilities: Parking Garden
Notes: ⊕ FREE HOUSE ♦ ⌁ ♥ 10

This 16th-century inn belongs to the celebrated chef-turned-restaurateur Marco Pierre White. His famed perfectionism is evident everywhere, from the immaculate styling that blends original 17th-century features with the refinement of white tablecloths and sparkling glassware, to the menu, which performs a similar trick, offering both traditional British food and time-honoured French classics. Your meal might open with a parfait of foie gras; calves' tongue with celeriac remoulade; or duck rillettes, followed by fish pie, roast venison Pierre Koffmann; or braised oxtail and kidney pudding. Tellingly, the desserts are described as 'puddings' and might include such familiar comforts as bread and butter pudding or rhubarb crumble. Good-value fixed-price menus are also a feature at lunchtime and on Sundays.

Recommended in the area

Highclere Castle; Hampshire Downs; Donnington Castle

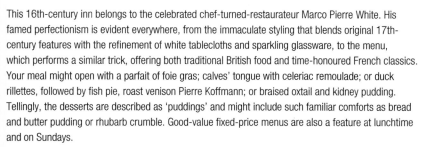

BUCKINGHAMSHIRE

South Africa Monument, Coombe Hill

The Crooked Billet

Address: 2 Westbrook End, Newton Longville,
BLETCHLEY, MK17 0DF
Tel: 01908 373936
Email: john@thebillet.co.uk
Website: www.thebillet.co.uk
Map ref: 3 SP83 **Directions:** M1 junct 13, follow
signs to Buckingham. 6m, signed at Buttledump rdbt
to Newton Longville **Open:** noon-2.30 5-11 (Sun
noon-4) **Closed:** Mon L ♿ ⏏ L Tue-Sat 12-2, Sun
12-4 **D** Mon-Sat 7-9.30 **Facilities:** Parking Garden **Notes:** ⊕ GREENE KING ♦♦ ♥ 300

While it retains much traditional charm, with original oak beams, open log fires and a large garden,
the top attraction is the food and wine offered by husband-and-wife team John and Emma Gilchrist.
Emma's weekly-changing menus are based on the finest ingredients, local where possible, and the
suppliers - right down to the 'people of Newton Longville for growing our vegetables and herbs' - are
all acknowledged in print. On offer is a range of sandwiches, wraps, burgers and goodies on toast,
and a seven-course 'whole table only' tasting menu. Falling somewhere between these two extremes
are main menu starters of garlic roasted hand-dived scallops with butternut squash purée, crisp sage
and lardons; house-cured sliced duck breast, pecorino shavings, white honey truffle , purple fig and
thyme. Then might come mild monkfish and king prawn curry, lemon and coriander rice with onion
fritter; or overnight roasted crispy pork belly braised Puy lentils, tarragon and baby onions. Desserts
include Muscat poached pear, tonka bean ice cream and a bar of 'Fruit & Nut'; or apple, blackberry and
almond tart, rosehip flavoured custard with blackberry ice cream. The cheese board has won heaps of
awards, as has John Gilchrist for compiling 'best wine' lists, including his 300-bin selection here.
Recommended in the area
Woburn Abbey; Bletchley Park; Leighton Buzzard Railway

The Royal Oak

Address: Frieth Road, BOVINGDON GREEN, Marlow, SL7 2JF
Tel: 01628 488611
Fax: 01628 478680
Email: info@royaloakmarlow.co.uk
Website: www.royaloakmarlow.co.uk
Map ref: 3 SU88
Directions: From Marlow, take A4155. In 300yds right signed
Bovingdon Green. In 0.75m pub on left
Open: all day all week 11-11 (Sun 12-10.30) **Closed:** 26 Dec
🍴 L Mon-Fri 12-2.30, Sat 12-3, Sun 12-4 D Sun-Thu
6.30-9.30, Fri-Sat 6.30-10 🍽 L Mon-Fri 12-2.30, Sat 12-3,
Sun 12-4 D Sun-Thu 6.30-9.30, Fri-Sat 6.30-10 **Facilities:**
Parking Garden **Notes:** ⊕ SALISBURY PUBS LTD ♟ 🐾 ☂ 19

Drive up the hill out of Marlow and you'll soon come across this old whitewashed pub. Sprawling
gardens, fragrant kitchen herbs and a sunny terrace suggest that it is well looked after. Red kites, which
were re-introduced to the Chilterns in 1989, now frequently soar majestically overhead. The interior is
both spacious and cosy, with a snug with wood-burning stove, a rose-red dining room and rich dark
floorboards. Plush fabrics and heritage colours create a warm background for the early evening regulars
gathered around a cryptic crossword, or playing a tense game of cards. The imaginative British food is a
big draw, not least because it derives from fresh, seasonal and, as far as possible, local produce. Fish,
of course, has to travel, but a belief in good food ethics means choosing new and interesting varieties
from sustainable sources. Other menu suggestions might include veal and rosemary sausage casserole
with Boston baked beans; and crispy pork belly with pig's cheeks on sticky red cabbage and cider
gravy. Real ales from Rebellion Brewery in Marlow Bottom keep beer miles to a minimum.

Recommended in the area

Cliveden (NT); Burnham Beeches; Hughenden Manor

The weir and All Saints church at Marlow on the River Thames

The Ivy House

Address: London Road, CHALFONT ST GILES, HP8 4RS
Tel: 01494 872184
Fax: 01494 872870
Email: ivyhouse@fullers.co.uk
Map ref: 3 SU99
Directions: On A413 2m S of Amersham & 1.5m N of Chalfont St Giles **Open:** all day all week ▣ **L** Mon-Fri 12-3, Sat-Sun all day **D** Mon-Fri 6-10, Sat-Sun all day ▣ **L** Mon-Fri 12-3, Sat-Sun all day **D** Mon-Fri 6-10, Sat-Sun all day **Facilities:** Parking Garden **Notes:** ⊕ FULLERS SMITH & TURNER ♦♦ ♉ ☻ 10

You can't miss the round-topped windows and distinctive full-length porch of this popular 17th-century brick and flint free house. It overlooks the Misbourne Valley, and within are beams, open fires, comfy armchairs, old pictures, wines by the glass, a good range of malts and always a new beer to sample. Food served in the bar, the former coach house and the restaurant includes ostrich fillet; chargrilled duck breast; steak with triple-cooked chunky chips; pan-fried pheasant breast; seafood pie.
Recommended in the area
Chiltern Open Air Museum; Bekonscot Model Village; Cliveden (NT)

The Red Lion

Address: CHENIES, Chorleywood,
Rickmansworth, WD3 6ED
Tel: 01923 282722
Fax: 01923 283797
Map ref: 3 TQ09
Directions: Between Rickmansworth & Amersham
on A404, follow signs for Chenies & Latimer
Open: all week **Closed:** 25 Dec **Facilities:** Parking
Garden **Notes:** ⊕ FREE HOUSE 🐾 🍷 10

Michael Norris has been at this popular hostelry for around twenty years, and under his expert direction the pub has achieved considerable renown. He is keen to stress that this is a pub that does food, not a restaurant that does beer, but that's not to say that the quality and range of food on offer is in any way an afterthought. Michael has put together a menu that has something for everyone, with a wide range of snacks, starters and main meals. Among the listings you'll find the ever-popular jacket potatoes; pasta carbonara; and a tasty beef, mustard and cheese pie, plus a number of more exotic dishes that might include Moroccan chicken breast with couscous; pork fillet with prunes; oxtail with root vegetables; and fresh tuna loin with roasted Mediterranean vegetables. Not so much exotic as downright unusual, the hot bacon and Milky Bar in a bap has its fans, too. But even with all this choice, it would be a shame not to try the famous Chenies lamb pie. Needless to say, the real ales on offer are kept in perfect condition and there are some good wines to choose from too. The Red Lion is not far outside the M25 at junction 18 and is well worth making a detour to enjoy its pleasant, country-pub atmosphere – the way that pubs used to be before piped music and fruit machines were invented – and the garden makes for enjoyable alfresco summer lunches.

Recommended in the area

Legoland; Bekonscot Model Village; Odds Farm Park Rare Breeds Centre

The Swan Inn

Address: Village Road, DENHAM, UB9 5BH
Tel: 01895 832085
Fax: 01895 835516
Email: info@swaninndenham.co.uk
Website: www.swaninndenham.co.uk
Map ref: 3 TQ08
Directions: From A40 take A412. In 200yds follow Denham Village sign on right. Through village, over bridge, last pub on left
Open: all day all week 11-11 (Sun 12-10.30)
Closed: 26 Dec ♿ **L** Mon-Fri 12-2.30, Sat 12-3, Sun 12-4 **D** Sun-Thu 6.30-9.30, Fri-Sat 6.30-10
🍴 **L** Mon-Fri 12-2.30, Sat 12-3, Sun 12-4 **D** Sun-Thu 6.30-9.30, Fri-Sat 6.30-10 **Facilities:** Parking Garden **Notes:** ⊕ SALISBURY PUBS LTD 👫 🐾 🍷 19

The Swan is probably everyone's idea of the traditional country inn – Georgian, double-fronted and covered in wisteria. The surprise, though, is that the secluded village of Denham is really no distance at all from the bright lights of both London and its premier airport at Heathrow. The interior is cosily welcoming, with a large log fire and pictures picked up at local auctions, while outside is a sunny terrace, and gardens large enough to lose the children in (only temporarily, of course). Though The Swan is still very much a pub, the quality of the food is a great attraction, with fresh, seasonal produce underpinning a menu that reinvigorates some old favourites and makes the most of market availability with daily specials. For a starter or light meal look to the 'small plates' section, where you'll find Marlow Rebellion (a local beer) steamed mussels with garlic herbs and onion rye bread; and pan-fried balsamic chicken livers on 'eggy bread' brioche with crispy pancetta. Among the main meals you'll find plenty of variety, from slow-cooked Chiltern lamb shoulder on smoked potato mash to Indian-spiced mackerel.

Recommended in the area

Burnham Beeches; Cliveden (NT); Dorney Court

The Nags Head

★★★★ ⊛ INN

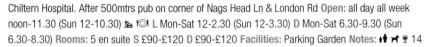

Address: London Road,
GREAT MISSENDEN, HP16 0DG
Tel: 01494 862200
Fax: 01494 862685
Email: goodfood@nagsheadbucks.com
Website: www.nagsheadbucks.com
Map ref: 3 SP80
Directions: 1m from Great Missenden on London Rd.
From A413 (Amersham to Aylesbury) turn left signed

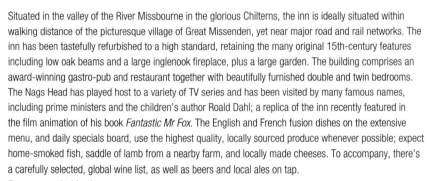

Chiltern Hospital. After 500mtrs pub on corner of Nags Head Ln & London Rd **Open:** all day all week noon-11.30 (Sun 12-10.30) 🍴 🍽 **L** Mon-Sat 12-2.30 (Sun 12-3.30) **D** Mon-Sat 6.30-9.30 (Sun 6.30-8.30) **Rooms:** 5 en suite **S** £90-£120 **D** £90-£120 **Facilities:** Parking Garden **Notes:** ♨ 🐾 ♊ 14

Situated in the valley of the River Missbourne in the glorious Chilterns, the inn is ideally situated within walking distance of the picturesque village of Great Missenden, yet near major road and rail networks. The inn has been tastefully refurbished to a high standard, retaining the many original 15th-century features including low oak beams and a large inglenook fireplace, plus a large garden. The building comprises an award-winning gastro-pub and restaurant together with beautifully furnished double and twin bedrooms. The Nags Head has played host to a variety of TV series and has been visited by many famous names, including prime ministers and the children's author Roald Dahl; a replica of the inn recently featured in the film animation of his book *Fantastic Mr Fox*. The English and French fusion dishes on the extensive menu, and daily specials board, use the highest quality, locally sourced produce whenever possible; expect home-smoked fish, saddle of lamb from a nearby farm, and locally made cheeses. To accompany, there's a carefully selected, global wine list, as well as beers and local ales on tap.

Recommended in the area

Roald Dahl Museum; Bekonscot Model Village; Whipsnade Zoo

The Rising Sun

Address: Little Hampden, GREAT MISSENDEN, HP16 9PS
Tel: 01494 488393 & 488360
Fax: 01494 488788
Email: sunrising@rising-sun.demon.co.uk
Website: www.rising-sun.demon.co.uk
Map ref: 3 SP80
Directions: From A413, N of Gt Missenden, take Rignall Rd on left signed Princes Risborough 2.5m. Turn right signed 'Little Hampden only'

Open: Tue-Sat 11-3, 6.30-10 (Sun 12-3) **Closed:** Sun eve & Mon ⓛ L Tue-Sun 12-2 D Tue-Sat 7-9
ⓘ L Tue-Sun 12-2 D Tue-Sat 7-9 **Facilities:** Parking Garden **Notes:** ⊕ FREE HOUSE ⓯ ⓣ ⓟ 10

Tucked away in The Chiltern Hills and just three miles from the Prime Minister's country retreat at Chequers, is The Rising Sun, a 250-year-old inn that was once frequented by previous PMs Harold Wilson and Ted Heath. It is close to the Ridgeway National Trail and reached down a single-track road, surrounded by beech woods and glorious scenery. A network of footpaths begins just outside the front door, making it the perfect base for country walks, and there are a number of cosy rooms to stay in. An attractive new feature is the landscaped garden area with comfortable armchair seating and tables for outside wining and dining. Rotisserie paprika-seasoned corn-fed chicken and chips is a speciality here. There's also a daily blackboard menu offering some good seafood, such as hot dressed crab with cheese and grain mustard sauce, and pan-fried skate wings with scallops, lemon and capers. Otherwise look out for the popular Sunday roasts, as well as dishes such as warm smoked chicken and bacon salad with peanut sauce, or roast shoulder of lamb with rosemary and honey. In winter, guests can enjoy hot mulled wine and warm spiced cider by the wood-burning stove and open fire.

Recommended in the area

Coombe Hill and Low Scrubs (NT); Waddesdon Manor (NT); Whipsnade Zoo

The Hand and Flowers

@ @ @

Address: 126 West Street, MARLOW, SL7 2BP
Tel: 01628 482277 **Fax:** 01628 401913
Email: theoffice@thehandandflowers.co.uk
Website: www.thehandandflowers.co.uk
Map ref: 3 SU88 **Directions:** M4 junct 9, A404
N into Marlow, A4155 towards Henley-on-Thames.
Pub on outskirts on right **Open:** 12-2.30 6.30-9.30
(Sun 12-3.30) **Closed:** 24-26 Dec, 31 Dec L, 1 Jan
D, Sun eve ⓑ ⓘ **L** Mon-Sat 12-2.30 **D** Mon-Sat
6.30-9.30, Sun 12-2.30 **Facilities:** Parking Garden **Notes:** ⊕ Greene King ♦ ♟ 10

Five years ago, Tom and Beth Kerridge reopened this 18th-century, whitewashed pub just outside
Marlow, and there seems to be no stopping its progress. The interior is an easygoing combination
of flagstone floors, beams, exposed stone walls, neutral colours, leather banquettes and cloth-free
tables. Tom is the chef, and he's frequently in the spotlight for his regularly changing, seasonal
menus of simple yet elegant modern British and rustic French food. Among dishes which have helped
him earn three AA Rosettes are starters of glazed omelette of smoked haddock and parmesan, and
creamy pumpkin soup, and seasonal favourites of slow-braised shin of Essex beef with glazed carrot,
red wine and beef dripping; and fillet of sea bream with root vegetable minestrone, pesto and crispy
squid. Round off with passionfruit and white chocolate trifle with coffee sorbet and mango; or lavender
pannacotta with heather honey, whisky jelly and honeycomb. The famous set lunch typically offers
croque madame, salmon croquette and rum baba with coconut sorbet, while on Sundays there are
roasts. The patio is a dining/drinking option if the weather's good. Two of the four stylish cottage suites
have private terraces with hot tubs. The Thames is close by for revitalising walks.
Recommended in the area
Cliveden (NT); Burnham Beeches; Hughenden Manor

The Old Queens Head

Address: Hammersley Lane, Tylers Green,
PENN, HP10 8EY
Tel: 01494 813371
Fax: 01494 816145
Email: info@oldqueensheadpenn.co.uk
Website: www.oldqueensheadpenn.co.uk
Map ref: 3 SU99
Directions: B474 through Beaconsfield New
Town towards Penn, 3m left into School Rd, left in
500yds into Hammersley Ln. Pub on corner opp
church **Open:** all day all week 11-11 (Sun 12-10.30) **Closed:** 26 Dec ⬛ **L** all wk 12-2.30, Sat 12-3,
Sun 12-4 **D** all wk 6.30-9.30, Fri & Sat 6.30-10 🍽 **L** all wk 12-2.30, Sat 12-3, Sun 12-4 **D** all wk
6.30-9.30, Fri & Sat 6.30-10 **Facilities:** Parking Garden **Notes:** ⊕ SALISBURY PUBS LTD ⭑ ⭒ ⭒ 19

The Old Queens Head exudes bags of character and atmosphere. The Dining Room, originally a barn,
dating from 1666, but with several later additions, now provides lots of cosy corners. Many hours
have been well spent at local auctions finding sympathetic old furniture and pictures, while warm
heritage colours blend with glowing dark floorboards, flagstones, rugs and classic fabrics. Although
first and foremost a pub, it is just as ready to serve a light bite at lunchtime, or a fabulous dinner,
special occasion or not. There's even free Wi-fi for those who have to work while eating. Experienced
staff provide good service and plenty of good old-fashioned hospitality. The food balances Classic
with Modern British, resulting in a menu with plenty of choice, such as Chiltern Hills venison and wild
mushroom suet pudding on purple sprouting broccoli with girolle and game jus; and grilled plaice on
lemon and thyme risotto with prawn beignet. A sunny terrace overlooks the large garden and the village
church of St Margaret's. There are great walks nearby in the ancient beech woodlands.
Recommended in the area
Bekonscot Model Village; West Wycombe; Legoland

The Windmill at Wicken Fen

The Three Horseshoes

Address: High Street, MADINGLEY, CB3 8AB
Tel: 01954 210221
Fax: 01954 212043
Email: thethreehorseshoes@huntsbridge.co.uk
Website: www.thethreehorseshoesmadingley.co.uk
Map ref: 3 TL36
Directions: M11 junct 13, 1.5m from A14 **Open:** all week
11.30-3 6-11 (Sun 6-9.30) ᴸ **L** Mon-Fri 12-2, Sat-Sun 12-2.30
D all wk 6.30-9.30 ⅠⓄⅠ **L** all wk 12-2.30 **D** Mon-Sat 6.30-9.30
Facilities: Parking Garden **Notes:** ⊕ FREE HOUSE ♦♦ ♥ 20

This is a picturesque thatched inn with a large garden that
stretches towards the local cricket pitch and open meadowland. Its proximity to Cambridge makes for
an eclectic clientele who lend a cosmopolitan air to the lively atmosphere. The busy bar is stocked to
please real ale enthusiasts with brews such as Adnams Bitter, Hook Norton Old Hooky, Smile's Best
and Cambridge Hobson's Choice, plus guest ales. The food is even more enticing. Chef-patron Richard
Stokes is a local, from the Fens, who has eaten his way around the world, and his success can be
gauged by the long queues for tables in the conservatory restaurant. His menu features seasonal Italian
cuisine, and there's a well-chosen wine list to accompany the intense flavours of the imaginative dishes.
A recent menu included pasta with brown shrimps, trevise, parsley, dried chilli, Vermouth and olive oil;
roast partridge stuffed with sage, mascarpone and garlic with braised Casteluccio lentils, cavolo nero,
carrots and Chianti; and pan-fried sea bass with local pink fur apple potatoes, girolle and trompette
mushrooms, Italian spinach and salsa verde. Desserts feature such Italian favourites as pannacotta,
zabaglione and chocolate truffle cake, with a selection of Italian cheeses as a savoury alternative.
Recommended in the area
Cambridge; Wimpole Hall and Home Farm; Duxford Imperial War Museum (Aircraft)

The Bell Inn Hotel

★★★ 79% ◉ HOTEL

Address: Great North Road, STILTON,
Peterborough, PE7 3RA
Tel: 01733 241066
Fax: 01733 245173
Email: reception@thebellstilton.co.uk
Website: www.thebellstilton.co.uk
Map ref: 3 TL18
Directions: From A1(M) junct 16 follow signs for
Stilton. Hotel on main road in village centre
Open: all week noon-2.30 6-11 (Sat-Sun noon-3 Sun 7-11) **Closed:** 25 Dec ⓑ **L** all wk 12-2.30
D all wk 6-9.30 ⑩ **L** Sun-Fri 12-2 **D** Mon-Sat 7-9.30 **Rooms:** 22 en suite (3 GF) **S** £73.50-£110.50
D £100.50-£130.50 **Facilities:** Parking Garden **Notes:** ⊕ FREE HOUSE ♥ 8

Historically an important stop on the Great North Road between London and York, this agreeable old
stone-built inn is one of the country's best surviving examples of a mid-17th-century coaching house.
The village is the birthplace of Stilton cheese and if you expect to find this delicacy well represented
here, you will - try pumpkin, Stilton and rosemary soup, for instance. The softly lit bistro, where
contemporary art complements the low ceilings and exposed beams, offers pasta with crab and chorizo,
for example, while in the first-floor, beamed restaurant, sip your aperitif in one of the leather armchairs
while choosing from the traditionally and internationally influenced menu. Typical would be roast Atlantic
cod fillet on scallion and lemon risotto; Dingley Dell pork belly with spinach, tomato, and cannellini bean
stew; and roasted local pheasant. Legend has it that from one of the restaurant windows Dick Turpin
jumped on to his horse Black Bess and escaped whoever was pursuing him. Those days have long gone
– today you can eat in the attractive courtyard without anyone demanding 'Your money or your life'.

Recommended in the area

Nene Valley Railway; Burghley House; Rutland Water

The gardens at Arley Hall

The Bhurtpore Inn

Address: Wrenbury Road, ASTON,
Nantwich, CW5 8DQ
Tel: 01270 780917
Email: simonbhurtpore@yahoo.co.uk
Website: www.bhurtpore.co.uk
Map ref: 6 SJ64
Directions: Just off A530 between Nantwich &
Whitchurch. Turn towards Wrenbury at x-rds in
village **Open:** 12-2.30 6.30-11.30 (Fri-Sat 12-12,
Sun 12-11) **Closed:** 25-26 Dec, 1 Jan 🍴 **L** Mon-Fri
12-2 **D** Mon-Fri 6.30-9.30 (Sat 12-9.30, Sun 12-9) **Facilities:** Parking Garden
Notes: 🍺 FREE HOUSE 🐾 🍷 11

The George family has a bit of a thing about this traditional village pub. In 1849 James George leased it from the local Combermere estate, from which descendant Philip George bought it in 1895, only to sell it six years later to a Crewe brewery. Ninety years later, in 1991, Simon and Nicky George were looking to buy their first pub and came across the boarded-up, stripped-out Bhurtpore. It ticked just about every box. Although it has been a pub since at least 1778, it was the 1826 Siege of Bhurtpore in India, where Lord Combermere had distinguished himself, that inspired its current name. With eleven real ales always available, a large selection of bottled beers and seven continental beers on tap, it is truly a free house. The award-winning food is fresh, home made and reasonably priced, both in the bar and the restaurant. Starters include spicy lamb samosas, and pork and black pudding patties with coarse grain mustard. Finish with spiced raisin and ginger pudding with toffee sauce. Behind the pub is a lawn with countryside views. At the centre of the local community, the pub is home to an enthusiastic cricket team, a group of cyclists known as the Wobbly Wheels and folk musicians.

Recommended in the area

Hack Green Secret Bunker; Cholmondeley Castle; Historic Nantwich; Stapeley Water Gardens

The Pheasant Inn

★★★★★ ≜ INN

Address: BURWARDSLEY, Nr Tattenhall, CH3 9PF
Tel: 01829 770434 **Fax:** 01829 771097
Email: info@thepheasantinn.co.uk
Website: www.thepheasantinn.co.uk
Map ref: 6 SJ55 **Directions:** A41 (Chester to
Whitchurch), after 4m left to Burwardsley. Follow
'Cheshire Workshops' sign **Open:** all week
🍴 L all wk (no food Mon 3-6) **D** all wk (no food
Mon 3-6) **Rooms:** 12 en suite (5 GF)
Facilities: Parking Garden **Notes:** ⊕ FREE HOUSE 👬 🛏 🍷 8

In a peaceful corner of Cheshire, yet this 300-year-old sandstone former farmhouse is just 15 minutes' drive from Chester. An alehouse from the mid-17th century, since the early 19th century only five families have been licensees. As well as the wooden-floored, heavy-beamed bar, you can take your drinks out into the stone-flagged conservatory, courtyard or terrace. The menu offers light-bites and deli-boards; a gastropub-style selection; and British and European fare. Stay over in one of the country-style bedrooms.

Recommended in the area

Beeston Castle; Cheshire Candle Workshops; Oulton Park

Albion Inn

Address: Park Street, CHESTER, CH1 1RN
Tel: 01244 340345
Email: christina.mercer@tesco.net
Website: www.albioninnchester.co.uk
Map ref: 5 SJ46
Directions: In city centre by Citywalls & Newgate
Open: 12-3, Tue-Fri 5-11, Sat 6-11, Sun 7-10.30,
Mon 5.30-11 **Closed:** 25-26 Dec, 1-2 Jan
🍴 L 12-2 **D** Mon-Sat 5-8 🍴 L 12-2 **D** Mon-Sat 5-8
Notes: ⊕ PUNCH TAVERNS 🛏 ♻

Many a young lad would have spent his last night in Civvy Street in what is now Chester's last Victorian corner pub, before heading for the Western Front in the First World War. Mike and Christina Mercer's traditional three-room interior - Vault, Snug and Lounge – evokes those times with Great War pictures, posters and advertisements. Regionally sourced 'trench rations' include boiled gammon and pease pudding; McConickies corned beef hash; filled Staffordshire oatcakes; fish pie; and a selection of club and doorstep sandwiches. Four cask ales are on tap, alongside malts and New World wines.

Recommended in the area

Roman Wall, Chester; Ness Gardens; Cholmondeley Castle

The Cholmondeley Arms

Address: CHOLMONDELEY, Malpas, SY14 8HN
Tel: 01829 720300
Fax: 01829 720123
Email: info@cholmondeleyarms.co.uk
Website: www.cholmondeleyarms.co.uk
Map ref: 6 SJ55
Directions: On A49, between Whitchurch
& Tarporley **Open:** all week 10am-11pm
(Sun 10am-10.30pm) **Closed:** 25 Dec ☕ **L** Mon-Fri
12-2.30, Sat-Sun 12-10 **D** Mon-Fri 6-10, Sat-Sun
12-10 **Facilities:** Wi-fi Parking Garden **Notes:** ⊕ FREE HOUSE ⅱ ⅺ ♈ 11

Set in the Cheshire countryside adjacent to Cholmondeley Castle, the Cholmondeley Arms is a friendly and relaxing gastro-pub. Whether you visit to sample the award-winning food or the CAMRA accredited real ales, it is sure to be an enjoyable experience. Relax by the open log fire after a walk in the surrounding hills, a trip to Cholmondeley Castle, a round of golf or a busy day at work. You can make use of our Wi-fi whether you are on business or a leisurely break at this quintessentially English pub.
Recommended in the area
Cholmondeley Castle Gardens; The Croccy Trail; Beeston Castle; The Sandstone Trail

---

The Davenport Arms

Address: Congleton Road, MARTON, SK11 9HF
Tel: 01260 224269
Fax: 01260 224565
Email: enquiries@thedavenportarms.co.uk
Website: www.thedavenportarms.co.uk
Map ref: 6 SJ86
Directions: 3m from Congleton on A34
Open: noon-3 6-mdnt (Fri-Sun noon-mdnt) **Closed:**
Mon L (ex BH) ☕ ⅰⓄⅰ **L** Tue-Sat 12-2.30, Sun 12-3
D Tue-Sat 6-9, Sun 6-8.30 **Facilities:** Parking
Garden **Notes:** ⊕ FREE HOUSE ⅱ ♈ 9

The Davenport is an 18th-century former farmhouse standing opposite a half-timbered church, built in 1343. The bar retains a traditional atmosphere with old settles and leather chesterfield armchairs. The flood-lit fresh water well is an unusual feature in the restaurant. Well kept real ales usually come from local brewers: Beartown Brewery, Weetwood Ales, Woodlands of Wrenbury and Macclesfield's Storm Brewing. All the food is prepared from fresh ingredients and locally sourced when possible.
Recommended in the area
Capesthorne Hall; Gawsworth Hall; Little Moreton Hall

Bridge Street, Chester

The Goshawk

Address: Station Road, MOULDSWORTH, CH3 8AJ
Tel: 01928 740900
Fax: 01928 740965
Website: www.thegoshawkpub.co.uk
Map ref: 6 SJ57
Directions: A51 from Chester onto A54. Left onto B5393 towards Frodsham. Enter Mouldsworth, pub on left opposite rail station
Open: all week noon-11 (Sun noon-10.30)
Closed: 25 Dec & 1 Jan **Facilities:** Parking Garden
Notes: ♦♦ ♀ 14

On the edge of the Delamere Forest, the Goshawk is just 15 minutes' drive from Chester. There is a good play area for children, and the decking outside overlooks a fine crown bowling green. The imaginative menu ranges from pub classics to more sophisticated fare. Everything is freshly prepared and you can eat in the bar, lounge or restaurant areas. A wide choice of wines from around the world is offered as well as real ales such as Timothy Taylors, Greene King and the changing casks of the week.

Recommended in the area

Go Ape at Delamere Forest; Mouldsworth Motor Museum; Sail Sports Windsurfing Centre

CORNWALL

Porthmeor Beach, St Ives

Trengilly Wartha Inn

★★★ ❀ INN

Address: Nancenoy, CONSTANTINE, TR11 5RP
Tel: 01326 340332
Fax: 01326 340332
Email: reception@trengilly.co.uk
Website: www.trengilly.co.uk
Map ref: 1 SW72
Directions: Follow signs to Nancenoy, left towards Gweek until 1st sign for inn, left & left again at next sign, continue to inn **Open:** all week 11-3 6-12 ᘖ **L** all wk 12-2.15 **D** all wk 6.30-9.30 ❀❙ **L** all wk 12-2.15 **D** all wk 6.30-12 **Rooms:** 8 en suite (2 GF) **S** £50-£65 **D** £80-£96 **Facilities:** Parking Garden **Notes:** ⊞ FREE HOUSE ⬤ ⬤ ⬤ 15

Trengilly Wartha is Cornish for 'settlement above the trees', the trees in question being those in the valley of Polpenwith Creek, an offshoot of the Helford River. This tucked-away, traditional inn stands in six acres of gardens and meadows, with a vine-shaded pergola and a family room in the conservatory. Since it's a free house, there's a good selection of real ales, over 40 malt whiskies and 150 wines, a good few by the glass. In the bar you can select from an imaginative range of meals, while in the Bistro, furnished with furniture crafted by local student cabinet-makers, there's a regulars' favourites menu, as well as a specials board, which three top chefs compete to fill. It ranges through local meats, game, fish and shellfish, modern vegetarian dishes, rich imaginative desserts and a Cornish cheeseboard with home-made biscuits. Typical starters are smoked pollock, grilled with herb butter; and sliced beetroot with goat's cheese, walnut and leaf salad. Main courses include confit of pork belly, slow-cooked in Cornish cider; fillet of red mullet with harissa cream sauce; monkfish cheeks with a rich cheese and mustard sauce; duck breast with braised cabbage and chilli plum sauce; and butternut squash gratin.

Recommended in the area

Mullion Cove; Pendennis Castle; St Michael's Mount (NT)

The Halzephron Inn

Address: GUNWALLOE, Helston, TR12 7QB
Tel: 01326 240406
Fax: 01326 241442
Email: halzephroninn@tiscali.co.uk
Website: www.halzephron-inn.co.uk
Map ref: 1 SW62
Directions: 3m S of Helston on A3083, right to Gunwalloe, through village. Inn on left
Open: all wk **Closed:** 25 Dec ᴸ **L** all wk 12-2 **D** all wk 7-9 ᴸ **L** all wk 12-2 **D** all wk 7-9 **Facilities:** Parking Garden **Notes:** ⊕ FREE HOUSE ⁛ ☗ 8

The name of this ancient inn derives from 'Als Yfferin', old Cornish for 'cliffs of hell', and this is an appropriate description of its situation on this hazardous but breathtaking stretch of coastline. Once a haunt of smugglers, the pub is located close to the fishing village of Gunwalloe and stands just 300 yards from the famous South Cornwall footpath. The only pub on the stretch between Mullion and Porthleven, today it offers visitors a warm welcome, a wide selection of ales and whiskies, and meals prepared from fresh local produce. These may be served outside, with views of the surrounding fields to the back or the ocean to the front, or inside, in a number of dining areas, from cosy nooks to a separate dining area or a family room (there's a thoughtful junior menu). Lunch and dinner bring a choice of fresh Cornish fare, accompanied by home-made granary or white rolls, plus daily-changing specials that might include roast monkfish tail wrapped in bacon on a seafood risotto, or seafood chowder. To follow there may be bread and butter pudding or hot chocolate fudge cake with Cornish cream. There's also a good wine list, with a choice of half-bottles.

Recommended in the area

Trevarno Gardens; Goonhilly Satellite Earth Station; RNAS Culdrose

The Crown Inn

★ ★ ★ INN

Address: LANLIVERY, Bodmin, PL30 5BT
Tel: 01208 872707
Email: thecrown@wagtailinns.com
Website: www.wagtailinns.com
Map ref: 1 SX05
Directions: Signed from A390. Follow brown sign about 1.5m W of Lostwithiel **Open:** all day all week
🍴 L all wk 12-2.30 D all wk 6.30-9 🍽 L all wk 12-2.30 D all wk 6.30-9 **Rooms:** 9 en suite (7 GF)
S £49.95-£79.95 **D** £49.95-£79.95 **Facilities:** Parking Garden **Notes:** ⊕ FREE HOUSE ❧ ⛟ ♟ 10

This charming pub was built in the 12th century for the men constructing St Brevita's church next door. Such great age means everything about it oozes history – its thick stone walls, granite and slate floors, glass-covered well, low beams, open fireplaces and distinctive bread oven. The bar serves beers from Sharps of Rock and Skinners of Truro, and ten wines by the glass from a reasonably priced wine list. With Fowey harbour not far away, the menu will undoubtedly offer fresh crab, scallops, mackerel and more, while other local produce includes meats from a butcher in Par, fruit and vegetables from a local grocer and dairy products from Lostwithiel. At lunchtime, try chef's smoked mackerel pâté, or a proper Cornish pasty. Dinner might begin with an appetiser of marinated olives and ciabatta bread, followed by a starter of locally smoked duck, Cornish charcuterie, or pan-seared scallops. Main courses include Greek-style salad; steaks with chips, onion rings and rocket and Parmesan salad; whole baked sea bass stuffed with lemon and fennel; and Laura's cheesy ratatouille. Some of the comfortable en suite rooms include children's beds, and in some dogs are welcome. The pretty front garden is lovely in warm weather.

Recommended in the area

Restormel Castle; Lanhydrock House (NT); China Clay Country Park

Hayle Beach

The Plume of Feathers

★★★★ INN

Address: MITCHELL, Truro, TR8 5AX
Tel: 01872 510387
Fax: 01637 839401
Email: enquiries@theplume.info
Website: www.theplume.info
Map ref: 1 SW85
Directions: Exit A30 to Mitchell/Newquay
Open: all day all week 9am-11/mdnt (25 Dec 11-5)
Rooms: 7 en suite (5 GF) **S** £53.75-£83.75 **D**

£75-£115 **Facilities:** Parking Garden **Notes:** 🛢 FREE HOUSE 👬 🐾 ♟ 7

Built in the 16th century, the Plume of Feathers has played host to various historical figures, including John Wesley and Sir Walter Raleigh. Today, thanks to its peaceful countryside location and loving restoration, it is the perfect place to relax over an award-winning real ale. The once-dilapidated stable barns now provide luxurious bedrooms, and the imaginative kitchen offers modern European food with classical British touches. The emphasis is on fish and the best Cornish ingredients.

Recommended in the area

The Eden Project; Truro; Newquay's beaches

The Bush Inn

Address: MORWENSTOW, Bude, EX23 9SR
Tel: 01288 331242
Website: www.bushinn-morwenstow.co.uk
Map ref: 1 SS21
Directions: Exit A39, 3m N of Kilkhampton, 2nd right into village of Shop. 1.5m to Crosstown. Inn on village green
Open: all day all week 11am-12.30am ⬛ L all wk D all wk ⬛ L all wk D all wk
Facilities: Parking Garden
Notes: ⬛ FREE HOUSE ⬛ ⬛ ⬛ 8

Said to be one of Britain's oldest pubs, the Bush Inn was originally built as a chapel in AD 950 for pilgrims en route to Spain. It became a pub some 700 years later and has provided sustenance for visitors for hundreds of years. Smugglers and wreckers were among them, drawn by the inn's dramatic and isolated clifftop location on the north Cornish coast; nowadays the views over the Tidna Valley and the Atlantic Ocean are just as stunning as they must have been then. The unspoilt interior features stone-flagged floors, old stone fireplaces, a Celtic piscina carved from serpentine set into a wall behind the cosy bar, and a 'leper's squint' – a tiny window through which the needy could grab scraps of food. Today the meals are very different, with the emphasis on fresh local produce, including beef from the inn's own farm. Local shoots provide the game, and seafood comes from home waters. In winter, warming dishes include red wine and blue cheese risotto and venison stew, all served with Cornish real ales and a variety of fine wines. In summer, diners can enjoy a plate of mussels or beer-battered pollock and chips in the garden, which contains sturdy wooden play equipment. There are three bed and breakfast rooms and self-catering accommodation is also available.

Recommended in the area

Clovelly; Morwenstow Church and Hawker's Hut (NT); Boscastle

The Pandora Inn

Address: Restronguet Creek, MYLOR BRIDGE,
Falmouth, TR11 5ST
Tel: 01326 372678
Fax: 01326 378958
Website: www.pandorainn.com
Map ref: 1 SW83
Directions: From Truro/Falmouth follow A39,
left at Carclew, follow signs to pub
Open: all day all week 10.30am-11pm
Facilities: Parking Garden **Notes:** ⊕ ST AUSTELL
BREWERY ⊕ ♀ ♀ 12

One of the best known inns in Cornwall, The Pandora is set by the water in the beautiful surroundings of Restronguet Creek. Parts of the thatched, cream-painted building date back to the 13th century, and its flagstone floors and low beamed ceilings suggest that little can have changed since. The atmosphere is splendidly traditional, with lots of snug corners, three log fires and a collection of maritime memorabilia. The inn is named after the good ship Pandora, sent to Tahiti to capture the Bounty mutineers. Unfortunately it was wrecked and the captain court-marshalled so, forced into early retirement, he bought the inn. A full range of drinks is served, including fine wines and beers from St Austell Brewery, HSD and Tribute. Meals are served in the bars or upstairs in the Sail Loft restaurant. When the sun shines, the tables and chairs set out on the new pontoon provide an experience akin to walking and eating on water. Food is taken seriously here, and the lunchtime and evening menus are supplemented by daily specials displayed on boards. Options range from sandwiches at lunchtime and afternoon teas to fine dining in the restaurant. Local seafood is a speciality of the house.

Recommended in the area

Trelissick Gardens (NT); National Maritime Museum; Pendennis Castle

Whipsiddery, Newquay

Lighthouse at St Anthony Head

The Victory Inn

Address: Victory Hill, ST MAWES, TR2 5PQ
Tel: 01326 270324
Fax: 01326 270238
Email: contact@victory-inn.co.uk
Website: www.victory-inn.co.uk
Map ref: 1 SW83
Directions: Take A3078 to St Mawes. Pub up Victory
Steps adjacent to harbour
Open: all day all week 11am-mdnt 🍺 L all wk 12-3
D all wk 6-9.30 🍴 L all wk 12-3 D all wk 6-9.15
Facilities: Garden **Notes:** 🛢 PUNCH TAVERNS 👫 🐕 🍷 8

This friendly fishermen's local, with spectacular harbour views, is named after Nelson's flagship, HMS
Victory, and is now an award-winning dining pub, offering the freshest of local seafood. The blackboard
specials change according to the day's catch, with dishes such as fresh crab salad; lobster thermidor;
cod and chips; crab and mushroom omelette; and trio of fish with squid ink risotto. There's also pub
grub and lunchtime snacks. In addition to real ales, there's a decent selection of wines by the glass.
Recommended in the area
The Eden Project; Falmouth Maritime Museum; St Mawes Castle

The Mill House Inn

Address: TREBARWITH, Tintagel, PL34 0HD
Tel: 01840 770200
Fax: 01840 770647
Email: management@themillhouseinn.co.uk
Website: www.themillhouseinn.co.uk
Map ref: 1 SX08
Directions: From Tintagel take B3263 S, right after
Trewarmett to Trebarwith Strand. Pub 0.5m on right
Open: 11-11 (Fri-Sat 11am-mdnt) (Sun noon-10.30)
Closed: 25 Dec 🛏 **L** Mon-Sat 12-2.30, Sun 12-3 **D**
all wk 6.30-8.30 ⚟ **D** all wk 6.30-9 **Facilities:** Parking Garden **Notes:** ⊕ FREE HOUSE ⅰ↟ 7

The Mill House dates back to 1760, and was a working mill until the 1930s. It is situated on the north
Cornish coast in a beautiful woodland setting, just half a mile from the surfing beach at Trebarwith
Strand, and a short distance from King Arthur's legendary castle. The Mill offers first class food and
accommodation (eight elegant rooms, all with en suite facilities) in a charming stone building. The
slate-floored bar with its wooden tables, chapel chairs and wood burning stove has a family friendly
feel. You may also choose to eat on the partly-covered tiered terraces (with heaters) at the front. A
new restaurant opened in July 2008 and is designed to blend in with the existing features of the Mill.
Traditional bar lunches such as snakebite-battered local haddock or a Cornish smoked fish platter are
followed by selections on the evening restaurant menu such as duo of Tintagel duck served with swede
and carrot purée or grilled local halibut with spinach and prawn ragout. Sharps and Tintagel Brewery
local ales together with an imaginative wine list complement the regularly changing menus, which
make use of the best locally sourced ingredients. The Mill House is licensed for wedding ceremonies
and is a perfect location for receptions, parties and conferences.

Recommended in the area

Trebarwith Surfing Beach; Tintagel Castle; Delabole Wind Farm

The clay works, St Austell

The Springer Spaniel

Address: TREBURLEY, Nr Launceston, PL15 9NS
Tel: 01579 370424
Email: enquiries@thespringerspaniel.org.uk
Website: www.thespringerspaniel.org.uk
Map ref: 1 SX37
Directions: On A388 halfway between Launceston & Callington **Open:** all week noon-2.30 6-10.30
🍴 L all wk 12-1.45 **D** all wk 6.15-8.45 🍽 L all wk 12-1.45 **D** all wk 6.15-8.45 **Facilities:** Parking Garden **Notes:** 🍺 FREE HOUSE 🍴 🐾 🍷 7

A friendly, traditional pub in the heart of the Cornish countryside offering delicious food, delectable ales, fine wines and great service. The old walls of The Springer Spaniel conceal a cosy bar with high-backed wooden settles, farmhouse-style chairs and a wood-burning stove to keep the chill out on colder days. There is a cosy candlelit restaurant, and for better weather a landscaped garden with outdoor seating. The menu features imaginative, contemporary dishes as well as traditional favourites and specialises in local, seasonal food including organic meat from the owners' farm.

Recommended in the area

Cotehele (National Trust); Mining Heritage Centre; Sterts Theatre, Upton Cross

CUMBRIA

Derwent Water, Lake District National Park

Drunken Duck Inn

★★★★★ ◎◎ INN

Address: Barngates, AMBLESIDE, LA22 0NG
Tel: 015394 36347
Fax: 015394 36781
Email: info@drunkenduckinn.co.uk
Website: www.drunkenduckinn.co.uk
Map ref: 5 NY30
Directions: From Kendal on A591 to Ambleside, then follow Hawkshead sign. In 2.5m inn sign on right, 1m up hill **Open:** all week **Closed:** 25 Dec ⓫ **L** all wk 12-4 **D** all wk 6-9.30 **Rooms:** 17 en suite (5 GF) **S** £90-£275 **D** £90-£275 **Facilities:** Parking Garden **Notes:** ⊕ FREE HOUSE ⁕♥ ♟ 20

This 17th-century inn is surrounded by 60 private acres of beautiful countryside. In spring, you can barely move for flowers, and all year round there are striking views of fells and lakes. Under the same family ownership since 1977, the Drunken Duck has been refurbished with a stylish mix of modern luxury and old world charm. Expect plenty of sofas to lounge in, a pretty residents' garden, and glamorous bedrooms. The bar, with its antique settles and log fires, serves beers from the inn's own Barngate Brewery. These have been named after much loved dogs: Cracker, Tag Lag and Chester's Strong and Ugly. The award-winning candlelit restaurant offers intelligent, modern British cuisine, with the same menu offered at lunch and dinner, supplemented by specials. Start with smoked haddock and pea risotto, or duck and spring onion confit with parmesan tuiles and chilli jam, followed by pan-fried Holker venison fillet with wild mushroom and foie gras croûte, rump of Kendal rough fell lamb with minted pea purée, Lyonnaise potatoes and rosemary jus, or hand-dived seared scallops. Desserts might include saffron scented brûlée with sesame caramel and mango salsa, or you could try the gourmet cheese list.

Recommended in the area

Lake District Visitor Centre; Armitt Museum; Windermere Steamboat Centre

The Wheatsheaf at Beetham

Address: BEETHAM, nr Milnthorpe, LA7 7AL
Tel: 015395 62123
Fax: 015395 64840
Email: info@wheatsheafbeetham.com
Website: www.wheatsheafbeetham.com
Map ref: 6 SD47 Directions: On A6 5m N of
junct 35 Open: 11am-11pm Closed: 25 Dec
♿ 🍽 L 12-2 D 6-9 Facilities: Parking Garden
Notes: ⊕ FREE HOUSE ♛ 12

Discreetly tucked away in the picturesque village of Beetham, this family-owned free house dates
back to 1609 and is very much a dining pub. It is the perfect base for exploring the Lake District and
Yorkshire Dales. The seasonally changing menu offers some of the best home cooking the region
has to offer. Traditional English fare is supplemented by daily specials created by the head chef, who
uses only the finest local ingredients. A typical dinner may include potted Morecambe Bay shrimps
followed by home-made steak, mushroom and Jennings Cumberland ale pie, finishing with sticky toffee
pudding. The cellar is well stocked with traditional cask ales and European and New World wines.
Recommended in the area
Levens Hall; Lakeland Wildlife Oasis; Leighton Hall

The Boot Inn

Address: BOOT, Eskdale Valley, CA19 1TG
Tel: 019467 23224
Fax: 019467 23337
Email: enquiries@bootinn.co.uk
Website: www.bootinn.co.uk
Map ref: 5 NY10
Directions: From A595 follow signs for Eskdale
then Boot
Open: all week Closed: 25 Dec 🍽 D all wk 6-8.30
Facilities: Parking Garden
Notes: ⊕ ROBINSONS ♟ 🐾

Whether you are in the bar with its crackling log fire, in the light and airy conservatory, or in the dining
room, which dates back to 1578, you can expect a warm welcome from Caroline, Sean and the friendly
staff at The Boot Inn. Enjoy a drink in the bar or the snug and plan a day in some of the best scenery
and walking areas in England. Traditional games, a pool table and a plasma screen TV are available in
the bar. There is a good selection of real ales, a comprehensive wine list and some good malt whiskies.
Recommended in the area
Muncaster Castle; La'al Ratty Steam Train; Whitehaven Rum Story; Eskdale, Lake District National Park

Brook House Inn

★★★★ ⇔ INN

Address: BOOT, Eskdale, CA19 1TG
Tel: 019467 23288
Fax: 019467 23160
Email: stay@brookhouseinn.co.uk
Website: www.brookhouseinn.co.uk
Map ref: 5 NY10
Directions: M6 junct 36, A590 follow Barrow signs.
A5092, then A595. Past Broughton-in-Furness then
right at lights to Ulpha. Cross river, next left signed
Eskdale & on to Boot. (NB not all routes to Boot are suitable in bad weather conditions)
Open: all week **Closed:** 25 Dec ⏃ **L** by arrangement **D** 6-8.30
Rooms: 7 en suite **S** £52.50-£60 **D** £72-£90 **Facilities:** Parking Garden
Notes: ⊕ FREE HOUSE ⟨⟩ ⚲ 10

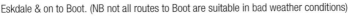

This family-owned country inn and restaurant is an ideal base for exploring Eskdale and the western fells of the Lake District. The scenery is picturesque and dramatic, with rugged mountains, tumbling waterfalls, lakes and tarns, and the River Esk winding its way through the woods. Delicious home-made food is available all day in the restaurant, bar or snug, from a menu complemented by blackboard specials. Main courses include beef and beer pie, and fettuccine with smoked salmon and prawns. Daytime salads and sandwiches made with home-made bread are also available. In the bar, well-kept real ales include Timothy Taylor Landlord, Jennings Cumberland, Hawkshead Bitter and a range of guest beers from other local brewers. On a one-a-day basis, a five-month stay would be necessary to sample each of the bar's 165 malt whiskies! Seven en suite bedrooms provide good quality accommodation and superb views. There is an annual beer festival in June.

Recommended in the area

Ravenglass & Eskdale Railway; Wastwater, Hardknott Fort; Scafell

The Sun Coniston

Address: CONISTON, LA21 8HQ
Tel: 015394 41248
Fax: 015394 41219
Email: info@thesunconiston.com
Website: www.thesunconiston.com
Map ref: 5 SD39
Directions: From M6 junct 36, A591, beyond
Kendal & Windermere, then A598 from Ambleside to
Coniston. Pub signed from bridge in village
Open: all day all week 11am-mdnt ⓑ L all wk 12-3
D all wk 6-9 **Facilities:** Parking Garden
Notes: ⊕ FREE HOUSE ⸱⸱ ⸱⸱ ⸱ 7

With a peaceful location at the foot of the mountains, The Sun Coniston offers a unique mix of bar, restaurant and inn, with the kind of comfortable informality and atmosphere that many attempt but few achieve. The 16th century pub is a favourite with thirsty walkers and tourists seeking peace from the village below. It boasts a wealth of classic Lakeland features including stone bar, floors and walls, exposed beams and a working range. The newly created first floor Boat Room is a new eating and drinking area, which is also home to an exhibition of rare Donald Campbell photographs. But at its heart is a very special bar with 8 guest real ales on hand-pull, 4 draft lagers, 20 plus malts and 30 plus wines. The menu has been created using locally sourced, seasonal ingredients to offer traditional British food as well as classic dishes with a twist. Depending on your mood, the freshly prepared food can be enjoyed in the bar, in the conservatory and outside on the front terrace.

Recommended in the area

Brantwood; Steam Yacht 'Gondola' (NT); Ravenglass & Eskdale Railway

The Punch Bowl Inn

★★★★★ ⊚⊚ INN

Address: CROSTHWAITE, Nr Kendal, LA8 8HR
Tel: 015395 68237
Fax: 015395 68875
Email: info@the-punchbowl.co.uk
Website: www.the-punchbowl.co.uk
Map ref: 6 SD49
Directions: M6 junct 36, A590 towards Barrow, A5074
& follow signs for Crosthwaite. Pub by church on left
Open: all week noon-mdnt **Rooms:** 9 en suite
S £93.75-£183.75 D £125-£310 **Facilities:** Parking Garden
Notes: ⊕ FREE HOUSE ♦♦ ♙ ♟ 16

The Punch Bowl is not only a bar and restaurant with excellent accommodation, it also serves as the village post office. The slatefloored bar, with open fires and original beams, is the perfect spot to enjoy a pint of Tag Lag from the Barngates Brewery. Leather chairs, gleaming wooden floors and a pale stone fireplace make for an elegant dining room. The award-winning menu features the local suppliers.

Recommended in the area

Sizergh Castle; Beatrix Potter country; Cartmel Race Course

Bower House Inn

★★ 74% HOTEL

Address: ESKDALE GREEN, Holmrook, CA19 1TD
Tel: 019467 23244
Fax: 019467 23308
Email: info@bowerhouseinn.co.uk
Website: www.bowerhouseinn.co.uk
Map ref: 5 NY10
Directions: 4m off A595, 0.5m W of Eskdale Green
Open: all day all week 11-11 ♙ L all wk D all wk
♙ D all wk 7-9 **Rooms:** 29 en suite (9 GF)
S £55-£75 D £61-£92 **Facilities:** Parking Garden **Notes:** ⊕ FREE HOUSE ♦♦ ♙

Located close to the main Cumbrian coast road in a scenic and unspoilt part of the Lake District, this fine 17th-century former farmhouse still provides a sanctuary for weary travellers. Inside it oozes traditional appeal, with its oak-beamed bar, warm fires and a warren of rooms. Hearty imaginative dishes, such as Morecambe Bay potted shrimps followed by roast venison with red wine and juniper sauce, are available in the charming restaurant. The inn also has a range of tasteful en suite bedrooms.

Recommended in the area

Ravenglass and Eskdale Railway; Muncaster Castle; Eskdale Water Mill

Highland Drove Inn and Kyloes Restaurant

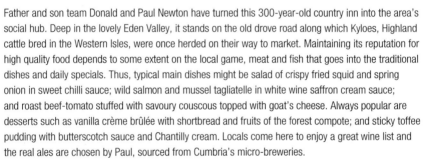

Address: GREAT SALKELD, Penrith, CA11 9NA
Tel: 01768 898349
Fax: 01768 898708
Email: highlanddroveinn@btinternet.com
Website: www.highland-drove.co.uk
Map ref: 6 NY53
Directions: Exit M6 junct 40, take A66 E'bound then
A686 to Alston. After 4m, left onto B6412 for Great Salkeld & Lazonby
Open: all week noon-2 6-late (Closed Mon L) 🍴 L Tue-Sun 12-2 D all wk 6-9 🍽 L Tue-Sun 12-2
D all wk 6-9 **Facilities:** Parking Garden **Notes:** ⊕ FREE HOUSE ⋔ 🐕 ♟ 25

Father and son team Donald and Paul Newton have turned this 300-year-old country inn into the area's social hub. Deep in the lovely Eden Valley, it stands on the old drove road along which Kyloes, Highland cattle bred in the Western Isles, were once herded on their way to market. Maintaining its reputation for high quality food depends to some extent on the local game, meat and fish that goes into the traditional dishes and daily specials. Thus, typical main dishes might be salad of crispy fried squid and spring onion in sweet chilli sauce; wild salmon and mussel tagliatelle in white wine saffron cream sauce; and roast beef-tomato stuffed with savoury couscous topped with goat's cheese. Always popular are desserts such as vanilla crème brûlée with shortbread and fruits of the forest compote; and sticky toffee pudding with butterscotch sauce and Chantilly cream. Locals come here to enjoy a great wine list and the real ales are chosen by Paul, sourced from Cumbria's micro-breweries.

Recommended in the area

Lake District National Park; Hadrian's Wall; Pennine Way

Queens Head Hotel

★★ 75% ❀ HOTEL

Address: Main Street, HAWKSHEAD, LA22 0NS
Tel: 015394 36271
Fax: 015394 36722
Email: enquiries@queensheadhotel.co.uk
Website: www.queensheadhotel.co.uk
Map ref: 5 SD39
Directions: M6 junct 36, A590 to Newby Bridge, 1st right, 8m to Hawkshead
Open: all week 11am-11.45pm Sun 12-11.45
🍴 **L** 12-2.30 Sun 12-5 **D** all wk 6.15-9.30
🍽 **L** 12-2.30 Sun 12-5 **D** all wk 6.15-9.30
Rooms: 13 en suite (2 GF) **S** £55-£60 **D** £75-£130
Facilities: Garden
Notes: ⊕ FREDERIC ROBINSON 🛉 🍷 11

This charming 16th-century hotel sits in the heart of historic Hawkshead, the village where William Wordsworth went to school and Beatrix Potter created Peter Rabbit. The surrounding area is a haven for walkers, and Esthwaite Water is a stone's throw away. Inside the hotel, you'll find low oak-beamed ceilings, wood-panelled walls, an original slate floor and a welcoming fire. As well as a range of well-appointed en suite bedrooms and self-catering accommodation, the hotel offers everything you could need for relaxed wining and dining. There's an extensive wine list and a selection of real ales, plus a full carte menu and an ever-changing specials board.
Recommended in the area
Hill Top (NT); Go Ape at Grizedale Forest Park; Brantwood House and Gardens

The Horse & Farrier Inn

Address: Threlkeld Village, KESWICK, CA12 4SQ
Tel: 017687 79688
Fax: 017687 79823
Email: info@horseandfarrier.com
Website: www.horseandfarrier.com
Map ref: 5 NY22
Directions: M6 junct 40 follow Keswick (A66) signs, after 12m turn right signed Threlkeld. Pub in village centre
Open: all day all week 7.30am-mdnt
Facilities: Parking Garden **Notes:** ⊞ JENNINGS BROTHERS PLC ♦♦ ➡ ⚑ 9

Within these whitewashed stone walls are all the essential features of an inn built over 300 years ago – slate-flagged floors, beamed ceilings, open fires. It stands in the picturesque village of Threlkeld, at the foot of 868-metre Blencathra, with views of the even higher Skiddaw in the west and Helvellyn to the south. The inn has an excellent reputation for good food in these parts, from hearty Lakeland breakfasts for those staying over, to meals served in either the bar, or the charming period restaurant. Making full use of local, seasonal produce, the kitchen offers a wide ranging menu. At lunch there are open sandwiches, baguettes and salads, as well as more substantial pan-fried 10oz steaks; poached smoked haddock; and spinach and ricotta cannelloni. The bar menu offers deep-fried breaded Whitby scampi; Mediterranean vegetable lasagne, and plenty more. At dinner, start with roasted fennel risotto; warm oriental duck leg confit; or duck liver and brandy pâté. Particular house specials include lamb shoulder, where the meat is slowly braised in Jennings Cumberland ale, and seared yellow fin tuna steak in olive oil and fresh lime marinade; or warm red onion and cherry tomato tartlet. Typical desserts include chocolate pudding with chocolate sauce and ice cream; and hot sticky toffee pudding.

Recommended in the area

Theatre by the Lake; Rookin House Adventure Centre; Keswick Golf Club

The Kings Head

Address: Thirlspot, KESWICK, CA12 4TN
Tel: 017687 72393
Fax: 017687 72309
Email: stay@lakedistrictinns.co.uk
Website: www.lakedistrictinns.co.uk
Map ref: 5 NY22
Directions: From M6 take A66 to Keswick then A591, pub 4m S of Keswick
Open: all week **Facilities:** Parking Garden
Notes: ⊕ FREE HOUSE ♦♦ ♠ ♟ 10

With 950-metre Helvellyn rearing up behind this 17th-century former coaching inn, it is not hard to describe the views as anything but truly sublime. Take our word for it, they really are. On sunny days, the garden is the most sought-after place to enjoy a meal or drink, although the wooden beams and inglenook fireplaces of the bar, restaurant and lounge areas could make it a tough call. Dark, strong Sneck Lifter is one of the Jennings beers on draught brewed in nearby Cockermouth. Favourites from the bar menu include home-made beefburgers, Waberthwaite Cumberland sausage, and peach, Blengdale Blue cheese and rocket salad, while soups and bloomer bread sandwiches are available all day. The elegant St John's Restaurant menu offers dishes such as home-cured gravadlax with celeriac rémoulade, followed by rack of lamb with roasted root vegetables, or monkfish tail fettucine with steamed mussels. Those with a sweet tooth will find it hard to resist sticky toffee pudding, or vanilla pod crème brûlée. The Lakeland Speciality Shop is well worth a visit for home-made preserves, Emma Bridgewater pottery, and local ale gift packs.

Recommended in the area

Lake District National Park; Thirlmere; Aira Force Waterfall

Queen's Head

★★★★ ⇔ INN

Address: Townhead, TROUTBECK,
Windermere, LA23 1PW
Tel: 015394 32174
Fax: 015394 31938
Email: feast@queensheadhotel.com
Website: www.queensheadhotel.com
Map ref: 6 NY40
Directions: M6 junct 36, A590/591, W towards
Windermere/Ambleside, at mini-rdbt onto A592
signed Penrith/Ullswater. Pub 3m on left **Open:** all day all week 8am-mdnt 🍺 ᵗ◎ᵗ 12-9
Rooms: 15 en suite (2 GF) **S** £70-£80 **D** £110-£130
Facilities: Parking **Notes:** ⊕ FREDERIC ROBINSON ᵢᵢ ⌐ 🍷 8

A classic 17th-century coaching inn, the Queen's Head offers stunning views across the Garburn
Pass. Just three miles from Windermere, it is little wonder that it is a magnet for ramblers. Today this
thriving pub, situated in the lovely, undulating valley of Troutbeck, continues to provide sustenance and
comfortable accommodation to its many visitors, both in the main building and in the converted barn.
The bars are full of nooks and crannies, and there are open fires and carved settles. With Robinson's
Brewery beers on the pumps, and a reputation for good food throughout the day, it draws regulars and
travellers alike. The menu offers such treats as home-made soups, fresh steamed mussels in white
wine, garlic and cream sauce, and home-made crumpet with goats' cheese to start, followed by a main
course of Queen's Head fish pie, South African bobotie, slow-braised lamb shank, or squash and Brie
risotto. A selection of mouthwatering desserts might also tempt you. There are excellent breakfasts for
those staying over.

Recommended in the area

Brockhole National Park Visitor Centre; The World of Beatrix Potter; Lake Windermere

Hutton-in-the-Forest, near Penrith

The Yanwath Gate Inn

Address: YANWATH, Penrith, CA10 2LF
Tel: 01768 862386
Email: enquiries@yanwathgate.com
Website: www.yanwathgate.com
Map ref: 6 NY52
Directions: Telephone for directions
Open: all day all week noon-11pm ⓖ **L** all wk
12-2.30 **D** all wk 6-9 ⓘ **L** all wk 12-2.30 **D** all
wk 6-9 **Facilities:** Parking Garden **Notes:** ⊕ FREE
HOUSE ⁂ ⌁ ⚑ 12

The delightful 17th-century inn takes its name from its original function as a tollgate. It has a growing
reputation for good food and has a beautiful garden with outdoor seating. At least three Cumbrian
ales are served here at any one time. For lunch the starter might be a bowl of mussels, soup of the
day or ham terrine followed by a main dish of fisherman's pie, venison burger or Cumberland sausage
with Yanwarth Gate black pudding. For dinner the mains include red bream, crisp belly pork, smoked
venison loin and an open lasagne of mushrooms and summer vegetables.
Recommended in the area
Rheged; Brougham Hall; steamer cruises on Ullswater

DEVON

Dartmoor National Park

The Turtley Corn Mill

★ ★ ★ ★ ⌂ INN

Address: AVONWICK, TQ10 9ES
Tel: 01364 646100
Fax: 01364 646101
Email: mill@avonwick.net
Website: www.avonwick.net
Map ref: 2 SX75
Directions: Please teleohone for directions
Open: all week Closed: 25 Dec
Rooms: 4 en suite S £89-£110 D £89-£110
Facilities: Parking Garden Notes: ⊕ FREE HOUSE ⊁ ☂ 9

Originally, this beautifully situated inn did what it says on the tin: it milled corn. Then for many years it was a chicken hatchery, before being turned into a pub in the 1970s. A complete renovation six years ago gave the pub a light, fresh style, made all the more enjoyable by an absence of music, gaming machines and pool tables; instead there's a far more rewarding supply of newspapers and books. The daily changing menu makes much of local produce, offering starters of ham hock terrine with toasted brioche; baked fig and goat's cheese salad; and home-made soup. Platters of local seafood, carved meat or West Country cheeses sit somewhere between starters and main courses of fish from the 'catch of the day' board; spicy veggie burger with guacamole and sour cream; Devon rib-eye steak with chunky-cut fries, field mushroom and vine tomatoes; Tunisian-style lamb and aubergine casserole with lemon couscous; and roasted potato and vegetable waffle with Mozzarella, plum tomatoes and basil and balsamic dressing. Or maybe a freshly made granary bread sandwich will suffice. King-sized beds occupy the four double en suite rooms; and there is an award-winning breakfast to enjoy. Within the six acres of grounds is a small lake with an island.

Recommended in the area

South Devon Heritage Coast; National Shire Horse Centre; Dartmoor National Park

The Masons Arms

★★ 80% ❀ HOTEL

Address: BRANSCOMBE, EX12 3DJ
Tel: 01297 680300
Fax: 01297 680500
Email: reception@masonsarms.co.uk
Website: www.masonsarms.co.uk
Map ref: 2 SY18
Directions: Turn off A3052 towards Branscombe, down hill, hotel at bottom of hill
Open: all week Mon-Fri 11-3 6-11 (Sat 11-11 Sun

12-10.30) ➧ L Mon-Fri 12-2, Sat-Sun 12-2.15 D all wk 7-9 ⦿ D all wk 7-9 **Rooms:** 21 en suite
S £80-£170 D £80-£170 **Facilities:** Parking Garden **Notes:** ⊕ FREE HOUSE ⋕ ⊶ ⏑ 14

Originally a cider house, this fine creeper-clad inn dates from 1360 and was at one time a well-documented haunt of smugglers. It is set in the picturesque village of Branscombe, just a 10-minute stroll from the beach, and there are wonderful walks in the area, including the South West Coast Path. The charming bar features stone walls, ancient ships' timbers, slate floors and a splendid open fireplace, which is used for spit roasts on a weekly basis, including Sunday lunchtime. The bar offers an extensive menu supplemented by daily specials, and the restaurant has an AA Rosette award for its fine dining. The menus draw on quality local produce, specialising in Branscombe crab and lobster, and feature such dishes as confit of aromatic duck leg with truffle oil mash, pear compôte and baby carrots. Outside there is a walled terrace with seating for around 100 people – very popular in the summer months – and if you are tempted to stay over, there are rooms in the original building and separate cottage rooms, all beautifully presented with designer fabrics and antique furniture. The Masons Arms welcomes dogs and water is provided for them.

Recommended in the area

Old Bakery, Manor Mill and Forge (NT); Jurassic Coast World Heritage Site; Donkey Sanctuary

The Sandy Park Inn

Address: CHAGFORD, Newton Abbott, TQ13 8JW
Tel: 01647 433267
Email: sandyparkinn@aol.com
Website: www.sandyparkinn.co.uk
Map ref: 2 SX78
Directions: From A30 exit at Whiddon Down, turn left towards Moretonhampstead. Inn 5m from Whiddon Down
Open: all day all week noon-11pm ⅃ L all wk 12-2.30 **D** all wk 6-9 **Facilities:** Parking Garden
Notes: ⊕ FREE HOUSE ⅋ ⅋ ⅋ 14

Everything about the 17th-century, thatched Sandy Park is how you'd want it to be. Dogs are frequently to be found slumped in front of the fire, horse-brasses and sporting prints adorn the walls, and the beamed bar attracts locals and tourists alike, all happily setting the world to rights with the help of a jolly good wine list and a choice of local brews, including Otter, St Austell Tribute and Sharp's Doom Bar. The Inn has built a local following for good quality pub food, sourced in and around Dartmoor, such as the roasting joints used for Sunday lunch, which began life less than two miles away. The bar offers a creative brasserie-style menu, with daily choices on the blackboard; the candlelit restaurant is equally appealing. Dishes to consider include pork and herb sausages handmade in Moretonhampstead; beer-battered cod and chips; pan-seared tuna with salad Niçoise; smoked haddock kedgeree; and John Dory with dry roasted tomatoes and warm buttered samphire. Vegetarians are not forgotten – check out the handmade spinach and goats' cheese filo parcels with basil and parmesan; or risotto with sauté courgettes and sweetcorn.

Recommended in the area

Dartmeet; Grimspound Bronze Age Settlement; Castle Drogo (NT)

The Old Thatch Inn

Address: CHERITON BISHOP, Nr Exeter, EX6 6HJ
Tel: 01647 24204
Email: mail@theoldthatchinn.f9.co.uk
Website: www.theoldthatchinn.com
Map ref: 2 SX79
Directions: 0.5m off A30, 7m SW of Exeter
Open: all week 11.30-3 6-11
Closed: 25-26 Dec, Sun eve 🍴 L all wk 12-2.30
D Mon-Sat 6.30-9 🍽️ **L** all wk 12-2.30 **D** Mon-Sat
6.30-9 **Facilities:** Parking Garden
Notes: 🛢️ FREE HOUSE 🚶 🐕 🍷 9

The Old Thatch Inn is a charming Grade II listed 16th-century free house located just inside the eastern borders of Dartmoor National Park, and half a mile off the A30. It once welcomed stagecoaches on the London to Penzance road and today it remains a popular halfway house for travellers on their way to and from Cornwall. For a time during its long history, the inn passed into private hands and then became a tea-room, before its licence was renewed in the early 1970s. Experienced owners David and head chef Serena London pride themselves on their high standards, especially when it comes to food, and all of the meals are prepared using fresh ingredients from the south-west, with seafood featuring strongly. Dishes change daily, depending on supplies, and examples include pan seared pigeon breast with a spinach mousse and mixed berry dressing; and baked fillet of seabass with a crayfish tail, lemon and thyme risotto. Diners can choose from a number of real ales and a good range of wines, with many available by the glass.

Recommended in the area

Castle Drogo (NT); Fingle Bridge, Dartmoor; Exeter

The Five Bells Inn

Address: CLYST HYDON, Cullompton, EX15 2NT
Tel: 01884 277288
Email: info@fivebellsclysthydon.co.uk
Website: www.fivebellsclysthydon.co.uk
Map ref: 2 ST00
Directions: B3181 towards Cullompton, right at Hele
Cross towards Clyst Hydon. 2m turn right, then sharp
right at left bend at village sign
Open: 11.30am-3 6.30-11pm **Closed:** 25 Dec,
Mon L 🍴 L Tue-Sun 11.30-2 D all wk 6.30-9
Facilities: Parking Garden **Notes:** ⊕ FREE HOUSE ♦♦ ☺ 8

Named after the number of bells in the village church, this beautiful white-painted, thatched former
farmhouse is still surrounded by rolling East Devon countryside. It became a pub around a century
ago, and in recent years accolades have been pouring in about the family-friendly atmosphere and the
dedication to real ales and good food from the owners, Roger and Di Shenton. For warmer days there's
a garden with a children's play area. The interior is welcoming, with old beams and an inglenook
fireplace, gleaming copper and brass, watercolours, books and games, and there are four eating
areas. Here you can choose from an interesting and well-balanced menu of dishes based on fresh local
ingredients such as prime West Country steaks and fresh fish. The traditional dishes might include
steak and kidney suet pudding, beef casserole, or plaice with chips and peas, and there are more
eclectic offerings – perhaps salmon with pesto crust and tomato salsa; breast of chicken with a Stilton
and apricot sauce; or citrus beef, leek and pickled kumquat pie in a potato pastry basket. There are
always vegetarian choices, the children's menu is particularly good and you can even get take-away
cod or sausage and chips. Real ales include Cotleigh Tawny Ale, Otter Bitter and O'Hanlon's.

Recommended in the area

Killerton Gardens; Exeter; Jurassic Coast World Heritage Site

The New Inn

★★★★ INN
Address: COLEFORD, Crediton, EX17 5BZ
Tel: 01363 84242
Fax: 01363 85044
Email: enquiries@thenewinncoleford.co.uk
Website: www.thenewinncoleford.co.uk
Map ref: 2 SS70
Directions: From Exeter take A377, 1.5m after
Crediton turn left for Coleford, continue for 1.5m
Open: all week 12-3 6-11 (Sun 7-10.30 winter)

Closed: 25-26 Dec ⓛ **L** all wk 12-2 **D** all wk 6.30-9.30 ⓘ **L** all wk 12-2 **D** all wk 6.30-9.30
Rooms: 6 en suite (1 GF) **S** £60-£65 **D** £85 **Facilities:** Parking Garden **Notes:** ⊕ FREE HOUSE ♦♦ ⚘ ♟ 10

Set in a little valley with a lovely garden, this pretty, 13th-century riverside cob and thatch inn has a
rambling interior, slate-floor, upholstered wall seats and roaring fires. The restaurant has been fashioned
from the old barns. Pop in for a ploughman's and a pint of Otter; River Exe moules marinière; beer-
battered fish and chips; or roasted duck breast with orange glaze. There are comfortable rooms available.
Recommended in the area
Tarka Line; Lydford Gorge; Castle Drogo (NT)

The Nobody Inn

★★★★ INN
Address: DODDISCOMBSLEIGH, Exeter, EX6 7PS
Tel: 01647 252394
Fax: 01647 252978
Email: info@nobodyinn.co.uk
Website: www.nobodyinn.co.uk
Map ref: 2 SX88 **Directions:** 3m SW of Exeter
Racecourse (A38) **Open:** 11-11 (Sun 12-10.30)
Closed: 25-26 & 31 Dec, 1 Jan ⓛ **L** Mon-Sat 12-2,
Sun 12-3 ⓘ **D** Mon-Thu 6.30-9, Fri-Sat 6.30-9.30,

Sun 7-9 **D** Mon-Thu 6.30-9, Fri-Sat 6.30-9.30, Sun 7-9 (Jan-Mar Thu-Sat only) **Rooms:** 5 en suite
1 pri fac **S** £45-£70 **D** £60-£95 **Facilities:** Parking Garden **Notes:** ⊕ FREE HOUSE ⚘ ♟ 20

Dating from around 1591, this is a charming free house, with low ceilings, blackened beams, inglenook
fireplace and antique furniture all contributing to the timeless and homely atmosphere. The great pub
food here is based around fresh local produce – as well as unusual local ales, there are over 300 wines
and 240 whiskies. The restaurant and bedrooms have been refurbished.
Recommended in the area
Exeter Quay; Crealy Adventure Park; Haldon Forest Park

The Holt

Address: 178 High Street, HONITON, EX14 1LA
Tel: 01404 47707
Email: enquiries@theholt-honiton.com
Website: www.theholt-honiton.com
Map ref: 2 ST10
Open: 11-3 5.30-mdnt **Closed:** 25, 26 Dec & 1 Jan, Sun & Mon 🍽 **L** all wk 12-2 **D** all wk 7-9.30
🍴 **L** all wk 12-2 **D** all wk 7-9.30
Notes: 🕴 🚜 🍷 9

There are three good reasons for pulling off the Honiton by-pass. One is to stop at The Holt. Second, it stocks the local Otter brewery's five beers, which you may enjoy downstairs on comfy sofas. And third is the light and airy upstairs dining area that has gained an AA Rosette. Proprietors Joe and Angus McCaig combine traditional and innovative ideas to create a comfortable and relaxed environment. Head Chef Josh McDonald Johnson produces everything from an open plan kitchen. Changing his menus every six to eight weeks to provide a multiplicity of local suppliers with the opportunity to showcase their produce. In addition to an enticing selection of tapas, lunchtime dishes might include salad of slow roasted pork cheek, grilled black pudding, Exmoor blue cheese and candied walnuts. Possible main courses in the evening include grilled fillet of bream, spiced courgette cake, glazed potatoes, baby onions and a saffron sauce, and a rabbit Wellington, smoked mash, Chantenay carrots, tarragon and cornichon sauce. Smoking Jacket Foods, the Holt's own smokery, appears at local food markets. Live music and film screenings ensure there is always something happening here.

Recommended in the area

Farway Countryside Park; Shute Barton House (NT); Pecorama Gardens and Grotto

Bickley Mill Inn

Address: KINGSKERSWELL,
Newton Abbot, TQ12 5LN
Tel: 01803 873201
Email: info@bickleymill.co.uk
Website: www.bickleymill.co.uk
Map ref: 2 SX86
Directions: From Newton Abbot on A380
towards Torquay. Right at Barn Owl Inn, follow
brown tourist signs
Open: all week **Closed:** 27-28 Dec & 1 Jan

L Mon-Sat 12-2 (Sun 12-2.30) D Mon-Sat 6.30-9.15 (Sun 6-8.30) L Mon-Sat 12-2 (Sun 12-2.30) D all wk 6.30-9.15 **Facilities:** Parking Garden **Notes:** ⊕ FREE HOUSE ♀♂ 🐾 ☂ 8

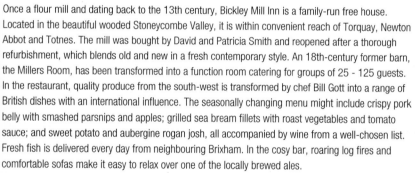

Once a flour mill and dating back to the 13th century, Bickley Mill Inn is a family-run free house. Located in the beautiful wooded Stoneycombe Valley, it is within convenient reach of Torquay, Newton Abbot and Totnes. The mill was bought by David and Patricia Smith and reopened after a thorough refurbishment, which blends old and new in a fresh contemporary style. An 18th-century former barn, the Millers Room, has been transformed into a function room catering for groups of 25 - 125 guests. In the restaurant, quality produce from the south-west is transformed by chef Bill Gott into a range of British dishes with an international influence. The seasonally changing menu might include crispy pork belly with smashed parsnips and apples; grilled sea bream fillets with roast vegetables and tomato sauce; and sweet potato and aubergine rogan josh, all accompanied by wine from a well-chosen list. Fresh fish is delivered every day from neighbouring Brixham. In the cosy bar, roaring log fires and comfortable sofas make it easy to relax over one of the locally brewed ales.

Recommended in the area

Dartmoor National Park; Paignton Zoo; Compton Castle (NT)

Castle Rock at the Valley of Rocks, nr Lynton, Exmoor National Park

The Harris Arms

Address: Portgate, LEWDOWN, EX20 4PZ
Tel: 01566 783331
Fax: 01566 783359
Email: info@theharrisarms.co.uk
Website: www.theharrisarms.co.uk
Map ref: 1 SX48
Directions: From A30 at Broadwoodwidger/Roadford Lake exit follow signs to Lifton then for Portgate
Closed: Mon & Sun eve 🏠 ⏴️ L Tue-Sun 12-2
D Tue-Sat 6.30-9 **Facilities:** Parking Garden
Notes: 🍺 FREE HOUSE ⛲ 🐕 ♟ 18

A 16th-century inn with wonderful views to Brent Tor, this establishment lives up to its promotional strapline: 'Eat Real Food and Drink Real Wine'. Located on the old A30 close to the boundary between Devon and Cornwall, it's an accessible spot for honest food with substance and style, plus real ales and excellent wines. Owners Rowena and Andy Whiteman have previously run vineyards in France and New Zealand, so their wine list, with over 150 wines, is both eclectic and extensive. The pub's excellent reputation, which reaches far beyond the local area, is built on exact cooking and locally-sourced ingredients. Example of a starter is roast breast of pigeon with beetroot risotto and red wine sauce, and main courses might include slow-roasted pork belly with spinach, apple sauce and black pudding and potato croquette; and pub classics such as home-cooked ham with eggs and chips. A children's menu is available. In warmer weather, enjoy a meal or drink outside on the decked patio.

Recommended in the area

Dartmoor National Park; Plymouth

Lynmouth harbour

The Ring of Bells Inn

Address: NORTH BOVEY, Newton Abbot, TQ13 8RB
Tel: 01647 440375
Fax: 01647 440746
Email: info@ringofbellsinn.com
Website: www.ringofbellsinn.com
Map ref: 2 SX78
Directions: 1.5m from Moretonhampstead off B3212. 7m S of Whiddon Down junct on A30
Open: all week **Closed:** 25 Dec ⓑ **L** all wk all day Etr-Oct, 12-2.30 Nov-Etr **D** all wk all day Etr-Oct, 6.30-9.30 Nov-Etr ⓘ **D** all wk 6.30-9.30 **Facilities:** Garden **Notes:** ⓦ FREE HOUSE ⓘ ⓘ ⓘ 12

This is one of Dartmoor's most historic inns, an attractive thatched property just off the village green. It was built in the 13th century for stonemasons working on the nearby church, and is still at the heart of the village's social life. Visitors are attracted by good Devon pub food and West Country ales, and there is certainly plenty to do and see in the area. Hearty appetites are catered for with classics like steak and ale pie, local bangers and mash, and lambs' liver and bacon, plus local rabbit in red wine.

Recommended in the area

Dartmoor National Park; Exeter; Dartmoor Railway

The Ship Inn

Address: NOSS MAYO, Plymouth, PL8 1EW
Tel: 01752 872387
Fax: 01752 873294
Email: ship@nossmayo.com
Website: www.nossmayo.com
Map ref: 2 SX54
Directions: 5m S of Yealmpton on River
Yealm estuary
Open: all day all week 🛏 †◎† **Facilities:** Parking
Garden Notes: ⊕ FREE HOUSE ♦♦ ♦ ♥ 10

Reclaimed English oak and local stone characterise this beautifully renovated 16th-century free house on the Yealm (sometimes pronounced Yam, apparently) estuary. The waterside location makes it an excellent walking and sailing destination - you can tie up your boat outside. Deceptively spacious inside, yet it remains cosy, thanks to the wooden floors, old bookcases, log fires and dozens of local pictures. From Dartmoor Brewery in Princetown, home of the prison, comes the whimsically named Jail Ale, plus Proper Job, Tribute Dartmoor and guest ales. Sit anywhere from the panelled library to a waterside table for a home-made snack or meal from the daily-changing bar or carte menus. A starter like leek and potato soup, or traditional crayfish tail cocktail with Marie Rose sauce, could be followed by pan-fried duck breast on potato rosti with plum sauce; Thai green chicken curry with rice; Cajun salmon fillet on creamed potatoes with roasted vine tomatoes; or pumpkin and pea risotto. Don't fall at the final hurdle by forgoing apple and berry crumble and custard; or chocolate mousse with shortbread. Interesting global wines, a decent list of malts, liqueurs and hot drinks complete the menu, which you can study while enjoying the great views from the waterside garden.

Recommended in the area

Saltram House (NT); Dartmoor Wildlife Park; National Shire Horse Centre

The Jack in the Green Inn

⬡⬡

Address: London Road, ROCKBEARE, Nr Exeter, EX5 2EE
Tel: 01404 822240
Fax: 01404 823445
Email: info@jackinthegreen.uk.com
Website: www.jackinthegreen.uk.com
Map ref: 2 SY09
Directions: From M5 take old A30 towards Honiton,
signed Rockbeare **Open:** all week 11-3 5.30-11 (Sun noon-11)
Closed: 25 Dec-5 Jan ⬛ **L** Mon-Sat 12-2 **D** Mon-Sat 6-9.30,
Sun 12-9 **Facilities:** Parking **Notes:** ⊕ FREE HOUSE ⊪ ♟ 12

There has been an inn on this site for several centuries, but
since Paul Parnell took over some 19 years ago, it has become an award-winning beacon of good
food in a contemporary and relaxed atmosphere. The inn is set in four acres of grounds and within its
whitewashed walls is a lounge bar furnished with comfy seating and dark wood tables, and a smart
restaurant. The simple philosophy here is to serve real food to real people, with a firm commitment
from the kitchen to sourcing the best and freshest local produce and preparing it to a consistently high
standard. Typical dishes on the bar menu include home made chicken liver parfait with redcurrant jelly;
'Posh' prawn cocktail with 'Bloody Mary' sauce; braised faggots, creamed potato and onion gravy; confit
Creedy Carver duck leg with creamed haricot beans. Throughout 2010 the inn is offering a 'Totally
Devon' 3-course menu experience. Current cask ales include Otter Ale, Doom Bar and Butcombe Bitter
plus three Devon ciders including St George's Temptation and Yarde Real Cider. Perfect for the summer
months is the new alfresco eating area for up to 60 people, and jazz fans should seek out the Friday
night events. Dogs are welcome in the courtyard, with water provided and a field for walking them.

Recommended in the area

Bicton Park; Escot Park; Crealy Adventure Park

The Victoria Inn

Address: Fore Street, SALCOMBE, TQ8 8BU
Tel: 01548 842604
Fax: 01548 844201
Email: info@victoriainn-salcombe.co.uk
Website: www.victoriainn-salcombe.co.uk
Map ref: 2 SX73
Directions: In town centre, overlooking estuary
Open: all day all week 11.30am-11pm (Fri-Sat
11.30am-11.30pm) **Closed:** 25 Dec pm 🍴 L all wk
12-2.30 D all wk 6-9 **Facilities:** Garden
Notes: 🛢 ST AUSTELL BREWERY 👬 🐾 🍷 12

Just a short stroll from the water's edge, this flower basket-fronted pub gets a very good press. At the rear, a 'secret' garden, sun terrace, large enclosed children's play area and even chickens to feed. In the bar, St Austell's range of real ales, a wide selection of wines and Champagnes by the glass, including the 'friendly' 250ml size, a choice of teas, coffees and cakes, the daily papers and free Wi-fi access. The menu reflects the enthusiasm of proprietors Tim Hore and Liz Sheldon for Devon-sourced, classic British pub dishes, such as a good choice of open sandwiches at lunchtime, and mains that include slow-roasted half shoulder of lamb with garlic, braised red cabbage and redcurrant sauce; sautéed pork fillet with rice, white wine and tarragon sauce; 'scrummy' fish pie with cheesy mash; paupiettes of lemon sole with cold water prawns and smoked salmon cream; and sweet potato and mixed bean balti with rice. Among the desserts is the indisputably traditional apple pie and custard, while chef's profiteroles with hot chocolate sauce are also up there with the classics. Dogs on a lead are welcome inside or out, and the really well behaved may be given a chewy treat.

Recommended in the area

Buckfast Abbey; Totnes Castle; Woodlands Leisure Park

East Dart River near Postbridge in Dartmoor National Park

The Blue Ball

★★★★ INN

Address:	Stevens Cross, Sidford,
	SIDMOUTH, EX10 9QL
Tel:	01395 514062
Fax:	01395 519584
Email:	rogernewton@blueballinn.net
Website:	www.blueballinn.net
Map ref:	2 SY18

Directions: M5 junct 30 exit to A3052. Through Sidford towards Lyme Regis, on left after village, approx 13m **Open:** all week **Closed:** 25 Dec eve 🍴 🍽 **L** all wk 12-3 **D** all wk 6-9 **Rooms:** 8 en suite (1 GF) **S** £60 **D** £95 **Facilities:** Parking Garden **Notes:** ⌑ PUNCH TAVERNS 👪 🐾 🍷 10

Run by the Newton family since 1912, but dating back to 1385, this thatched, cob- and flint-built old inn was destroyed by fire in March 2006 and rebuilt with tremendous care to recapture its original atmosphere. A central bar covers the main seating areas, while outside is an attractive garden. You will find pub food favourites and ales served by hand pump. There are eight comfortable bedrooms.

Recommended in the area

Crealy Adventure Park; Seaton Tramway; South West Coast Path

Dukes

★★★★ 🛏 INN

Address: The Esplanade, SIDMOUTH, EX10 8AR
Tel: 01395 513320
Fax: 01395 519318
Email: dukes@hotels-sidmouth.co.uk
Website: www.hotels-sidmouth.co.uk
Map ref: 2 SY18
Directions: M5 junct 30 onto A3052, take 1st exit to Sidmouth on right then left onto Esplanade
Open: all week 🛏 L Sun-Thu 12-9. Fri-Sat 12-9.30 D Sun-Thu 12-9, Fri-Sat 12-9.30 🍽 L Sun-Thu 12-9. Fri-Sat 12-9.30 D Sun-Thu 12-9. Fri-Sat 12-9.30 **Rooms:** 13 en suite S £35-£45 D £70-£120 **Facilities:** Parking Garden **Notes:** 🍺 FREE HOUSE 🚶 🐕 🍷 16

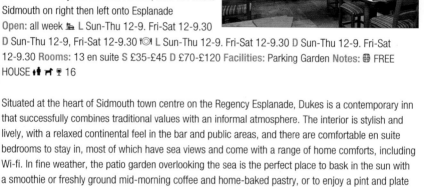

Situated at the heart of Sidmouth town centre on the Regency Esplanade, Dukes is a contemporary inn that successfully combines traditional values with an informal atmosphere. The interior is stylish and lively, with a relaxed continental feel in the bar and public areas, and there are comfortable en suite bedrooms to stay in, most of which have sea views and come with a range of home comforts, including Wi-fi. In fine weather, the patio garden overlooking the sea is the perfect place to bask in the sun with a smoothie or freshly ground mid-morning coffee and home-baked pastry, or to enjoy a pint and plate of your choice at lunchtime. Branscombe and O'Hanlons are among the real ale choices on offer, and over a dozen wines are served by the glass. Traditional English-style dishes vie with the specials board, where seafood from Brixham and Lyme Bay, and prime meats from West Country farms will be found. The head chef and his team aim to produce dishes that will suit all tastes: potted crab, crispy duck confit and home-made banoffee pie are typical examples.

Recommended in the area

Jurassic Coast; Crealy Great Adventure Parks; Exeter Cathedral

The Tower Inn

Address: Church Road, SLAPTON, Kingsbridge, TQ7 2PN
Tel: 01548 580216
Email: towerinn@slapton.org
Website: www.thetowerinn.com
Map ref: 2 SX84
Directions: Off A379 S of Dartmouth, turn left at Slapton
Sands **Closed:** Mon in winter ﹩ ⭐ **L** all wk 12-2 **D** all wk 7-9
Facilities: Parking Garden **Notes:** ⊞ FREE HOUSE ⁙ ⚐ ♟ 8

The Tower is a 14th-century inn set in an historic village in
Devon's lovely South Hams, approached down a narrow lane. Its
name comes from the ruined tower overlooking the pub's walled
garden. Inside is a fascinating series of interconnecting rooms,
with stone walls, beams, pillars and pews, flagstone floors, scrubbed oak tables and log fires. Food at
lunchtime ranges from sandwiches to full meals, and a separate evening menu is served by candlelight.
Food is sourced locally whenever possible, including fresh fish landed at Start Bay. There is an excellent
range of traditional beers, plus local cider and mulled wine in winter.

Recommended in the area

Slapton Sands; Slapton Ley Nature Reserve; Cookworthy Museum of Rural Life

---

The Golden Lion Inn

Address: TIPTON ST JOHN, Sidmouth, EX10 0AA
Tel: 01404 812881
Email: info@goldenliontipton.co.uk
Website: www.goldenliontipton.co.uk
Map ref: 2 SY09
Open: 12-2.30 6-11 **Closed:** (Sun eve Sep-Mar)
﹩ **L** all wk 12-2 **D** Mon-Sat 6.30-8.30 ⭐ **L** Sun
Mar-Sep 7-8.30 **Facilities:** Parking Garden
Notes: ⊞ HEAVITREE ♟ 10

This inviting village pub, run by a French/Cornish husband-and-wife team, has a pleasingly eclectic
decor, with art deco prints sitting alongside Tiffany lamps and paintings by Cornish artists. Yet it
maintains its traditional atmosphere thanks to low wooden beams, stone walls and a log fire. The food
is equally pleasing, combining rustic Mediterranean and British cuisine as seen in dishes such as pork
tenderloin with prunes and Armagnac. Daily specials might include fresh fish and seafood landed at
nearby Sidmouth or braised oxtail. Vegetarians have plenty to choose from, and there's a lighter lunch
menu too, again based on good, local produce.

Recommended in the area

Bicton Park and Gardens; Sidmouth Regency town; Ottery St Mary Church

Widecombe in the Moor in Dartmoor National Park

The Durant Arms

★★★★ ⊜ INN

Address: Ashprington, TOTNES, TQ9 7UP
Tel: 01803 732240
Website: www.durantarms.co.uk
Map ref: 2 SX86
Directions: Exit A38 at Totnes junct, to Dartington & Totnes, at 1st lights right for Kingsbridge on A381, in 1m left for Ashprington
Open: all week ⓑ **L** all wk 12-2 **D** all wk 7-9.15
🍽 **L** all wk 12-2 **D** all wk 7-9.15
Rooms: 8 en suite (2 GF) **Facilities:** Parking Garden
Notes: ⊕ FREE HOUSE ⦿ ⇥ ♟ 8

A locally renowned dining pub set in a pretty South Hams village, the Durant Arms dates from the 18th century and was originally the counting house for the neighbouring 500-acre Sharpham Estate. Sharpham wines and cheese are among the culinary delights, offered alongside a choice of real ales and dishes cooked to order, using local produce where possible.

Recommended in the area

Sharpham Vineyard & Cheese Dairy; Elizabethan town of Totnes; River Dart

The White Hart

Address: Dartington Hall, TOTNES, TQ9 6EL
Tel: 01803 847111
Fax: 01803 847107
Email: bookings@dartingtonhall.com
Website: www.dartingtonhall.com
Map ref: 2 SX86 **Directions:** Near A38, on A384, 2m from Totnes **Open:** all week 11-11 (Sun noon-10.30) **Closed:** 24-27 Dec ⏰ **L** all wk 12-2 **D** all wk 6-9 🍴 **L** all wk 12-2 **D** all wk 6-9
Facilities: Parking Garden
Notes: 🍺 FREE HOUSE ♨ ♟ 8

The White Hart is tucked away in the corner of the courtyard of 'the most spectacular mansion in Devon', the 14th-century Dartington Hall, famed for its advancement of the arts. Surrounding it are landscaped gardens, rolling farmland, an ancient deer park and woodland, through which the River Dart heads for Totnes and the sea. In the informal bar, chunky beams, flagstone floors and log fires are balanced by light-oak furniture to create a stylish blend of old and new, while the restaurant, originally the hall's kitchen, retains its medieval architecture, original tapestry and huge fireplace. Here, you'll discover a menu prepared with diligently sourced, ethically produced ingredients from South Devon, even from the estate itself, such as single-suckled beef, grass-reared lamb, and additive-free and free-range chickens and eggs. Fish is sourced daily at the local fish market and interesting local cheeses come from speciality makers. Dishes might include Dartington beefburger, caramelised onions and melted Cheddar served with French fries and salad; local mussels cooked with curried leeks, cream and coriander; and aubergine, spinach and chickpea tagine with lemon-minted couscous. Overnight guests can wake to birdsong and views of the South Devon countryside. Walks wind through the gardens and along the Dart.

Recommended in the area

Dartington Cider Press Centre; South Devon Heritage Coast; Dartmoor National Park

Cridford Inn

Address: TRUSHAM, Newton Abbot, TQ13 0NR
Tel: 01626 853694
Email: reservations@vanillapod-cridfordinn.com
Website: www.vanillapod-cridfordinn.com
Map ref: 2 SX88
Directions: A38 take junct for Teign Valley, turn right follow signs Trusham for 4m
Open: all week 11-3 6-11 (Sat 11-11 Sun noon-10.30) ⓑ **L** all wk 12-2 **D** all wk 7-9.30 🍽 **L** Sun 12-1.30 **D** Mon-Sat 7-9.30
Facilities: Parking Garden **Notes:** ⊕ FREE HOUSE ♦♦ 🍷 8

Award-winning chef Ian Nixon and his wife, Tracey, run this ancient bar and the Vanilla Pod restaurant, which stand where a smallholding mentioned in the Domesday Book used to be. It was built as a Devon longhouse, under whose roof humans and animals lived in close harmony around a central open fire, now replaced by more conventional heating arrangements. The beamed bar contains what is thought to be the country's earliest surviving domestic example of a medieval window frame, as well as a good selection of local ales, wines, traditional pub grub and specials. The fine-dining contemporary restaurant offers starters that include wild mushroom soup with herb oil and truffle foam; ham hock terrine, poached egg and chips; and pan-fried Brixham scallops with pea and pancetta risotto. Among the main courses are seared sirloin steak with onion rings, buttered spinach and forest mushroom jus; pan-fried chicken breast and slow-roasted chicken shank with sweetcorn fritter, pea purée and thyme jus; trio of fish fillets on shellfish bisque; and tomato, pepper and aubergine terrine with smoked applewood dressing. Don't leave without tasting Ian's signature vanilla pod chocolate cup. There is a family dining area too.

Recommended in the area

Canonteign Falls; Belvedere Castle; Haldon Forest and Go Ape

The Digger's Rest

Address: WOODBURY SALTERTON, EX5 1PQ
Tel: 01395 232375
Fax: 01395 232711
Email: bar@diggersrest.co.uk
Website: www.diggersrest.co.uk
Map ref: 2 SY08
Directions: 2.5m from A3052. Signed from Westpoint
Open: all week 11-3 6-11 (Sat-Sun all day in summer)
Facilities: Parking Garden
Notes: ⊕ FREE HOUSE ♥ 13

The Digger's Rest is everything you would expect of a cosy country free house. Originally a Devon cider house, this 500-year-old building has thick walls of stone and cob with heavy beams under a thatched roof and a real log fire. The menu features simple fresh food expertly prepared to order. The emphasis here is on using fresh fish and local meats, supporting good farming husbandry and buying local and West Country organic produce where available. The menu, which includes pub classics, changes to reflect seasonal availability of raw ingredients and there is also a specials board and children's menu with proper food which kids actually like. The philosophy of buying locally also extends to the drinks range with an interesting wine list created by a local wine merchant. Real ales feature Otter Bitter from Devon and guest appearances from other local and award-winning brewers. Whether you want a pint, coffee, glass of wine, snack or a full meal, you will find a warm welcome at The Digger's Rest.

Recommended in the area

Jurassic Coast; Powderham Castle; Fairlynch Museum

Rose & Crown

Address: Market Street, YEALMPTON, PL8 2EB
Tel: 01752 880223
Fax: 01752 881058
Email: info@theroseandcrown.co.uk
Website: www.theroseandcrown.co.uk
Map ref: 2 SX55
Open: all week ᵬ L all wk 12-2.30 D all wk
6.30-9.30 ⍟ L all wk 12-2.30 D all wk 6.30-9.30
Facilities: Parking Garden
Notes: ⚬ ⌁ ⍟ 8

Now under new ownership, just a ten minute drive from Plymouth city centre is this very stylish village pub for eating and drinking. The decor includes an attractive mix of tables and old dining chairs, with some good quality sofas, and a large fire place. The absence of curtains and other soft furnishings mean the acoustics are generally lively. This pub has a sensibly thought through balance between the contemporary and the traditional. The terraced garden, with a charming fountain, is a lovely spot in the warmer months. There is a good range of wines, but real ales are taken seriously too. The food on offer is a smart mix of modern pub food with restaurant presentation and quality. The regular-changing à la carte menu tends to include fish, game, meat and vegetarian dishes – all sourced as locally as possible. A 2-course set lunch for £10 (3 courses for £13) is always popular. There is a new function room opposite – suitable for wedding receptions, other celebrations, meeting room etc.

Recommended in the area

Kitley Caves; South West Coast Path; Dartmoor National Park

DORSET

Sunset at Kimmeridge Bay

Gaggle of Geese

Address: BUCKLAND NEWTON, DT2 7BS
Tel: 01300 345249
Email: gaggle@gaggleofgeese.co.uk
Directions: On B3143 N of Dorchester
Map ref: 2 ST60
Open: all wk 11.30-3 6-11.30 (Sun 11.30-11.30, Sat 11.30-11.30 in summer) Closed 1 wk Jan, 25 Dec 🍽 L served Mon-Sat 12-2, Sun 12-3 booking required **D** served Sun-Thu 7-9, Fri-Sat 7-9.30 booking required ⭐ **L** served Mon-Sat 12-2, Sun 12-3 booking required **D** served Sun-Thu 7-9, Fri-Sat 7-9.30 booking required **Facilities:** Parking Garden
Notes: ⊕ FREE HOUSE 👬 🐎 🍷 10

Mark and Emily Hammick, who also run the European Inn at Piddletrenthide, bought this village pub in 2008 and renovated it. The makeover resulted in the creation of a back-to-basics style of bar, one that with its comfy sofas and log fire rather resembles someone's front room. But in whose front room could you order a West Country real ale or cider, a glass of wine, or even a scotch egg? Tall candles and fresh flowers adorn the deep red dining room, where the daily changing menu offers a wide selection of classic British dishes, a typical main course being slow-roasted, stuffed pork shoulder with pan haggerty and curly kale, and chocolate brownie with vanilla ice cream a regular dessert. Being local farmers as well as publicans, Mark and Emily use good traceable local produce where possible, including meat from Mark's parents' farm, fruit, vegetables and game from villagers, and house white wine from nearby Sherborne, a commitment that earns them accreditation to the Direct from Dorset scheme. Attached to the pub is a skittle alley, while the adjoining five acres of land include a croquet lawn, an orchard, and paddocks where charity goose and poultry auctions are held.

Recommended in the area

Cerne Abbas Giant; Jurassic Coast; Minterne Magna House

Durdle Door

The Anchor Inn

Address: High Street, BURTON BRADSTOCK, DT6 4QF
Tel: 01308 897228
Email: info@dorset-seafood-restaurant.co.uk
Website: www.dorset-seafood-restaurant.co.uk
Map ref: 2 SY48
Directions: 2m SE of Bridport on B3157 in centre of Burton Bradstock **Open:** all week **Closed:** 1 Jan 🍺
🍽 **L** all wk 12-2 **D** all wk 6-9.30 **Facilities:** Parking
Notes: 🍺 PUNCH TAVERNS ♦ ⛟ ☕ 10

This 300-year-old coaching inn is just inland from a stretch of the Jurassic Coast World Heritage Site, and near the amazing shingle feature known as Chesil Beach. In keeping with its name, the pub is full of marine memorabilia, fishing tools and shellfish adorning the walls. The house speciality is fish and seafood, and there are 20 main fish courses on offer, plus Catch of the Day. Look out for whole crab, lobster, mussels and dived scallops plus plaice, skate wing, Dover sole and halibut. Meat dishes include a range of chargrilled steaks and roasted crispy duck. There is a selection of fine wines available.
Recommended in the area
Coastline from Chesil Beach to Lyme Regis; West Bay Harbour; Abbotsbury Sub-Tropical Gardens

Dorset

The Acorn Inn

★★★★ ❀ INN

Address: EVERSHOT, Dorchester, DT2 0JW
Tel: 01935 83228
Fax: 01935 83707
Email: stay@acorn-inn.co.uk
Website: www.acorn-inn.co.uk
Map ref: 2 ST50
Directions: A303 to Yeovil, Dorchester Rd, on A37
right to Evershot **Open:** all day all week 11-11

🍴 **L** all wk 12-2 **D** all wk 7-9 🍽 **L** all wk 12-2 **D** all
wk 7-9 **Rooms:** 10 en suite **S** £65-£80 **Facilities:** Parking Garden **Notes:** ⊕ FREE HOUSE 🛉 🐾 🍷 7

Thomas Hardy immortalised this 16th-century, stone-built coaching inn as the 'Sow and Acorn' in *Tess of the d'Urbervilles*, and in later years notorious 'hanging' Judge Jeffreys is thought to have used the main hall to hold court. The inn is set in the pretty village of Evershot (Hardy's Evershead) in a designated Area of Outstanding Natural Beauty. There are two oak-panelled bars, and log fires blaze in carved Hamstone fireplaces. Meals and drinks can be taken in the bar, restaurant, outside on the patio or in the garden. Three of the bedrooms feature four-poster beds, and two are suitable for families. All rooms have refurbished, en suite bathrooms and are equipped with satellite TV, Wi-fi and facilities for making hot drinks. All food is sourced locally whenever possible from sustainable sources and responsible suppliers, allowing the inn to take full advantage of the fantastic seafood, game and vegetables on their doorstep. The varied carte menu in the restaurant changes frequently according to the seasonally available ingredients, and the bar menu offers hearty wholesome dishes to accompany the real ales and ciders; there's also the daily-changing special board. The award-winning Evershot Village Bakery supplies the excellent breads.

Recommended in the area

Mapperton House and Gardens; Jurassic Coast World Heritage Site; Dorchester

91

The European Inn

Address: PIDDLETRENTHIDE, Dorchester, DT2 7QT
Tel: 01300 348308
Email: info@european-inn.co.uk
Website: www.european-inn.co.uk
Map ref: 2 SY79
Directions: 5m N of Dorchester on B3143
Closed: 25 Dec, 1 Jan, last 2 wks Jan,
Sun eve & Mon ⓛ L all wk 12-2 D Mon-Sat 7-9
⏺ L all wk 12-2 D Mon-Sat 7-9
Facilities: Parking Garden
Notes: ⊕ FREE HOUSE ⅋ 禰 ⛾ 9

This name of this dog-friendly village pub might appear to celebrate the final ratification of last year's Lisbon Treaty, but no, it dates from 1860, when its landlord returned from the Crimean War. Today's owners, Mark and Emily Hammick, also run the European's sister inn, the Gaggle of Geese at Buckland Newton. Pleasing customers is their priority, whether they want just a pint of Palmers Copper and a packet of crisps at the small, slate-topped bar, or a fine three-course dinner with wine in the restaurant. Here a cheery waitress greets you as you head for your table set with fresh flowers and tall candles, and peruse the short menu. It changes almost daily, with many ingredients sourced locally to produce indisputably British dishes, such as starters of gratin of Portland crab; and home-smoked duck breast with blackcurrant jam; main courses of line-caught fillet of Abbotsbury sea bass with caper jus vinaigrette; and fillet steak with pan haggerty. Desserts include mulled wine-poached pear with mulled wine sorbet; and apple crumble and custard. Sandwiches are available at lunchtimes, two roasts on Sundays. When the sun shines, the deck area becomes a delightful drinking and dining spot.

Recommended in the area

Thomas Hardy's Cottage (NT); Tank Museum, Bovington; Chesil Beach

The Cricketers

Address: SHROTON OR IWERNE COURTNEY,
Blandford Forum, DT11 8QD
Tel: 01258 860421
Fax: 01258 861800
Email: cricketers@heartstoneinns.co.uk
Website: www.heartstoneinns.co.uk
Map ref: 2 ST81
Directions: 7m S of Shaftesbury on A350, turn right after Iwerne Minster. 5m N of Blandford Forum on A360, past Stourpaine, in 2m left into Shroton. Pub in village centre
Open: all week 11-3 6-11 (Sat-Sun 11-11 summer only)
L all wk 12-2.30 D Mon-Sat 6-9.30 L all wk 12-2.30
D Mon-Sat 6-9.30 **Facilities:** Parking Garden
Notes: ⊕ FREE HOUSE ⁂

The Cricketers lies at the foot of Hambledon Hill in the heart of the beautiful Dorset countryside, with The Wessex Ridgeway nearby. At The Cricketers you will find great pub food, a selection of real ales, and a warm welcome from hosts Andy and Natasha and their team. Daily deliveries of fresh fish, meat and local produce, combined with a choice of well kept real ales, mean that The Cricketers is the perfect choice for food or just to enjoy a quiet pint. Although proud of their food, The Cricketers is a real village pub and customers are equally welcome to drop by for a pint of real ale or a glass of wine. The pub lies between the cricket pitch and the village green. A right of way passes through the pub garden which provides a delightful spot for weary walkers to take refreshment. Andy and Natasha are proud of their long association with Shroton Cricket Club from which the pub takes its name.

Recommended in the area

Cavalcade of Costume Museum; Gold Hill Museum and Garden; Royal Signals Museum

The ruins of Christchurch Castle

Rose & Crown Trent

Address: TRENT, Sherborne, DT9 4SL
Tel/Fax: 01935 850776
Email: dine@roseandcrowntrent.co.uk
Website: www.roseandcrowntrent.com
Map ref: 2 ST51 **Directions:** Just off A30 between
Sherborne & Yeovil **Open:** 12-3 6-11 (Sat-Sun
12-11) **Closed:** Mon ⓑ ⓞ **L** Tue-Sun 12-3
D Tue-Sat 6-9 **Facilities:** Parking Garden
Notes: ⊕ WADWORTH ♥ ⚘ ⚑ 8

Heather Kirk and Stuart Malcom are well into their stride at this picturesque rural gem. Built in the 14th century for the builders of the village church spire, its rustic charm is now due in no small measure to its thatched roof, beams, large fireplaces and flagstone floors. The Trent Barrow Room is the perfect place to retire once the drinks have been brought. Quality local produce is the key to tasty light bites and tapas, or more substantial offerings such as chargrilled sirloin steak with fondant potatoes and roast vine tomato; and sun-blushed tomato, wild mushroom and spinach tartlet. There is an Early Doors Sausage menu at £8.95 between 6-7pm, Tuesday to Friday. Alfresco dining can be enjoyed in the beer garden.
Recommended in the area
Fleet Air Arm Museum, Yeovilton; Montacute House; (NT); Tintinhull House & Garden (NT)

Statue, Bowes Museum, Barnard Castle

The Bridge Inn & Restaurant

Address: Whorlton Village, BARNARD CASTLE, DL12 8XD
Tel: 01833 627341 **Fax:** 01833 627995
Email: info@thebridgeinnrestaurant.co.uk
Website: www.thebridgeinnrestaurant.co.uk
Map ref: 7 NZ01
Open: noon-2 6.30-11 (Sun 5.30-10)
Closed: 24 Dec eve, 25-26 Dec, Mon-Tue
L Tue-Fri 12-2 **D** Mon-Sat 6.30-11
Facilities: Parking Garden **Notes:** ⊕ ♦♦ 🐾

Leaving behind some of the North East's finest restaurants, chef Paul O'Hara and his family came here "to fuse together the creativity and excitement of the city with great quality local produce that's freshly available right here on my doorstep". Transformation of The Bridge is evident in the good real ales, extensive wine list and wide choice of food. A typical meal might be smoked eel fillet, roast beetroot and horseradish cream; pot-roast pheasant with bacon and chestnuts; or a blackboard special such as poached fillet of wild sea bass, monkfish tails and scallops with spring onion risotto.
Recommended in the area
Yorkshire Dales National Park; Rokeby Park; High Force Waterfall

Rose & Crown

★★ ◉◉ HOTEL
Address: ROMALDKIRK, Barnard Castle, DL12 9EB
Tel: 01833 650213
Fax: 01833 650828
Email: hotel@rose-and-crown.co.uk
Website: www.rose-and-crown.co.uk
Map ref: 7 NY92 **Directions:** 6m NW from Barnard Castle on B6277 **Open:** 11-11 **Closed:** 23-27 Dec **L** 12-1.30 **D** 6.30-9.30 🍴 **L** Sun 12-1.30 **D** 7.30-8.45
Rooms: 12 en suite (5 GF) **S** £89 **D** £140-£200
Facilities: Parking **Notes:** ⊕ FREE HOUSE ♦♦ 🐾 ♀ 14

An 18th-century coaching inn overlooking one of three village greens, the stocks and pump. Next door is the Saxon church known as The Cathedral of the Dale. Dine in the bar, with open fire, carriage lamps, old settle and prints; the candlelit oak-panelled restaurant is all white linen and silver cutlery, or in the brasserie with its warm red walls. You will find well-executed classic British fare with modern and regional influences on the menu.
Recommended in the area
Yorkshire Dales National Park; Cauldron Snout Waterfall; Hamsterley Forest

ESSEX

Jubilee Fountain in Halstead

Axe & Compasses

Address: High St, ARKESDEN, CB11 4EX
Tel: 01799 550272
Fax: 01799 550906
Map ref: 3 TL43
Directions: From Buntingford take B1038 towards
Newport. Then left for Arkesden
Open: all week noon-2.30 6-11 (Sun noon-3
7-10.30) 🛏 L all wk 12-2 D all wk 6.45-9.30
🍽 L all wk 12-2 D all wk 6.45-9.30 Facilities:
Parking Garden Notes: ⊕ GREENE KING ♟ 14

Picture postcard perfect, this historic inn is located in the narrow main street of a beautiful village. A
stream called Wicken Water runs alongside, criss-crossed by footbridges leading to white, cream and
pink colour-washed thatched cottages. The central section of the inn – the thatched part – dates from
1650, but the building has since been extended to utilise the old stable block, which accommodated
horses until the 1920s, and into a 19th-century addition that now houses the public bar. The beamed
interior is full of character and includes the welcoming bar, a comfortable and softly lit restaurant, and
a cosy lounge furnished with antiques, and displaying horse brasses and old agricultural implements.
During winter there may well be a warming fire blazing in the hearth, and in summer there is further
seating outside on the patio. Beer lovers will enjoy the real ales on tap, which include Greene King IPA,
Abbot Ale and Old Speckled Hen. For those who prefer the juice of the vine, there is a wine list that's
split almost evenly between France and the rest of the world. The restaurant offers a full carte, while an
extensive blackboard menu is available in either the lounge or bar. Dishes include pan-fried duck breast
with black cherries and cherry brandy; whole grilled lemon sole; medallions of beef fillet and rösti potato
with soft green peppercorns, brandy and cream.

Recommended in the area
Audley End House & Gardens; Imperial War Museum Duxford; Mountfitchet Castle

Ruins of Abbey and Parish Church at Waltham Abbey

The Cricketers

Address: CLAVERING, Saffron Walden, CB11 4QT
Tel: 01799 550442
Fax: 01799 550882
Email: info@thecricketers.co.uk
Website: www.thecricketers.co.uk
Map ref: 4 TL43
Directions: From M11 junct 10, A505 E. Then A1301, B1383. At Newport take B1038 **Open:** all day all week **Closed:** 25-26 Dec 🍴 **L** all wk 12-2 **D** all wk 6.30-9.30 🍴 **L** all wk 12-2 **D** all wk 6.30-9.30 **Facilities:** Parking Garden **Notes:** ⊞ FREE HOUSE ♦♦ ♱ 10

A 16th-century country inn run by Sally and Trevor Oliver since 1976. Look no further than the nearby cricket pitch for the reason behind the pub's name and the cricketing memorabilia in the beamed, log fire-warmed bar and restaurant. Seasonal menus and daily specials include lots of fresh fish, properly hung meats and, for children, organic salmon and free-range chicken breast. Famous son Jamie supplies vegetables, herbs and leaves from his certified organic garden. The extensive wine list changes regularly.

Recommended in the area
Audley End House; Imperial War Museum Duxford; Cambridge

The Swan at Felsted

Address: Station Road, FELSTED,
Dunmow, CM6 3DG
Tel: 01371 820245
Fax: 01371 821393
Email: info@theswanatfelsted.co.uk
Website: www.thegreatpubcompany.co.uk
Map ref: 4 TL62
Directions: Exit M11 junct 8 onto A120 signed
Felsted. Pub in village centre
Open: all week noon-3 5-11 (Sun noon-6)

▆ **L** Mon-Sat 12-2.30, Sun 12-4 **D** Mon-Sat 6-9.30 ⍟ **L** Mon-Sat 12-2.30, Sun 12-4
D Mon-Sat 6-9.30 **Facilities:** Parking Garden **Notes:** ⊕ GREENE KING ⁂ ⌁ ☻ 9

Ideally situated for exploring the stunning north Essex countryside, and only a short drive from Stansted
Airport, the Swan is an imposing building and was for many years the village bank. It was rebuilt after
a disastrous fire in the early 20th century, and the interior decoration has a fresh, contemporary feel.
A pretty courtyard garden to the rear provides a tranquil, sheltered eating area overlooked by the village
church, and during winter a roaring log fire greets guests as they cross the threshold. The kitchen has a
great commitment to quality local produce, with dishes ranging from pork sausages, creamy mash and
red onion gravy, or Swan bacon and cheese burger, to slow roasted lamb neck in a port, mushroom
and baby onion sauce with dauphinoise potatoes or oven roasted cod, olive oil mash, local asparagus
and nut brown butter. Fine wines, including a good selection by the glass, and well-kept cask ales also
help to achieve a fine balance between the traditional English pub and a high quality restaurant.
A stylish function room with its own entrance and bespoke menus is available for private parties of
up to 20 people.

Recommended in the area

Hatfield Forest National Nature Reserve; Mountfitchet Castle Experience; Paycockes House

Beth Chatto Gardens

Bell Inn & Hill House

Address: High Road, HORNDON ON THE HILL,
SS17 8LD
Tel: 01375 642463
Fax: 01375 361611
Email: info@bell-inn.co.uk
Website: www.bell-inn.co.uk
Map ref: 4 TQ68
Directions: M25 junct 30/31 signed Thurrock
Open: all week **Closed:** 25-26 Dec ⓑ **L** all wk
12-1.45 **D** all wk 6.30-9.45 ⓘ⚹ **L** Mon-Sat 12-1.45,
Sun 12-2.30 **D** all wk 6.30-9.45 **Facilities:** Parking Garden
Notes: ⊕ FREE HOUSE ⚹ 🐾 🍷 16

When the present family acquired this coaching inn in 1938 it had no running water or electricity. Today there are plenty of mod cons, but the restoration has retained such features as the courtyard balcony where luggage was lifted from coach roofs. There's a good range of real ales, a lengthy wine list, and dishes such as poached leg of lamb with olive polenta among the intriguing food options.
Recommended in the area
Tilbury Fort; Hadleigh Castle; Southend Museum, Planetarium and Discovery Centre

The Compasses at Pattiswick

Address: Compasses Road, PATTISWICK, Braintree, CM77 8BG
Tel: 01376 561322
Fax: 01376 564343
Email: info@thecompassesatpattiswick.co.uk
Website: www.thegreatpubcompany.co.uk
Map ref: 4 TL82
Directions: From Braintree take A120 E towards Colchester.
After Bradwell 1st left to Pattiswick **Open:** all week 12-3 5.30-11
(Sat 5.30-mdnt, Sun noon-4.30, Sun eve in summer) 🍴 **L** all wk
12-3 **D** Mon-Thu 6-9.30, Fri-Sat 6-9.45 🍽 **L** Mon-Sat 12-3,
Sun 12-4.30 **D** Mon-Thu 6-9.30, Fri-Sat 6-9.45
Facilities: Parking Garden **Notes:** ⊕ FREE HOUSE 🍴 🐾 🍷 12

Tucked away in delightful countryside, this renovated gastro-pub offers a contemporary take on country style, with a flagstone floor in the bar, an open fire and rustic furniture. The menu of light bar meals and à la carte dishes is packed with quality produce, including a rich selection of game from the surrounding woods. Dishes range from traditional pub classics, such as beer battered fish and chips, to leg of lamb steak with creamy roasted garlic mash and red wine jus, along with daily specials. Similarly, the children's menu concentrates on simple classics popular with younger guests. The balance between bar, restaurant and private dining room enables the Compasses to cater for any occasion, and it is popular with locals, walkers and cyclists as well as those willing to travel in search of quality. Outside, extensive patios offer separate areas allowing families a clear view of the children's play area, while locals can enjoy the glorious Pattiswick sunsets with a well-kept pint of Woodforde's Wherry, from Norfolk, or one of a range of local ales from Nethergate Brewery.

Recommended in the area

Paycockes House; Beth Chatto Gardens; Colchester Zoo

Cotswold Water Park

The Old Passage Inn

★ ★ ★ ★ ◉◉ 🍷 RESTAURANT WITH ROOMS

Address: Passage Road, ARLINGHAM, GL2 7JR
Tel: 01452 740547
Fax: 01452 741871
Email: oldpassage@ukonline.co.uk
Website: www.theoldpassage.com
Map ref: 2 SO71
Directions: 5m from A38 adjacent M5 junct 13
Open: 11-3 6-finish (all day Easter-Sep) **Closed:** 25 Dec,
Sun eve & Mon ¶◎¶ **L** Tue-Sat 12-2.30, Sun 12-3 **D** Tue-Sat 7-9
Rooms: 3 en suite **S** £70-£130 **D** £90-£130
Facilities: Parking Garden **Notes:** ⊕ FREE HOUSE ♦♦ ⌁ 🍷 14

The 'old passage' in the name refers to the ford and later ferry service that crossed the River Severn here. The rich harvest of salmon and elvers that once came from the river is now sadly depleted, but chef Mark Redwood's seafood menu features local, sustainable ingredients, such as freshwater crayfish, whenever possible. Fresh lobster from Pembrokeshire (sometimes from Cornwall) is always available from the tank, and freshly shucked oysters and Fruits de Mer are specialities. The simple but innovative menus often change daily to reflect what is available, but might include such dishes as roast tranche of turbot served with parsley new potatoes and hollandaise. The large dining room has a fresh and airy appeal, and in summer you can eat out on the garden terrace, with views across a bend in the river towards Newnham-on-Severn and the distant Forest of Dean. The three stunning en suite bedrooms enjoy the same views and enable guests to enjoy not only an exceptional breakfast, but also take full advantage of the excellent wine list at dinner, which includes plenty of half bottles and wines by the glass, and features wines from the Three Choirs Vineyard at Newent.

Recommended in the area

Wildfowl and Wetlands Trust, Slimbridge; Owlpen Manor; Berkeley Castle

Coates, the restored entrance to the Thames & Severn Canal tunnel

Owlpen in The Cotswolds

The Queens Arms

Address: The Village, ASHLEWORTH, GL19 4HT
Tel: 01452 700395
Map ref: 2 SO82
Directions: From Gloucester N on A417 for 5m.
At Hartpury, opp Royal Exchange turn right at Broad
St to Ashleworth. Pub 100yds past village green
Open: noon-3 7-11 **Closed:** 25-26 Dec & 1 Jan,
Sun eve (ex BH wknds) ॾ L all wk 12-2 D Mon-Sat
7-9 ᵀᴼᴵ L all wk 12-2 D Mon-Sat 7-9 **Facilities:**
Parking Garden **Notes:** ⊕ FREE HOUSE ⬤ ⬤ 14

Hailing from South Africa, experienced restaurateurs Tony and Gill Burreddu bought The Queens
Arms in 1998. They have created a warm, homely atmosphere with the emphasis on imaginative,
locally sourced food, well kept ales and an excellent wine list. All the food is home made including the
delicious desserts. Alongside traditional favourites such as steak and kidney pie and salmon fishcakes,
specialities might include slow roasted belly of pork, lamb noisettes with wild mushroom sauce, fresh
halibut with asparagus and beurre blanc, and South African dishes of Bobotie and tomato Bredie.
Recommended in the area
Ashleworth Tithe Barn; Gloucester Docks and Museum; Slimbridge Wildfowl & Wetlands Trust

The Red Hart Inn at Awre

Address: AWRE, nr Newnham-on-Severn,
GL14 1EW
Tel: 01594 510220
Map ref: 2 SO70
Directions: E of A48 between Gloucester
& Chepstow, access is from Blakeney
or Newnham villages
Closed: 23 Jan-5 Feb, Mon (winter)
Facilities: Parking Garden
Notes: ⊕ FREE HOUSE ♦ ♥ ♀ 11

Close to the wide, meandering River Severn, this traditional free house was built in 1483 for workmen renovating the nearby 10th-century church. The charming interior ticks all the boxes under the Historic Features heading, including flagstone floors, stone fireplaces, lots of exposed beams, and an original working well, which is now attractively illuminated. It's the kind of atmospheric place where you can enjoy half of Wye Valley Butty Bach, real cider or a glass of wine, and suddenly a meal seems a good option. That being the case, rest assured that food is taken seriously here - so much so that a list of all local growers and suppliers appears on each table. Among the favourite dishes are Gloucester Old Spot sausages with mash and onion gravy; local beef steak and ale casserole with mustard mash; pan-roasted breast of chicken with dauphinoise potatoes, mushrooms and smoked bacon sauce; and chargrilled pork loin with glazed apples, mashed potato and Awre's Severn cider sauce. The four desserts - crème brûlée, chocolate torte with Bailey's pannacotta; syrup sponge pudding and custard; and apple cheesecake with crumble topping and caramel sauce - can be enjoyed individually or taken all together on one 'Awresome' plate. Being close to the river, the inn is in an ideal spot to walk off lunch.

Recommended in the area

Forest of Dean; Symonds Yat; Goodrich Castle

The Kings Head Inn

★★★★ ❀ INN

Address: The Green, BLEDINGTON, Chipping Norton, OX7 6XQ
Tel: 01608 658365
Fax: 01608 658902
Email: info@kingsheadinn.net
Website: www.kingsheadinn.net
Map ref: 3 SP22
Directions: On B4450 4m from Stow-on-the-Wold
Open: all week **Closed:** 24-25 Dec **Rooms:** 12 en suite (3 GF)
Facilities: Parking Garden **Notes:** ⊕ FREE HOUSE ₹ 8

This award-winning 16th-century inn is set off the village green, complete with a little brook and crossed by a rustic bridge. Much of the original building has survived complete with low ceilings, sturdy beams, flagstone floors, exposed stone walls and big open fireplaces. Solid oak furniture, and in the winter, warm roaring fires in the inglenook, result in that unmistakeable English country pub look. But this is no museum piece, and in recent years the pub has acquired considerable renown for its excellent beer, the quality of the food, its 12 comfortable rooms and a wine list with more than 40 bins. All of the food on the menu is prepared in-house and is organic and locally sourced as far as is practical. A meal could begin with tiger prawns cooked in lemongrass, ginger and garlic; home-made duck spring roll with sweet chilli sauce; or chargrilled courgette, watercress and cous cous salad with harissa dressing. This might be followed by grilled mustard and herb chicken breast with purple sprouting broccoli and chorizo parmentier potatoes, chargrilled tuna steak with ginger and leek salad, or spicy green vegetable curry.

Recommended in the area

Blenheim Palace; Cotswold Wildlife Park; Hook Norton Brewery

Eight Bells

Address: Church Street, CHIPPING CAMPDEN,
GL55 6JG
Tel: 01386 840371
Fax: 01386 841669
Email: neilhargreaves@bellinn.fsnet.co.uk
Website: www.eightbellsinn.co.uk
Map ref: 3 SP13
Directions: M40 Junct 15
Open: noon-11 (Sun noon-10.30) **Closed:** 25 Dec
🍺 🍽 L Mon-Thu 12-2, Fri-Sun 12-2.30
D Mon-Thu 6.30-9, Fri-Sat 6.30-9.30, Sun 6.30-8.45
Facilities: Garden **Notes:** ⊕ FREE HOUSE 🚶 🐎 🍷 8

This beautiful 14th-century Cotswold stone inn was built to house stonemasons working on the nearby church and to store the eight church bells. There is an atmospheric bar and a candlelit dining room with oak beams, open fires and a priest's hole. Traditional ales and ciders are served and there's a daily-changing menu of freshly prepared local food. Outside is a courtyard garden and a terrace.
Recommended in the area
The Cotswold Way; Hidcote Manor (NT); Stratford-upon-Avon

The Tunnel House Inn

Address: COATES, Cirencester, GL7 6PW
Tel: 01285 770280
Fax: 01285 700040
Email: bookings@tunnelhouse.com
Website: www.tunnelhouse.com
Map ref: 2 SO90
Directions: From Cirencester on A433 towards
Tetbury, in 2m turn right towards Coates,
follow brown signs to Canal Tunnel & Inn
Open: all week **Closed:** 25 Dec 🍺 12-9.30
🍽 12-9.30 **Facilities:** Parking Garden **Notes:** ⊕ FREE HOUSE 🚶 🐎

The Tunnel House Inn, steeped in history and enjoying a glorious rural location, is reached down a bumpy track by Sapperton Tunnel on the Thames and Severn Canal. The garden is ideal for relaxing with a drink or a meal, while log fires warm the welcoming bar in winter months. A children's play area and spectacular local walks add to its popularity. The monthly-changing menu features good home-cooked dishes such as Gloucester Old Spot sausages with mash, red onion marmalade and gravy.
Recommended in the area
Thames and Severn Canal; Westonbirt Arboretum; Corinium Museum, Cirencester

The Green Dragon Inn

★★★★ ⟅⟆ INN

Address: Cockleford, COWLEY,
Cheltenham, GL53 9NW
Tel: 01242 870271 **Fax:** 01242 870171
Email: green-dragon@buccaneer.co.uk
Website: www.green-dragon-inn.co.uk
Map ref: 2 SO91
Directions: Telephone for directions
Open: all week ⟅⟆ **L** Mon-Fri 12-2.15, Sat 12-2.30,
Sun 12-3 **D** all wk 6-8.30 ⟅⟆ **L** Mon-Fri 12-2.15,
Sat 12-2.30, Sun 12-3 **D** all wk 6-8.30 **Rooms:** 9 en suite (4 GF) **S** £70 **D** £95-£150
Facilities: Parking Garden **Notes:** ⊕ BUCCANEER ⟅⟆ ⟅⟆ ⟅⟆ 9

A handsome stone-built inn dating from the 17th century, the Green Dragon is located in the hamlet of Cockleford at the heart of the picturesque Cotswolds. It is a popular retreat for those who appreciate good food, fine wine and real ales. The fittings and furniture are the work of Robert Thompson, the Mouse Man of Kilburn (so-called for his trademark mouse) who lends his name to the Mouse Bar, with its stone-flagged floors, beamed ceilings and crackling log fires. Nine cottage-style, en suite bedrooms are available, including a suite. All rooms are equipped with direct dial telephones and TVs, and breakfast is included, along with the newspaper of your choice. The menu takes in lunchtime sandwiches, children's favourites, and starters/light meals such as smoked halibut on Thai marinated vegetable tagliatelle or Caesar salad. The daily specials board might offer local Cockleford trout with garlic and caper butter, or pavé of venison on sweet potato mash with a wild mushroom sauce. The choice of real ales includes Hook Norton, Directors, Butcombe and a monthly changing guest beer. Additional features are the heated dining terrace and the function room/skittle alley.

Recommended in the area

Holst Birthplace Museum; Gloucester Cathedral; Witcombe Roman Villa

The Inn at Fossebridge

★★★★ 🛏 INN

Address: FOSSEBRIDGE, nr Cheltenham, GL54 3JS
Tel: 01285 720721
Fax: 01285 720793
Email: info@fossebridgeinn.co.uk
Website: www.fossebridgeinn.co.uk
Map ref: 3 SP01 **Directions:** From M4 junct 15,
A419 towards Cirencester, then A429 towards Stow.
Pub approx 7m on left **Open:** all day all week noon-
mdnt (Sun noon-11.30) 🛏 🍽 **L** all wk 12-3

D Mon-Sat 6.30-10, Sun 6.30-9.30 **Rooms:** 8 en suite **S** £110-£120 **D** £110-£160
Facilities: Parking Garden **Notes:** ⊕ FREE HOUSE 🛉 🐾 ♟ 8

This attractive family-run free house, which sits in the heart of the Coln Valley, has a rich history. It was
once a coaching inn, which some say was used by smugglers. Formerly known as the Lord Chedworth's
Arms, it is now a quintessential Cotswold dining pub with rooms. The four-acre grounds are home to
deer, foxes, badgers and kingfishers, and there's a lake and the River Coln running through. Today
the inn successfully combines original features such as exposed beams, stone walls, open fires and
flagstone floors with high levels of comfort and service. Samantha Jenkins is the general manager and
daughter of the owner, Robert Jenkins. The atmospheric Bridge Bar and Restaurant is located in the
oldest part of the building and is a great place to enjoy the wide selection of beers, ales, wines, spirits
and soft drinks; some produced in the Cotswolds. Under the care of French head chef, the inn's varied
bar and restaurant menus offer dishes made from local produce, from light snacks to main courses such
as shallow-fried Billingsgate cod with chips and mushy peas or best end of lamb, fondant potatoes, fine
beans wrapped in bacon. There are eight luxury bedrooms and Lakeside Cottage in the grounds.

Recommended in the area

Chedworth Roman Villa (NT); Warwick Castle; Oxford

The Weighbridge Inn

Address: MINCHINHAMPTON, GL6 9AL
Tel: 01453 832520
Fax: 01453 835903
Email: enquiries@2in1pub.co.uk
Website: www.2in1pub.co.uk
Map ref: 2 SO80
Directions: Between Nailsworth & Avening on B4014
Open: all day all week noon-11 (Sun noon-10.30)
Closed: 25 Dec & 10 days Jan ⌷ L all wk 12-9.30
D all wk 12-9.30 ⓘ L all wk 12-9.30 D all wk

12-9.30 **Facilities:** Parking Garden **Notes:** ⊕ FREE HOUSE ⓧ ⓧ ⓧ 16

By the side of the old packhorse road to Bristol, now a footpath and bridleway, stands this part-17th-century classic Cotswold inn. The weighbridge that once was here used to serve the local woollen mills, weighing the raw materials on arrival, and again when the finished cloth left for markets in Bristol, Bath and London. An illustration on the cover of the restaurant menu shows how it looked when the horse-drawn vehicles lined up to have their cargoes weighed, while memorabilia from the mills themselves and rural artefacts from the area are displayed around the pub. In the bar and restaurant you'll find a good choice of real ales, wines and traditional home-prepared hearty fare, including the inn's 'famous 2-in-1' pies. First produced here more than 30 years ago, these double delights contain a filling of your choice, such as salmon in a creamy sauce, or steak and kidney, in one half, while the other can be packed with cauliflower cheese, broccoli mornay or root vegetables to give a variety of combinations. Other main courses include lamb shank, seafood bake, chicken Maryland, and spinach and mushroom lasagne. Outside, the patios and sheltered landscaped gardens offer good views of the Cotswolds.

Recommended in the area

Westonbirt Arboretum; Woodchester Mansion; Chavenage House

The Ostrich Inn

Address: NEWLAND, nr Coleford, GL16 8NP
Tel: 01594 833260
Fax: 01594 833260
Email: kathryn@theostrichinn.com
Website: www.theostrichinn.com
Map ref: 2 SO50
Directions: Follow Monmouth signs from Chepstow (A466), Newland signed from Redbrook
Open: all week **Facilities:** Garden
Notes: ⊕ FREE HOUSE ⋔ ⋔

A 13th-century free house in a pretty village close to two Areas of Outstanding Natural Beauty, the Forest of Dean and the Wye Valley. It was constructed for the workmen who built All Saints church opposite, known locally as the Cathedral of the Forest. The pub's name probably came from the ostrich emblem used by the Probyn family, one-time local landowners. An unusual feature is the priest hole, alongside the more predictable wooden beams and log fire warming the large lounge bar, where landlady Kathryn Horton serves up to eight regular and guest real ales. You eat in the small, intimate restaurant, the larger bar, the walled garden or on the patio, choosing dishes such as freshly prepared rack of Welsh lamb with merguez sausage and smoked belly pork in rich Madeira sauce; monkfish and tiger prawns in rich chive butter cream sauce, Gruyère mashed potato and dressed salad leaves; or creamy wild mushroom and wilted rocket risotto, lemon and white truffle oil and wild mushroom scented pepper. In the bar expect 'fulfilling' soup, pastas, sizzling ribs, and three cheese 'certainly not a quiche' tart. With a reference to an affordable wine list, The Ostrich can rest its case.

Recommended in the area

Clearwell Caves; Dick Whittington Family Leisure Park; National Diving and Activity Centre, Chepstow

Cloisters at Gloucester Cathedral

The Puesdown Inn

★★★★ ⑧⑧ INN

Address: Compton Abdale, NORTHLEACH,
Cheltenham, GL54 4DN
Tel: 01451 860262 **Fax:** 01451 861262
Email: inn4food@btopenworld.com
Website: www.puesdown.cotswoldinns.com
Map ref: 3 SP11 **Directions:** On A40 between
Oxford & Cheltenham, 3m W of Northleach
Closed: Sun eve & Mon eve ♨ ⑩ L all wk 12-3
D Tue-Sat 6-10.30 **Rooms:** 3 en suite (3 GF)
S £50-£79.50 D £79.50-£89.50 **Facilities:** Parking Garden **Notes:** ⊕ FREE HOUSE ⋔ ⋌ ⬥ 15

A former coaching inn, with oak flooring, log fires, cosy sofas and chef-patron John Armstrong's
excellent modern British, lunch and dinner menus. At lunchtime, there's pub favourites like steak and
ale pie, while dinner might offer baked scallop infused with Pernod and thyme, and Old Spot black
pudding; lamb with dauphinoise potatoes; and traditional stone-baked pizzas from a state-of-the-art
oven. Bedrooms offer king-size beds and storm showers. There is also a patio and large garden.
Recommended in the area
Cotswold Farm Park; Bourton-on-the-Water Model Village; Hailes Abbey (NT)

The Bell at Sapperton

Address: SAPPERTON, Cirencester, GL7 6LE
Tel: 01285 760298
Fax: 01285 760761
Email: thebell@sapperton66.freeserve.co.uk
Website: www.foodatthebell.co.uk
Map ref: 2 SO90
Directions: From A419 halfway between Cirencester & Stroud
follow signs for Sapperton. Pub in village centre near church
Open: all week 11-2.30 6.30-11 (Sun 12-10.30) 🍴 **L** all wk
12-2.15 **D** all wk 7-9.15 **Facilities:** Parking Garden
Notes: ⊕ FREE HOUSE 🚻 🍷 20

Regular diners come to this contemporarily-styled Cotswold pub,
located in an idyllic and historic village close to the source of the River Thames, for Paul Davidson and
Pat LeJeune's regularly-changing menus. These are based on produce from an impressive line-up of
West Country and Welsh Borders suppliers. If you want just a drink, there are plenty of wines by the
glass, while Paul's passion for real ales ensures his Uley Old Spot and Otter Bitter are always in tip-top
condition. Although the Bell could hardly be further from the sea, it enjoys a reputation for the freshest
fish and seafood, so check the chalkboards for the day's catch, which might include wild salmon,
turbot, brill, and scallops (a wider selection is offered at weekends). The daily changing lunchtime menu
features both light dishes, such as grilled sardines on red peppers with olive oil dressing, and more
substantial ones, such as bacon chop with free-range fried egg and Chesterton Farm black pudding.
Evening choices are home-cured salt cod croquette with pickled chicory, tomato and tarragon dressing;
chargrilled Hereford rib-eye steak with roast tomato and mushrooms; and butternut and mascarpone
risotto infused with truffle oil and salad leaves.

Recommended in the area

Cotswold Water Park; Westonbirt Arboretum; The Cotswolds

Hailes Abbey

The Swan at Southrop

@@

Address: SOUTHROP, Nr Lechlade, GL7 3NU
Tel: 01367 850205
Fax: 01367 850517
Email: info@theswanatsouthrop.co.uk
Website: www.theswanatsouthrop.co.uk
Map ref: 3 SP10
Directions: Off A361 between Lechlade & Burford
Open: all week L 12-3 D 6-10.30 L 12-3 D 6-10.30 **Notes:** FREE HOUSE 10

A beautifully kept, foliage-covered, early 17th-century Cotswold inn on the village green. The interior is light and airy in summer, yet in the colder months, with log fires burning, you couldn't wish for a cosier place. In the quarry-tiled snug, old Penguin paperbacks line the mantelpiece over the open fire, while in the restaurant modern art lines the white walls. Antony Worrall-Thompson protégé Sebastian Snow and his wife Lana relaunched the Swan in September 2008; he cooks 'turf to table' food, while Lana looks after front of house. Menus include a carte, a simpler bar menu and a weekend roast.

Recommended in the area

Bibury; Buscot Park; Cotswold Water Park

Bear of Rodborough Hotel

★★★ 77% HOTEL

Address: Rodborough Common, STROUD, GL5 5DE
Tel: 01453 878522
Fax: 01453 872523
Email: info@bearofrodborough.co.uk
Website: www.cotswold-inns-hotels.co.uk/bear
Map ref: 2 SO80
Directions: From M5 junct 13 follow signs for Stonehouse then Rodborough
Open: all week **Rooms:** 46 en suite **Facilities:** Parking Garden **Notes:** ⊕ FREE HOUSE ⚬ 🛱 ☌ 6

Set at the top of a steep hill and surrounded by 300 acres of National Trust land, The Bear of Rodborough is situated in the historic south west corner of the Cotswolds. This 17th-century former coaching inn has 46 bedrooms and is worth seeking out for all sorts of reasons: comfortable accommodation, open log fires, stone walls and solid wooden floors, and provides a luxurious retreat where you can enjoy fine food and drink while relaxing in a homely, friendly atmosphere. The delightful Yorkstone terrace area and the walled croquet lawn and gardens provide the perfect spot for relaxing with friends or just catching the sun in the afternoon or on a warm summer's evening. The restaurant with its stone-arched dining room is a great setting for the contemporary English cuisine with strong traditional influences, which uses the finest fresh ingredients, many produced locally. The seasonal menu might include caramelised loin of Old Spot pork wrapped in Parma ham or roasted pumpkin and parmesan risotto. Enjoy fine traditional British ales in the Grizzly Bar, where there is an extensive menu if you wish to lunch or dine in a more relaxed atmosphere.

Recommended in the area

Owlpen Manor; Westonbirt Arboretum; Stroud House Gallery

Gumstool Inn

Address: Calcot Manor, TETBURY, GL8 8YJ
Tel: 01666 890391
Fax: 01666 890394
Email: reception@calcotmanor.co.uk
Website: www.calcotmanor.co.uk
Map ref: 2 ST89
Directions: 3m W of Tetbury **Open:** all week 11.30-2.30 5.30-11 **L** all wk 11.30-2 **D** all wk 7-9.30 **L** all wk 12-2 **D** all wk 7-9.30 **Facilities:** Parking Garden **Notes:** FREE HOUSE 12

The cheerful and cosy Gumstool is part of Calcot Manor Hotel, set in 220 acres of Cotswold countryside. As a free house, Gumstool stocks a good selection of real ales, mostly from the West Country, and an excellent choice of wines. The food is top-notch gastro-pub quality – no wonder, as it comes from the same kitchen as its 'big sister', the hotel's Conservatory restaurant, meticulously supervised by Executive Chef Director Michael Croft. There is a pretty sun terrace outside, while dark winter evenings are warmed with cosy log fires.

Recommended in the area

Westonbirt Arboretum; Slimbridge Wetlands Centre; Tetbury

The Farriers Arms

Address: Main Street, TODENHAM, Moreton-in-Marsh, GL56 9PF
Tel: 01608 650901
Email: info@farriersarms.com
Website: www.farriersarms.com
Map ref: 3 SP23
Directions: Right to Todenham at N end of Moreton-in-Marsh. 2.5m from Shipston on Stour
Open: all week noon-3 6-11 (Sun noon-3 6.30-11) **L** Mon-Sat 12-2, Sun 12-2.30 **D** Mon-Sat 6-9, Sun 6.30-9 **Facilities:** Parking Garden **Notes:** FREE HOUSE 11

Just three miles from Moreton-in-Marsh, stands this pretty, traditional Cotswold pub, next door to the old village smithy. The Farriers Arms dates from 1650 and has all the features you'd associate with a country local: a large inglenook fireplace with a wood-burning stove, exposed stonework, hop-hung beams and polished flagstone floors. To complete the picture there is a great choice of real ales on offer along with excellent food served in both the bar and restaurant. For warmer days there is a beautiful terraced garden.

Recommended in the area

Batsford Arboretum; Chastleton House; Cotswold Falconry Centre

Dunham Massey Hall, Altrincham

The Victoria

Address: Stamford Street, ALTRINCHAM, WA14 1EX
Tel: 0161 613 1855
Email: the.victoria@yahoo.co.uk
Map ref: 6 SJ78
Directions: From rail station, cross main road, turn right. 2nd left onto Stamford St
Open: all day all week noon-11 (Sun noon-6) **Closed:** 26 Dec & 1 Jan 🍺 **L** Mon-Sat 12-3 **D** Mon-Sat 5.30-9 🍽 **L** Mon-Sat 12-3, Sun 12-4 **D** Mon-Sat 5.30-9 **Notes:** 👪 🍷 9

Situated in the Stamford quarter of Altrincham, tucked away behind the main shopping street, the Victoria has been carefully restored as a traditional food-led tavern. This small, one-roomed pub now offers a wood-panelled dining area to one side, and a more casual bar area on the other. As well as the main menu, which changes every six to eight weeks according to seasonal availability and majors on locally sourced ingredients, there's a lighter lunch menu. Starters might include Morecambe Bay brown shrimp and battered prawn cocktail; Bury black pudding Scotch egg topped with locally smoked bacon; or Blacksticks Blue cheese and broad bean rice pudding. Among the main courses may be naturally raised Cumbrian pink veal and mushroom steamed pudding; and oven-roasted monkfish on a bed of pease pudding. On Sunday, a traditional roast is also available, usually including locally raised rib of beef. The wine list features over 30 carefully chosen bottles, while there are a range of hand-pulled cask ales, as well as many non-alcoholic drinks from the temperance bar, such as Dandelion and Burdock. The search is on for products no longer seen on menus, and future delights may include dishes such as tripe, smoked eel and pressed tongue.

Recommended in the area

Dunham Massey Hall Park and Garden (NT); Altrincham Market; Altrincham Ice Dome

The Spinnaker Tower, Portsmouth

The Wellington Arms

◉◉

Address: Baughurst Road, BAUGHURST, RG26 5LP
Tel: 0118 982 0110
Email: info@thewellingtonarms.com
Website: www.thewellingtonarms.com
Map ref: 3 SU56 **Directions:** M4 junct 12
follow Newbury signs on A4. At rdbt left signed
Aldermaston. Through Aldermaston. Up hill,
at next rdbt 2nd exit, left at T-junct, pub 1m on
left **Closed:** Mon, Sun eve, Tue L ⏺ L Wed-Sun

12-2.30 D Tue-Sat 6.30-9.30 **Facilities:** Parking Garden **Notes:** ⊕ PUNCH TAVERNS ♦♦ ⌁ ♟ 12

The Wellington Arms is an exceptionally pretty whitewashed building, set amid well-tended gardens,
surrounded by fields and woodland. This is Jason King and Simon Page's first venture in the pub
trade and after four years their elegantly furnished dining room has a well-deserved reputation for its
impressive daily-changing menus and very good value lunches. The board is chalked up daily with
many of the pub's home-grown favourites; crispy fried, pumpkin flowers stuffed with ricotta, parmesan
and lemon zest on young leaves; roast rack of home-reared Saddleback pork with crackling, sticky red
cabbage and roast new potatoes; jelly made from their own elderflower cordial with strawberries and
thick cream. Further evidence of the commitment to quality are the pub's three Langstroth beehives,
200 free-range, rare breed hens, eight pedigree Saddleback and Tamworth pigs, herb and vegetable
gardens, home-made jams, chutneys and pickles together with careful sourcing of organic and home-
grown produce. Fish is delivered direct from the market in Brixham and English meat comes from
Vicars family butchers in Reading. From Australia there's an exclusive range of Aesop soaps and hand
cream, Husk herbal teas and pink salt flakes from the Murray River area, all available to buy.
Recommended in the area
The Vyne (NT); Basing House; Roman Silchester

The Sun Inn

Address: Sun Hill, BENTWORTH,
Alton, GU34 5JT
Tel: 01420 562338
Map ref: 3 SU64
Directions: Telephone for directions
Open: all week
Facilities: Parking Garden
Notes: ⊕ FREE HOUSE ♦♦ ⚥ ♛ 6

This delightful, flower-adorned, 17th-century free house on the village outskirts always seems to be pleasantly busy, which might make you wonder why some pubs always seem to be empty. Well, the Sun Inn does have some considerable advantages - it was built as two cottages, which helps to explain today's series of interconnecting, original brick- and wood-floored rooms, each with a log fire, furnished with scrubbed, candlelit tables, pews and settles, and decorated with hanging hops and old photographs. You enter the middle room, which is the bar, where eight, yes eight, real ales, mostly from Hampshire and neighbouring counties, are lined up for beer drinkers' delectation. The home-prepared food listed on the blackboards is of the hearty and traditional kind that customers from the Sun's rural hinterland must relish, such as beef Stroganoff; a range of meat and vegetarian curries; liver and bacon; cheesy haddock bake; filled Yorkshire puddings; braised steak in red wine and mushroom sauce; and Mediterranean lamb. They're pretty keen too on game in season, including pheasant dishes and venison cooked in Guinness with pickled walnuts. The desserts are home made too. Outside, there are tables and a pretty sunken garden, sheltered by tall hedges and reached via a rustic archway.

Recommended in the area

Jane Austen's House, Chawton; Gilbert White's House & Oates Museum, Selborne; Watercress Line

King John's Hunting Lodge at Wilk's Water

The Red Lion

Address: Rope Hill, BOLDRE, Lymington, SO41 8NE
Tel: 01590 673177 **Fax:** 01590 674036
Website: www.theredlionboldre.co.uk
Map ref: 3 SZ39
Directions: From M27 junct 1 through Lyndhurst & Brockenhurst towards Lymington, follow Boldre signs
Open: 11-3 5.30-11 (Sun noon-4 6-10.30) ► †⊙¶ **L** Mon-Sat 12-2.30, Sun 12-3.30 **D** Mon-Sat 6-9.30, Sun 6-9 (Sun 12-9 Summer) **Facilities:** Parking Garden **Notes:** ⊕ FREE HOUSE †† ⌁ ¶ 18

A proper New Forest Pub mentioned in the Domesday Book, although today's inn dates from the 15th century. Incorporating original stables and old cottages, the interior has a cosy, rambling feel with low beams, fires and authentic copper and brasses. Offering fresh locally sourced food, the pub belongs to the Associate Members of The New Forest Marque for using and promoting New Forest produce. Dishes are traditional and home made, often featuring local venison, game and seafood, plus old fashioned home-made puddings. Enjoy monthly Pie and Pudding Evenings for £10.
Recommended in the area
Bucklers Hard; Hurst Castle; Beaulieu

Carnarvon Arms

Address: Winchester Road, WHITWAY, Burghclere,
Newbury, RG20 9LE
Tel: 01635 278222
Fax: 01635 278444
Email: info@carnarvonarms.com
Website: www.carnarvonarms.com
Map ref: 3 SU45
Directions: M4 junct 13, A34 S to Winchester. Exit
A34 at Tothill Services, follow Highclere Castle signs.
Pub on right

Open: all week ♨ ⵣ L Mon-Sat 12-2.30, Sun 12-6 **D** Mon-Thu 6.30-9, Fri-Sat 6.30-9.30, Sun
6.30-8.30 **Facilities:** Parking Garden **Notes:** ⵣ ⵣ ⵣ 15

This stylish country inn was built in the mid-1800s as a coaching inn for travellers to nearby Highclere
Castle, which has been the home of the Earls of Carnarvon since the late 17th century. Now completely
refurbished, the inn's interior strongly reflects its history, in particular its relationship with one of the
20th century's most famous archaeologists, the 5th Earl, who in 1922 discovered Tutankhamun's tomb
in the Valley of the Kings. In the dining room, with its impressive vaulted ceiling, Egyptian-inspired wall
motifs pay homage to his work; in the friendly bar rich leather upholstery is offset by natural colours.
The kitchen team oversees excellent modern British cooking interlaced with plenty of pub classics, all
with a strong emphasis on local seasonal produce, and menus change accordingly. Examples of what
to expect are pan-fried scallops with buttered samphire and herb fish cream, rump of English lamb with
fine beans, sun-blushed tomatoes and rosemary sauce, and Mr Parsons' local sausages with mash and
shallot sauce. Comfortable private rooms are available for business meetings, corporate events and
private parties.
Recommended in the area
Newbury Races; Watermill Theatre; Kennet & Avon Canal

The East End Arms

Address: Main Road, EAST END, nr Lymington, S041 5SY
Tel/Fax: 01590 626223
Email: manager@eastendarms.co.uk
Website: www.eastendarms.co.uk
Map ref: 3 SZ39
Directions: From Lymington towards Beaulieu (past Isle of Wight ferry), 3m to East End **Open:** all week 🍽 **L** all wk 12-2.30 **D** Mon-Sat 7-9.30 **Facilities:** Parking Garden **Notes:** FREE HOUSE

The East End Arms Pub and Restaurant cleverly combines serious food with local tradition. The emphasis is on fresh local ingredients and a varied menu which is changed daily. The is an abundance of charm and character with roaring log fires in the winter and a pretty courtyard garden for the summer. A recent addition to the pub is five en suite bedrooms. This traditional New Forest pub is owned by the former Dire Straits bass guitarist, John Illsley, and is idyllically situated between Lymington and Beaulieu.

Recommended in the area

Bucklers Hard; Hurst Castle; Beaulieu Motor Museum

The Chestnut Horse

Address: EASTON, Winchester, S021 1EG
Tel: 01962 779257
Fax: 01962 779037
Website: www.thechestnuthorse.com
Map ref: 3 SU53
Directions: From M3 junct 9 take A33 towards Basingstoke, then B3047. Take 2nd right, then 1st left **Open:** all week noon-3.30 5.30-11 (Sun eve closed winter) **L** all wk 12-2.30 **D** Mon-Sat 6-9.30 🍽 **L** all wk 12-2 **D** Mon-Sat 6-9.30
Facilities: Parking Garden **Notes:** HALL & WOODHOUSE 9

This 16th-century dining pub has a well-earned local reputation for the quality of its food. Old tankards and teapots hang from the low-beamed ceilings in the two bar areas, where a large open fire is the central focus in winter. The candlelit restaurants are equally inviting: the light, panelled Green Room, and the darker low-beamed Red Room with a wood-burning stove. Menus might include pork tenderloin, garlic roast potatoes, purées of beetroot and orange or Bombay crusted hake fillet and lemon confit potatoes.

Recommended in the area

Watercress Steam Railway; River Itchen (walking, fishing); Intech Science Museum

The Bugle

Address: High Street, HAMBLE-LE-RICE, SO31 4HA
Tel: 023 8045 3000
Fax: 023 8045 3051
Email: manager@buglehamble.co.uk
Website: www.buglehamble.co.uk
Map ref: 3 SU40
Directions: M27 junct 8, follow signs to Hamble. In village centre turn right at mini-rdbt into one-way cobbled street, pub at end
Open: all week ♿ **L** Mon-Thu 12-2.30, Fri 12-3, Sat 12-10, Sun 12-9 **D** Mon-Thu 6-9.30, Fri 6-10, Sat 12-10, Sun 12-9 **Notes:** ♦♦ ♊ 8

The Bugle is at the heart of village life with its charming waterside location and river views. The Grade II listed building features natural flagstone floors, exposed beams and brickwork, a solid oak bar and real open fires. In addition to the restaurant area, a private dining room, the Captain's Table, is available upstairs, accommodating up to 12 guests. The seasonal menu is based on fresh, top quality ingredients, using local produce wherever possible, with meals served alongside well-kept local real ales, wine and speciality rums. The menu offers a good range of bar bites such as salt 'n' pepper squid and devilled whitebait. For something a bit more substantial, there's Hampshire free-range beef burger, relish and skinny chips; south coast day boat sole with lemon and parsley butter and new potatoes. Fresh seafood and other home-made dishes are offered from the daily specials board, and there's a tempting range of desserts. At weekends, The Bugle's traditional roasts are popular. Alfresco dining with river views is possible, plus there are heated umbrellas if the weather's not quite at its best. Dogs are allowed, but not in the restaurant.

Recommended in the area

Hamble River boat trips; Royal Victoria Country Park; Netley Abbey

Squabb Woods at Romsey

The Vine at Hannington

Address: HANNINGTON, Tadley, RG26 5TX
Tel: 01635 298525
Fax: 01635 298027
Email: info@thevineathannington.co.uk
Website: www.thevineathannington.co.uk
Map ref: 3 SU55
Directions: Hannington signed from A339 between Basingstoke & Newbury **Open:** 12-3 6-11 (Sat-Sun all day) **Closed:** 25 Dec, Mon & Sun eve in Winter
🍴 **L** Tues-Fri 12-2, Sat-Sun 12-2.30 **D** all wk 6-9
🍽 **L** Tues-Fri 12-2, Sat-Sun 12-2.30 **D** all wk 6-9 **Facilities:** Parking Garden **Notes:** 👫 🐕 🍷 10

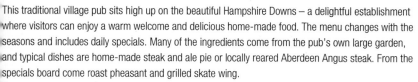

This traditional village pub sits high up on the beautiful Hampshire Downs – a delightful establishment where visitors can enjoy a warm welcome and delicious home-made food. The menu changes with the seasons and includes daily specials. Many of the ingredients come from the pub's own large garden, and typical dishes are home-made steak and ale pie or locally reared Aberdeen Angus steak. From the specials board come roast pheasant and grilled skate wing.

Recommended in the area

Highclere Castle; The Wayfarers Walk; Milestones Museum, Basingstoke

The Plough Inn

Address: LONGPARISH, Andover, SP11 6PB
Tel: 01264 720358
Email: eat@theploughinn.info
Website: www.theploughinn.info
Map ref: 3 SU44
Directions: From M3 junct 8 take A303 towards
Andover. In approx 6m take B3048 towards
Longparish **Closed:** 25 Dec, Sun eve
Facilities: Parking Garden
Notes: ⊕ ENTERPRISE INNS ♦♦ ⚐ 🍷 10

Parish records date this charming village inn to 1721, although it has certainly seen some changes since then. A convenient mile from the A303, it stands, quite literally, on the Test Way - the path cuts through the car park. The Test itself, one of Britain's finest trout rivers, is close enough for its resident ducks to waddle over to be fed by diners in the garden. Inside it is warm and comfortable, with flagstone and oak floors, leather chairs, soft furnishings and open log fires, any remaining spaces filled with fishing memorabilia and bric-a-brac. Lunch choices include roasted Mediterranean vegetable and goat's cheese salad; smoked salmon; pasta of the day; beer-battered fish and chips; liver and bacon with wholegrain mustard mash; and grilled halloumi, tomato and olive polenta with creamed leeks. The dinner menu has some additional items, such as 10oz rib-eye and sirloin steaks; fresh local trout fillets with sautéed tarragon gnocchi; and pan-fried chicken supreme with chorizo, lentil and borlotti bean cassoulet. A typical dessert would be baked blueberry and white chocolate cheesecake with damson jam. As for wine, it would be a picky customer indeed who couldn't find something suitable on the well put-together list.

Recommended in the area

Hawk Conservancy; Stonehenge; Mottisfont Abbey

The Fox

Address: NORTH WALTHAM,
Basingstoke, RG25 2BE
Tel: 01256 397288
Email: info@thefox.org
Website: www.thefox.org
Map ref: 3 SU54
Directions: From M3 junct 7 take A30 towards
Winchester. Village signed on right. Take 2nd signed
road **Open:** all day all week 11-11 **Closed:** 25 Dec
L all wk 12-2.30 Sun 12-3 **D** all wk 6-9.30
Sun 6.30-8.30 **Facilities:** Parking Garden **Notes:** FREE HOUSE 14

It is well worth leaving the tedium of the M3 for this free house and restaurant in a country lane just off the motorway's junction 7. It was once three 17th-century farm cottages, as becomes evident when you see the exposed beams and open fires. In the restaurant the fresh flowers look lovely, while in the cosy Village Bar are beers from Brakspear, Ringwood and the Hobgoblin, at least ten bottled ciders, and fourteen wines by the glass. Not for consumption, though, is the collection of miniatures - more than 1,100 so far and counting (further contributions are always welcome). The bar and monthly changing restaurant menus and daily blackboard specials make full use of local game and other produce, including vegetable and herbs from the garden and daily deliveries of fresh fish from the coast. Specialities include a superb cheese soufflé and main courses of Shetland mussels steamed in white wine and garlic; pork tenderloin medallions; halibut fillet stuffed with salmon mousseline; and wild mushroom Stroganoff. Regular 'special menu' evenings – Burns Supper and St George's Day, for example – are always popular. Meals can be served in the large garden, which includes a children's play area.

Recommended in the area

The Vyne; Winchester Cathedral; Stonehenge

The Bush

Address: OVINGTON, Alresford, SO24 0RE
Tel: 01962 732764
Fax: 01962 735130
Email: thebushinn@wadworth.co.uk
Website: www.wadworth.co.uk
Map ref: 3 SU53
Directions: A31 from Winchester, E to Alton & Farnham, approx 6m turn left off dual carriageway to Ovington. 0.5m to pub
Open: all day all week **Facilities:** Parking Garden
Notes: ⊞ WADWORTH 🐾 ♟ 12

A rose-covered vision of a bygone age, The Bush is as delightful as it is hard to find, tucked away just off a meandering lane and overhung by trees. Once a refreshment stop on the Pilgrim's Way linking Winchester and Canterbury, these days the pub is more likely to attract walkers exploring the Itchen Way. A gentle riverside stroll along the Itchen, which flows past the pretty garden, will certainly set you up for a leisurely drink or a lingering meal. The pub's interior is dark and atmospheric; there's a central wooden bar, high backed seats and pews, stuffed animals on the wall and a real fire. Ales on offer include Wadworth 6X, IPA and Malt & Hops, JCB, Horizon, Old Timer and guest beers. The regularly-changing menu makes good use of local produce. Choices range from bar snacks, sandwiches and ploughman's lunches through to satisfying gastro-pub meals, taking in the likes of organic smoked trout mousse with warm toast, and slow-roasted belly pork on braised Savoy cabbage with organic cider jus. Finish with a traditional pudding such as Eton mess or rhubarb crumble. Not surprisingly, film crews love this location.

Recommended in the area

Avington Park; Winchester Cathedral; Mid-Hants Railways

Eyeworth Pond at Fritham

The Rose & Thistle

Address: ROCKBOURNE, Fordingbridge, SP6 3NL
Tel: 01725 518236
Email: enquiries@roseandthistle.co.uk
Website: www.roseandthistle.co.uk
Map ref: 3 SU11
Directions: Follow Rockbourne signs from A354 (Salisbury to Blandford Forum road), or from A338 at Fordingbridge follow signs to Rockbourne **Open:** all week 🛏 **L** all wk 12-2.30 **D** Mon-Sat 7-9.30 🍽 **L** all wk 12-2.30 **D** Mon-Sat 7-9.30 **Facilities:** Parking Garden **Notes:** ⊞ FREE HOUSE ♦♦ 🚶 ♟ 12

Nestling in one of the most picturesque villages in the county, on the edge of the New Forest, the Rose & Thistle has everything you'd expect from the quintessential English pub: a tranquil setting, flowers around the door and a beautiful old building dating back to the 16th century. It has a welcoming low-ceilinged interior with oak beams and furniture, fresh flowers, magazines and an open fireplace. In summer, you can enjoy the delightful country garden. Well-kept real ales – Fuller's London Pride, Timothy Taylor Landlord and Palmers Copper Ale – are on offer, along with Scrumpy (cider), a carefully selected wine list and other drinks. Fresh seasonal food is cooked to order and includes fish such as skate, turbot and Cornish crab when available. The restaurant menu, available at lunch and dinner, offers dishes such as venison steak with sloe gin and blackberries, pork belly with crab apple gravy, and tagliatelle with feta, spinach and sun blush tomatoes. Lighter lunch choices might include scrambled eggs with crispy proscuitto, locally-made pork and sausages with wholegrain mustard mash, and chickpea and butternut squash crumble; the Sunday lunch of rare roast sirloin of beef is also very popular. Desserts are all home made and an extensive local cheeseboard is delicious.

Recommended in the area

Rockbourne Roman Villa and Trout Fishery; Breamore House; Salisbury

The Plough Inn

Address: Main Road, SPARSHOLT, Nr Winchester, SO21 2NW
Tel: 01962 776353
Fax: 01962 776400
Map ref: 3 SU43
Directions: From Winchester take B3049 (A272) W,
left to Sparsholt, Inn 1m
Open: all week **Closed:** 25 Dec
Facilities: Parking Garden
Notes: ⊕ WADWORTH ♦♦ ⚞ ♟ 14

Set in beautiful countryside, just a stone's throw from
Winchester, this inn is a great place to refresh yourself after a
walk in the nearby Farley Mount Country Park. Owners Richard
and Kathryn Crawford have a simple philosophy: to serve customers with good quality food and drink
in a friendly atmosphere. The Plough was built about 200 years ago as a coach house for Sparsholt
Manor, but within 50 years it had already become an alehouse. Since then it has been much extended,
yet from the inside it all blends together very well, helped by the farmhouse-style furniture and the
adornment with agricultural implements, stone jars and dried hops. The Wadworth brewery supplies all
of the real ales, and there's a good wine selection. The left-hand dining area is served by a blackboard
menu offering such light dishes as feta and spinach filo parcels with a Thai pesto dressing or a beef,
ale and mushroom pie with vegetables. To the right, a separate board offers meals that reflect a more
serious approach – perhaps breast of chicken filled with mushrooms on a garlic and bacon sauce; lamb
shank with braised red cabbage and rosemary jus; and several fish dishes. Booking is always advisable.
Recommended in the area
Winchester Cathedral; Mottisfont Abbey (NT); Sir Harold Hillier Gardens and Arboretum

The Wykeham Arms

Address: 75 Kingsgate Street,
WINCHESTER, SO23 9PE
Tel: 01962 853834
Fax: 01962 854411
Email: wykeham.arms@fullers.co.uk
Website: www.fullershotels.com/rte.asp?id=129
Map ref: 3 SU42
Directions: Near Winchester College & Winchester Cathedral
Open: all day all week 11-11 (Sun 11-10.30)
 L Mon-Sat 12-3 L all wk 12-3 D all wk 6-9.30
Facilities: Parking Garden **Notes:** FULLERS 18

The 18th-century 'Wyk' stands beyond the cathedral, in the oldest part of the city. A top hostelry indeed, and well worth negotiating some narrow streets for (although its car park is for residents only). It stands on the corner of delightful Canon Street, now a well-to-do conservation area, but in the 19th century a notorious red-light district. An immediate neighbour is the famous college after whose 14th-century founder, William of Wykeham, it is named. Please turn off your mobile before entering the L-shaped bar, warmed by three wood-burning fires, with old college desks to sit at, and walls and ceilings blanketed with memorabilia, curiosities and framed lists of Old Wykehamists, their names Latinised. Fuller's range of real ales is partnered by a comprehensive wine list, a sensible number available by the glass. Eat in the bar or one of the bijou side rooms on famous Wyk Pie; South Coast king scallops with celeriac purée and crispy pancetta; or confit rabbit leg and pan-fried loin with sauté potatoes, creamed leeks and red wine jus. Dark chocolate nemesis is a memorable dessert. Beautifully appointed en suite bedrooms are both in the pub and in the 16th-century Saint George building opposite.

Recommended in the area

Gurkha Museum; Wolvesey Castle; City Mill (NT)

River Wye at Hereford

The Riverside Inn

Address: AYMESTREY, nr Leominster, HR6 9ST
Tel: 01568 708440
Fax: 01568 709058
Email: theriverside@btconnect.com
Website: www.theriversideinn.org
Map ref: 2 SO46
Directions: On A4110, 18m N of Hereford
Open: 11-3 6-11 (Sun 12-3 6-10.30) **Closed:** 26
Dec & 1 Jan, Mon lunch, Sun eve in winter
L Tue-Sun 12-2 **D** Mon-Sat 7-9 L Tue-Sun
12-2 **D** Mon-Sat 7-9 **Facilities:** Parking Garden **Notes:** FREE HOUSE 7

Alongside the lovely River Lugg, overlooking an old stone bridge, this delightful black-and-white inn is surrounded by wooded hills and meadowland. Anglers will certainly appreciate the mile of private fly fishing for brown trout and grayling on the river here. It is located halfway along the Mortimer Way, making it great for walkers, too, and there are a number of circular walks in the vicinity. Walking packages are offered at the inn, with accommodation and free transport provided to and from the start/ finish points. The interior of the building, with its low beams and log fires, provides a relaxing atmosphere, reflecting the 400 years of hospitality that have been carried out on this spot. Richard and Liz Gresko are the current hosts, who take a serious approach to food. Locally-grown produce is used wherever possible, including vegetables, salads and herbs from their own gardens, and home-made preserves. The type of cuisine here is English, but with a new and interesting twist. Real ales and ciders from local brewers match bar food specialities such as grilled organic chicken, wilted kale and red wine jus, while the restaurant menu might include tenderloin of local pork stuffed with apricot, prune and pistachios. On a summer's day, sit outside in the terraced and landscaped garden, watching the river flow by.

Recommended in the area

Hergest Croft Gardens; Berrington Hall, Ashton; Croft Castle

Eastnor Castle

Stockton Cross Inn

Address: KIMBOLTON, Leominster, HR6 0HD
Tel: 01568 612509
Email: info@stocktoncrossinn.co.uk
Website: www.stocktoncrossinn.co.uk
Map ref: 2 SO56
Directions: On A4112, 0.5m off A49, between Leominster & Ludlow
Closed: Sun & Mon eve ᴸ L Tue-Sun 12-2 D Tue-Sun 7-9 ˡᴼˡ L Tue-Sun 12-2 D Tue-Sun 7-9
Facilities: Parking Garden
Notes: 🛢 FREE HOUSE ꟊ ♚ 6

Stockton Cross is a 16th-century drovers' inn with real log fires, its picturesque black and white exterior regularly photographed by tourists and for calendars etc. Its peace and beauty are belied by the historical fact that alleged witches were once hanged here. There is a serious interest in good food, with much produce locally sourced to provide an interesting and varied menu. The relaxed and friendly atmosphere, real ales and fine wines add to the charm, and there is also a pretty country garden.

Recommended in the area

Hergest Croft Gardens; Croft Castle; Berrington Hall (NT)

The Saracens Head Inn

★★★★ INN

Address: SYMONDS YAT (EAST), HR9 6JL
Tel: 01600 890435
Fax: 01600 890034
Email: contact@saracensheadinn.co.uk
Website: www.saracensheadinn.co.uk
Map ref: 2 SO51
Directions: From Ross-on-Wye take A40 to
Monmouth. In 4m take Symonds Yat East turn. 1st
right before bridge. Right in 0.5m. Right in 1m

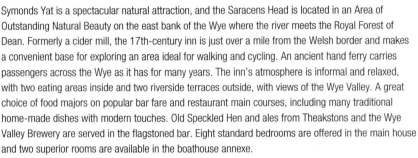

Open: all week 11-11 **Closed:** 25 Dec 🍽 **L** all wk 12-2.30 **D** all wk 6.30-9 🍽 **L** all wk 12-2.30
D all wk 6.30-9 **Rooms:** 10 en suite (1 GF) **S** £50-£70 **D** £79-£130 **Facilities:** Parking Garden
Notes: ⊕ FREE HOUSE 🍴 🐾 ☎ 7

Symonds Yat is a spectacular natural attraction, and the Saracens Head is located in an Area of
Outstanding Natural Beauty on the east bank of the Wye where the river meets the Royal Forest of
Dean. Formerly a cider mill, the 17th-century inn is just over a mile from the Welsh border and makes
a convenient base for exploring an area ideal for walking and cycling. An ancient hand ferry carries
passengers across the Wye as it has for many years. The inn's atmosphere is informal and relaxed,
with two eating areas inside and two riverside terraces outside, with views of the Wye Valley. A great
choice of food majors on popular bar fare and restaurant main courses, including many traditional
home-made dishes with modern touches. Old Speckled Hen and ales from Theakstons and the Wye
Valley Brewery are served in the flagstoned bar. Eight standard bedrooms are offered in the main house
and two superior rooms are available in the boathouse annexe.

Recommended in the area

Goodrich Castle; Symonds Yat Rock; Forest of Dean

The Mill Race

Address: WALFORD, Ross-on-Wye, HR9 5QS
Tel: 01989 562891
Email: enquiries@millrace.info
Website: www.millrace.info
Map ref: 2 SO52
Directions: From Ross-on-Wye take B4234 to Walford. Pub 3m on right after village hall
Open: all week 11-3 5-11 (Sat-Sun all day)
L Mon-Fri 11-2, Sat 10-2.30, Sun 12-2.30
D Mon-Sat 6-9.30, Sun 6-9 **L** Mon-Fri 12-2, Sat-Sun 12-2.30 **D** Mon-Sat 6-9.30, Sun 6-9 **Facilities:** Parking Garden **Notes:** ⊕ FREE HOUSE 13

In the beautiful Wye Valley, the award-winning Mill Race is a friendly village gastro-pub whose original stone floors and Welsh slate floor are well complemented by a modern interior. The blazing fire literally ensures a warm welcome, while the large deck offers outdoor dining and views towards Goodrich Castle. The bar serves a selection of local ales and ciders, and the extensive wine list offers thirteen by the glass. An environmentally responsible approach to local food sourcing, including from the pub's own farm, lies behind a regularly changing menu of simple, well-prepared food. Lunch might be vegetarian quiche; free-range chicken, leek and bacon pie; Mill Race burger; or a choice of steaks. Dinner possibilities include Wye Valley battered fish with hand-cut chips; Madgetts duck breast with black pudding risotto; roast saddle of rabbit with sun-blushed tomato mash; and field mushroom and garlic tagliatelle with parmesan. There always seems to be something going on at the Mill Race, with Indian, game and music nights, and even one devoted to Britain's only vodka - distilled in Herefordshire! The pub makes a good base for a variety of local walks, including the challenge-free, one-mile Woodland Walk, which partly follows a disused railway line.

Recommended in the area

Symonds Yat; International Centre for Birds of Prey; Hereford Cathedral

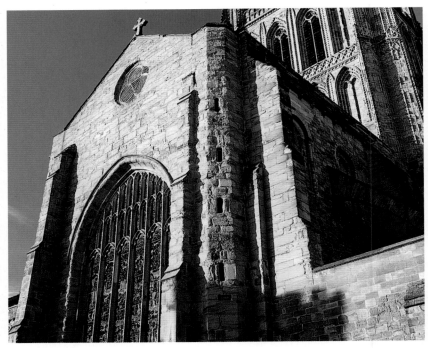

Hereford Cathedral

Rhydspence Inn

★★★★ INN

Address: WHITNEY-ON-WYE, Hereford, HR3 6EU
Tel: 01497 831262
Fax: 01497 831751
Email: info@rhydspence-inn.co.uk
Website: www.rhydspence-inn.co.uk
Map ref: 2 SO24
Directions: N side of A438, 1m W of Whitney-on-Wye **Open:** all week 11-2.30 7-11 🍴 L all wk 11-2 D all wk 7-9 🍽 L all wk 11-2 D all wk 7-9 **Rooms:** 7 en suite **Facilities:** Parking Garden **Notes:** ⊕ FREE HOUSE ⁛

Dating from 1380, this charming inn was probably built for travellers and pilgrims heading for Hereford Cathedral. Later, drovers and their animals rested here en route to faraway markets. Meals and snacks are served in the bars in the heavily beamed Tudor part, while in the elegant dining room expect roast duck breast with pink grapefruit and sambuca sauce; or grilled sea bass fillets on crushed potato with lemon, parmesan and sage butter. Gaze at the Welsh hills from the landscaped terraces and gardens.

Recommended in the area

Hay-on-Wye 'Booktown'; Offas' Dyke Path; Brecon Beacons National Park

The River Wye at Symonds Yat

Mill Wood in Much Hadham

The Bricklayers Arms

Address: Hogpits Bottom, FLAUNDEN,
Nr Hemel Hempstead, HP3 0PH
Tel: 01442 833322
Fax: 01442 834841
Email: goodfood@bricklayersarms.com
Website: www.bricklayersarms.com
Map ref: 3 TL00
Directions: M25 junct 18 onto A404 (Amersham road). Right at
Chenies for Flaunden **Open:** all week 12-11.30 (25 Dec 12-3)
🏠 🍴 **L** Mon-Sat 12-2.30, Sun 12-3.30 **D** Mon-Sat 6.30-9.30,
Sun 6.30-8.30 **Facilities:** Parking Garden **Notes:** ⊕ FREE
HOUSE ⁑ 🐕 🍷 12

This picturesque, 18th-century listed country pub is an ivy-clad, flint building situated in a lovely village at the end of winding lanes that snake between Chipperfield and Latimer. The interior has low wooden beams, exposed brickwork and real log fires, and a warm welcome from Alvin and Sally Michaels is guaranteed. Over the past six years, The Bricklayers Arms has gained an excellent reputation for its traditional English and French fusion menu created by the highly trained and award-winning chef, Claude Paillet. The same menu can be enjoyed throughout the restaurant and pub seven days a week, with dishes including the famous, home-smoked fish plate; home-made terrines; traditional Tring Ale battered cod; 21-day aged fillet steak, and fillet of locally reared Worcestershire Black Spot pork. There's always a choice of fresh fish dishes and vegetarian options on the menu plus tantalising specials of the day. A carefully selected wine list of over 140 varieties to suit all budgets and tastes is available, as well as beers and local ales on tap. If you're thinking of calling in for the ever popular Sunday lunch, be sure to book in advance.

Recommended in the area

Chenies Manor House; Berkhamsted Castle; Ashridge Estate (NT)

Alford Arms

Address: Frithsden, HEMEL HEMPSTEAD, HP1 3DD
Tel: 01442 864480
Fax: 01422 876893
Email: info@alfordarmsfrithsden.co.uk
Website: www.alfordarmsfrithsden.co.uk
Map ref: 3 TL00
Directions: From Hemel Hempstead on A4146 take 2nd left at Water End. In 1m left at T-junct, right after 0.75m. Pub 100yds on right
Open: all day all week 11-11 (Sun 12-10.30)
Closed: 26 Dec 🍽 L Mon-Fri 12-2.30, Sat 12-3, Sun 12-4 **D** Mon-Thu 6.30-9.30, Fri-Sat 6.30-10, Sun 7-9.30 **Facilities:** Parking Garden **Notes:** 🌐 SALISBURY PUBS LTD 🛏 🛩 ⚐ 19

An attractive Victorian pub in the unruffled hamlet of Frithsden, surrounded by National Trust woodland. The flower-filled garden overlooks the village green, and historic Ashridge Forest is nearby. Cross the threshold and in the dining room and bar you'll pick up on the warm and lively atmosphere, derived partly from the buzz of conversation, partly from the discreet background jazz, and partly from the rich colours and eclectic mixture of old furniture and pictures, mostly acquired from Tring salerooms. The seasonal menu and daily specials balance modern British with more traditional fare, mostly prepared from fresh, local produce. A good choice of 'small plates' ranges from rustic breads with roast garlic and olive oil, to oak-smoked bacon on bubble and squeak with hollandaise sauce and poached egg. Main meals with a similarly imaginative approach include Moroccan spiced lamb shank on sweet potato mash, pan juices and cumin yoghurt; Cornish fish stew with saffron potatoes, rouille and gruyère; and pumpkin gnocchi with roast beetroot, porcini, watercress and walnut pesto. Puddings are interestingly tweaked too, such as crispy banana and almond spring roll with lemongrass caramel.

Recommended in the area

Berkhamsted Castle; Walter Rothschild Zoological Museum; Whipsnade Wild Animal Park

Moor Place at Much Hadham

The Fox and Hounds

Address: 2 High Street, HUNSDON, SG12 8NH
Tel: 01279 843999
Fax: 01279 844077
Email: info@foxandhounds-hunsdon.co.uk
Website: www.foxandhounds-hunsdon.co.uk
Map ref: 3 TL41
Directions: From A414 between Ware & Harlow take B180 in Stanstead Abbotts N to Hunsdon
Open: noon-4 6-11 **Closed:** Sun, Mon eve
🍴 **L** Tue-Sun 12-3 **D** Tue-Sat 6.30-9.30

🍽 **L** Sun 12-3 **D** Fri-Sat 7-9.30 **Facilities:** Parking Garden **Notes:** ⊕ FREE HOUSE ♦♦ 🐾 🍷 10

This welcoming pub is set in a pretty village surrounded by Hertfordshire countryside. It has a comfy, laid-back bar featuring a log fire, leather sofas and local ales. There's a large separate dining room and an outside terrace in the large garden. Chef owner James Rix, who trained under some of the industry's top chefs, has quickly made a name for himself at this family-run establishment, with a seasonal menu that combines classics with modern touches, and changes twice a day.

Recommended in the area

Henry Moore Foundation; Paradise Wildlife Park; Lee Valley Park

The Cabinet Free House and Restaurant

Address: High Street, Reed, ROYSTON, SG8 8AH
Tel: 01763 848366
Email: thecabinet@btconnect.com
Website: www.thecabinetatreed.co.uk
Map ref: 3 TL34
Directions: 2m S of Royston, just off A10
Open: 12-3 6-12 (Sat-Sun all day) **Closed:** Mon,
1 Jan ▣ **L** 12-3 **D** 6-9 ▣ **L** 12-3 **D** 6-9 **Facilities:** Parking Garden
Notes: ⊕ FREE HOUSE ▪▪ ▪ ☺ 12

Set foot in Reed and you'll be transported back to the days of old when the houses were surrounded by moats and the public house was the social hub of the village. The word 'cabinet' in the pub's name came into use in the 16th century to describe a small room used as a study, retreat or meeting place. This ties in with the age of this country inn and restaurant, which has a white-painted clapboard exterior, an open fire, shotguns and a delightful bar and snug with an original brick laid floor. There is an air of informality which is reflected on the menus where you will find the sort of dishes the owners themselves like to eat. Alongside the carte there are good value set lunch menus, including one dedicated to roasts on Sundays. Food is prepared from the best local produce, and the dishes draw inspiration from around the world. A meal might begin with River Farm smoked mackerel pâté, horseradish and toast, followed by 21-day aged Tilbury Meadows fillet of beef, roasted beetroot, mustard mash, feta and almond pesto. To round things off, there could be the ever popular apple and raspberry crumble with, of course, 'proper' custard.

Recommended in the area

Imperial War Museum, Duxford; City of Cambridge; Shuttleworth Collection

Rochester Cathedral

Leeds Castle

Griffins Head

Address: CHILLENDEN, Canterbury, CT3 1PS
Tel: 01304 840325
Fax: 01304 841290
Map ref: 4 TR25
Directions: A2 from Canterbury towards Dover, then B2046. Village on right
Open: all week **Closed:** Sun pm ⧫ L 12-2 D 7-9
Facilities: Parking Garden
Notes: ⊞ SHEPHERD NEAME ⚑ 10

Dating from 1286, this Kentish Wealden hall has great historical character, with beamed bars and inglenook fireplaces. Fine Kentish ales from Shepherd Neame and home-made food have helped the old inn to make its mark with visitors as well as locals, among them Kent's cricketing fraternity. The menu is typically English and specialises in game from local estates in season and locally caught fish when possible. Outside there's a very pretty garden where drinkers can linger at their leisure, and a bat and trap pitch (an ancient relative of cricket, still popular in Kent). A vintage car club meets here on the first Sunday of every month.

Recommended in the area

Canterbury; Wingham Bird Park; Howlett's Wild Animal Park

The Plough at Ivy Hatch

Address: High Cross Road, IVY HATCH, TN15 0NL
Tel: 01732 810100
Email: theploughpubco@tiscali.co.uk
Map ref: 4 TQ55
Directions: Off A25 between Borough Green &
Sevenoaks, follow signs to Ightham Mote
Open: all week noon-3 6-11 (Sat noon-11 Sun 10-6)
🥘 L Mon-Sat 12-2.45, Sun 12-6 **D** Mon-Sat 6-9.30
🍽 L Mon-Sat 12-2.45, Sun 12-6 **D** Mon-Sat 6-9.30
Facilities: Parking Garden
Notes: ⊕ FREE HOUSE ♦♦ ♟ 8

Deep in the countryside, this tile-hung village pub is a perfect spot for a lingering lunch or supper. The aim of Miles and Anna Medes is to make it the centre of the community; their driving passion is to source the best locally produced farm products and present them as classic dishes on a British- and European-influenced menu that they update daily, with nothing frozen or pre-made brought in. Typical starters are plum tomato and basil soup, and crayfish tail cocktail with tomato and cucumber salsa; for main courses consider pan-fried gurnard fillets with crushed new potatoes, beetroot purée, white wine and caviar sauce; or roast rump of Oakdale Farm lamb with dauphinoise potatoes and Savoy cabbage; or roast butternut squash and garlic risotto. For dessert, there's brandy-roasted peaches with mascarpone; and white chocolate cheesecake with coffee ice cream. A 'small lunch' could be a North Atlantic prawn and Marie Rose sandwich, or a home-made steakburger. The wine list is extensive, beers are from Harveys and Westerham breweries, and juices come from local producer Owletts Farm. There is a dining terrace at the front and a beautiful drinks garden surrounded by cob nut trees. With many good walks in the area don't worry about your boots as walkers are very welcome.

Recommended in the area

Ightham Mote; Knole House and Park; Oldbury Hill & Styants Wood

The Bottle House Inn

Address: Coldharbour Road, PENSHURST,
Tonbridge, TN11 8ET
Tel: 01892 870306
Fax: 01892 871094
Email: info@thebottlehouseinnpenshurst.co.uk
Website: www.thebottlehouseinnpenshurst.co.uk
Map ref: 4 TQ54
Directions: From Tunbridge Wells take A264 W, then
B2188 N. After Fordcombe left towards Edenbridge
& Hever. Pub 500yds after staggered x-rds **Open:**

11-11 (Sun 11-10.30) **Closed:** 25 Dec **Facilities:** Parking Garden **Notes:** ⊕ FREE HOUSE ♦♦ 🐾 🍷 8

A well-regarded dining pub, The Bottle House was built as a farmhouse in 1492, and in 1806 a licence
was obtained to sell ales and ciders. It was registered as an alehouse at each subsequent change of
hands, at a time when hop-growing was the major local industry. The pub was said to be the originator
of the ploughman's lunch, made with bread from the old bakery next door and cheese donated by
Canadian soldiers billeted nearby. The building was completely refurbished in 1938 and granted a
full licence; it was reputedly named after all the old bottles discovered during these works. Today,
low beams and a copper-topped counter give the bar a warm, welcoming atmosphere. Choose from
the range of Harveys and Larkins hand-pumped beers and eight wines by the glass. The menu has
something for everyone, starting with grilled green lip mussels stuffed with Welsh rarebit, or deep-fried
sesame-coated brie and breaded mozzarella with plum and apple chutney. Lighter meals and shares
are also available and may include smoked fish platter or linguini in creamy basil pesto sauce. For main
courses enjoy trio of Kentish sausages with mustard mash; oven-roasted skate wing with cracked black
pepper crust; or braised lamb shank with mint and rosemary gravy.

Recommended in the area

Hever Castle; Royal Tunbridge Wells; Penshurst Place & Gardens

The Coastguard

Address: St Margaret's Bay,
ST MARGARET'S AT CLIFFE, CT15 6DY
Tel: 01304 853176
Email: thecoastguard@talk21.com
Website: www.thecoastguard.co.uk
Map ref: 4 TR34
Directions: 2m off A258 between Dover & Deal, follow St
Margaret's at Cliffe signs. Through village towards sea **Open:**
all day all week 11-11 (Sun 11-10.30) ⓛ **L** all wk 12.30-2.45
D all wk 6.30-8.45 ⓘ **L** all wk 12.30-2.45 **D** all wk 6.30-8.45
Facilities: Parking Garden **Notes:** ⊕ FREE HOUSE ⓲ ⓱

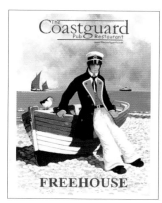

Britain's 'nearest pub to France' stands a stone's throw from
the edge of the English Channel, with the famous White Cliffs of Dover as its backdrop and views
across the world's busiest waterway from the outdoor tables. In the 19th century St Margaret's Bay
was threatened with a proposal that would have transformed it from a quiet fishing village to a seaside
resort; the plan was shelved, and the village happily stayed desirable enough to attract several famous
residents and visitors, including Lord Byron, Max Beerbohm, Noel Coward, Ian Fleming and Peter
Ustinov. The extensive bar stocks real ales from local micro-breweries, British and European bottled
beers, wines from Kent and a range of single malts, some from now-closed distilleries. The menu
changes daily, even during opening hours, depending upon the weather and what's available (nothing
is kept in the freezer for reheating). For that reason you will only find a sample menu on the website if
you look before you leave home; just be certain when you actually arrive that you'll find award-winning,
locally caught fish and seafood, beef from a local farm, fresh salads and individual savoury tarts.
The bread is baked in-house and the highly regarded cheeseboard attracts accolades year after year.

Recommended in the area

Dover Castle; Walmer Castle; South Foreland Heritage Coast

The Beacon

★ ★ ★ ★ INN

Address: Tea Garden Lane, Rusthall,
nr ROYAL TUNBRIDGE WELLS, TN3 9JH
Tel: 01892 524252 **Fax:** 01892 534288
Email: beaconhotel@btopenworld.com
Website: www.the-beacon.co.uk
Map ref: 4 TQ53
Directions: From Tunbridge Wells take A264
towards East Grinstead. Pub 1m on left
Open: all day all week Mon-Sat 11-11 (Sun
12-10.30) 🍺 🍽 **L** Mon-Thu 12-2.30, Fri-Sun 12-9.30 **D** Mon-Thu 6.30-9.30, Fri-Sun 12-9.30
Rooms: 3 en suite **S** £68.50 **D** £97 **Facilities:** Parking Garden **Notes:** ⊕ FREE HOUSE 🍴 ♟ 12

High up on a sandstone outcrop just 1.5 miles from Tunbridge Wells, The Beacon has one of the best
views in southeast England. Formerly a grand country home, it retains impressive architectural features,
including stained glass, moulded ceilings and an oak-panelled bar in which you can select from a
fine range of beers and wine to complement the food. As members of Kentish Fare, the proprietors
are strongly committed to using county-produced ingredients, and in the restaurant you can choose
from starters such as local pork terrine with apple chutney and crisp sage, or pressed English goat's
cheese and eggplant with piquant tomato relish. Your meal could continue with slow-roasted shoulder
of English mutton, fondant potato and caper and parsley sauce, crisp line-caught fillet of sea bass with
ginger and soy, ribbon courgettes and lemony rice. Try to save room for dessert, notably natural yogurt
and rose water panacotta with rhubarb compote, or brioche bread and butter pudding with Baileys and
chocolate. Walk off your meal in the 17 acres of grounds, which include lakes, woodland paths and a
chalybeate spring. There's also a lovely terrace that's perfect for a pre-dinner drink in summer.

Recommended in the area

Royal Tunbridge Wells; Penshurst Place & Gardens; Spa Valley Railway

LANCASHIRE

The Bridestones Rocks

The Forest of Bowland at Slaidburn

The Red Pump Inn

Address: Clitheroe Road, BASHALL EAVES, BB7 3DA
Tel: 01254 826227
Email: info@theredpumpinn.co.uk
Website: www.theredpumpinn.co.uk
Map ref: 6 SD64 **Directions:** 3m from Clitheroe,
follow Whitewell & Bashall Eaves signs **Open:** 12-3
6-11 (Sat 12-11 Sun 12-9) **Closed:** Mon (ex BH)
🏨 🍴 **L** Tue-Sat 12-2, Sun 12-7.30 **D** Tue-Sat 6-9,
Sun 12-7.30 **Facilities:** Parking Garden
Notes: ⊕ FREE HOUSE ♦♦ ♟ 10

With superb views, The Red Pump Inn is an owner-run free house that maintains a commitment to high standards and environmentally-friendly sustainability. The short but fresh menu is compiled to reflect the passion for superb food held by the owners and their chefs. Extra-matured local beef features on the weekly steak night, and Fridays bring a celebration of seafood. Herbs and vegetables come from the garden, and bread, sausages and desserts are home made. Local, regional and national cask ales are kept in tip-top condition and there's an impressive wine list.

Recommended in the area

Forest of Bowland; Gawthorpe Hall; Pendle Hill

Clog and Billycock

Address: Billinge End Road, Pleasington, BLACKBURN, BB2 6QB
Tel: 01254 201163
Email: enquiries@theclogandbillycock.com
Website: www.theclogandbillycock.com
Map ref: 6 SD62
Directions: M6 junct 29 onto M65 junct 3, follow signs for Pleasington
Open: all week noon-11 (Sun noon-10.30) **Closed:** 25 Dec
L Mon-Sat 12-2, Sun 12-8.30 (Afternoon bites Mon-Sat 2-5.30) **D** Mon-Fri 6-9, Sat 5.30-9, Sun 12-8.30
Facilities: Parking Garden
Notes: ⊕ FREE HOUSE ♦♦ ✦ ♛ 8

The Clog and Billycock has been part of Pleasington's history for over 150 years, although this new venture opened only in 2008. Its name comes from the attire of an early landlord (a billycock is black felt hat, a predecessor of the bowler). Set in the quaint village of Pleasington, the building has undergone an expensive renovation, and the result is a warm and relaxing pub in which to enjoy Thwaites ales, draught ciders, fine wines and superb food. Sharrock's Lancashire cheese on toast with local cured streaky bacon makes an excellent light lunch, while the ploughman's highlights the pub's real food objectives, consisting of an impressive plate of Blackstick's Blue, Sandham's Creamy Lancashire, honey roast ham, Forager's collared pork, pickled free-range egg, celeriac and walnut salad, home-made pickles, piccalilli and organic bread. Hot options from chef Nigel Haworth's locally sourced menu may include cornfed Goosnargh chicken with chunky chips and garlic and herb sauce; Simpson's Dairy rice pudding could complete a meal to remember. Children are welcomed with fun educational sheets and competitions, as well as equally well thought-out children's meals.

Recommended in the area

Pleasington Priory; Pleasington Old Hall Wood and Wildlife Garden; Witton Country Park

The Highwayman

Address: BURROW, Nr Kirkby Lonsdale, LA6 2RJ
Tel: 01524 273338
Email: enquiries@highwaymaninn.co.uk
Website: www.highwaymaninn.co.uk
Map ref: 6 SD67
Directions: M6 junct 36, A65 to Kirkby Lonsdale. Then A683 S. Burrow approx 2m
Open: all week noon-11 (Sun noon-10.30)
Closed: 25 Dec ☒ L Mon-Sat 12-2, Sun 12-8.30 (Afternoon bites Mon-Sat 2-5.30)
D Mon-Fri 6-9, Sat 5.30-9, Sun 12-8.30
Facilities: Parking Garden **Notes:** ⁙ ⌁ ⚑ 8

Starting life as a coaching inn during the 18th century, a legend surrounds this establishment regarding its use as a midnight haunt of notorious Lancashire highwaymen. The inn is set in a delightful country area close to the historic market town of Kirkby Lonsdale, popular for its pretty cottages, quaint streets and attractive shops and tea rooms. The refurbished Highwayman has a stone-floored interior with solid wood furniture and welcoming open fires. There is also a beautifully landscaped terraced garden, planted to attract local butterflies and birds. Thwaites cask ales, ciders and guest beers are served alongside a list of fine wines, and the menus are a tribute to regional specialities and local producers and suppliers. Typical dishes are Port of Lancaster Smokehouse kipper fillet, with boiled egg and watercress salad; Lakeland farmers' Herdwick mutton pudding, capers, parsley mash and black peas; and Cartmel sticky toffee pudding with butterscotch sauce and vanilla ice cream. Don't miss the tri-counties cheeseboard, with the best from Lancashire, Yorkshire and Cumbria. The children's menu offers real food in smaller portions, and seasonal fun sheets are available to keep younger customers amused.

Recommended in the area

Sizergh Castle; Levens Hall; White Scar Caves

The Assheton Arms

Address: Downham, CLITHEROE, BB7 4BJ
Tel: 01200 441227
Fax: 01200 440581
Email: asshetonarms@aol.com
Website: www.assheton-arms.co.uk
Map ref: 6 SD74
Directions: A59 to Chatburn, then follow Downham signs
Open: all week ⓛ L Mon-Sat 12-2, Sun 12-9
D all wk 6-9 **Facilities:** Parking
Notes: ⊕ FREE HOUSE ⅰ♠ ♞ ♟ 22

Pendle Hill looms over the village, whose houses, thanks to the Assheton family, which owns it, are delightfully free of TV aerials and dormer windows; there aren't any village name road signs either. Even the original stocks remain, so imagine how TV drama producers love it as a location. The stone-built pub was renamed in 1950 after Ralph Assheton, who became Lord Clitheroe in 1955 in recognition of his contribution during the Second World War. The family coat of arms on the sign above the door features a man holding a scythe incorrectly; the reason involves the English Civil War - any local will tell you the tale. In the single bar and sectioned rooms you'll find solid oak tables, wingback settees, the original 1765 fireplace, and a large blackboard listing the daily specials. Be pleasantly surprised this far from the coast by the range of seafood (according to season), including oysters, mussels, scallops and lobster; pan fried monkfish, and sea bream. Other dishes are Mrs Whelan's Burnley black pudding with piccalilli and mustard; bacon and cranberry casserole; traditional fish and chips; and, the one that in this neck of the woods would be conspicuous by its absence, Lancashire hot pot.

Recommended in the area

Forest of Bowland; Samlesbury Hall; Yorkshire Dales National Park

Cartford Country Inn & Hotel

Address: Little Eccleston, PRESTON, PR3 0YP
Tel: 01995 670166
Email: info@thecartfordinn.co.uk
Website: www.thecartfordinn.co.uk
Map ref: 6 SD52
Directions: Off A586
Open: all week **Closed:** 25 Dec
Facilities: Parking
Notes: ⊕ FREE HOUSE ⫯♦

The refurbished Cartford Inn is a 17th-century coaching inn nestling on the banks of the River Wyre on Lancashire's Fylde Coast; it combines traditional features with contemporary style. As a result of the extensive refurbishment the owners, Patrick and Julie Beaume have achieved a unique ambience where a warm welcome is always assured. An open wood fire welcomes guests in the bar lounge area where there are several cosy corners to enjoy a quiet drink. Food, from an informal snack to a three-course meal, is served throughout the lounge, alcoves and games room (where dominoes, cards, chess, backgammon and other board games are available). Alternatively the same menu is available in the first-floor restaurant, Mushrooms, for those seeking a more traditional dining experience. There is also a charming beer garden overlooking the River Wyre with stunning views of the surrounding countryside with Beacon Fell and the Trough of Bowland as a backdrop. The inn offers seven individually decorated, en suite bedrooms. Although in the heart of the Fylde Coast countryside, the Cartford is less than ten minutes from the M55 junction 3 and an equal distance from nearby Blackpool.

Recommended in the area

Blackpool; Wyre Estuary Country Park; Marsh Mill

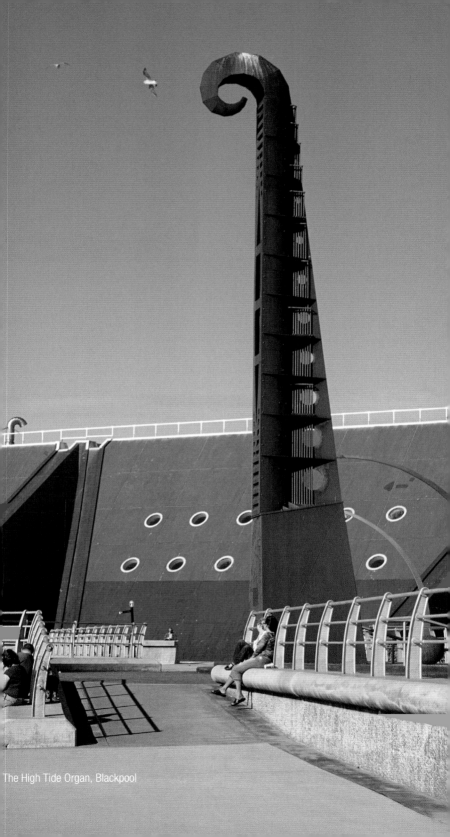

The High Tide Organ, Blackpool

The Three Fishes

Address: Mitton Road, Mitton, WHALLEY, BB7 9PQ
Tel: 01254 826888
Fax: 01254 826026
Email: enquiries@thethreefishes.com
Website: www.thethreefishes.com
Map ref: 6 SD73
Directions: M6 junct 31, A59 to Clitheroe.
Follow signs for Whalley, take B6246 for 2m
Open: all day all week **Closed:** 25 Dec ♨ **L** Mon-Sat
12-2, Sun 12-10.30 (Afternoon bites Mon-Sat 2-5.30) **D** Mon-Fri 6-9, Sat 5.30-9, Sun 12-10.30
Facilities: Parking Garden **Notes:** ⊕ FREE HOUSE ⋔ 🍷 13

The Three Fishes is over 400 years old and has been a pub for most of that time, providing refreshment to travellers on the old road from the 16th-century bridge at Lower Hodder and the ferry at Mitton. The place was supposedly named after the three fishes pendant in the coat of arms of John Paslew, last abbot of nearby Whalley Abbey (look above the entrance to see them carved in stone). The tiny hamlet of Mitton is set on a limestone rise above the River Ribble and is surrounded by beautiful countryside. The pub prides itself on its genuine Lancashire hospitality, real ales, and the best food ever in its long history. The menu demonstrates a passionate commitment to regional food, with dishes such as Morecambe Bay shrimps, served with blade mace butter and toasted muffin; heather reared Bowland lamb Lancashire hotpot; and aged sirloin of Ribble Valley beef with proper chips. You might finish your meal with Lancashire curd tart with organic lemon cream, or the excellent Lancashire cheese board with biscuits and fireside chutney. Photographs of local 'food hero' producers and suppliers line the walls, in tribute to their contribution to the success of the Three Fishes.

Recommended in the area

Stonyhurst College; Clitheroe Castle; All Hallows Medieval Church

The Forest of Bowland at Whitewell

The Inn at Whitewell

★★★★★ ⊛ INN

Address: Forest of Bowland, WHITEWELL,
Nr Clitheroe, BB7 3AT
Tel: 01200 448222
Fax: 01200 448298
Email: reception@innatwhitewell.com
Website: www.innatwhitewell.com
Map ref: 6 SD64
Directions: From B6243 follow Whitewell signs
Open: all week 11-11 ☕ **L** all wk 12-2 **D** all wk
7.30-9.30 **D** all wk 7.30-9.30 **Rooms:** 23 en suite (1 GF) **S** £77-£165 **D** £105-£203
Facilities: Parking Garden **Notes:** ⊕ FREE HOUSE 🐾 🍷 20

Commanding wonderful views this delightful 16th-century inn, a former deer keeper's cottage, is set high up on the banks of the River Hodder in the Forest of Bowland. The bar — just one area where the family passion for antiques is evident — serves local real ales, and organic beers and ciders from around the world, and impressive food at lunchtime and evening. For formal dining, try the riverside restaurant.
Recommended in the area
Ribchester Roman Museum; Browsholme Hall; Yorkshire Dales National Park

Castle ruins at Ashby-de-la-Zouch

Old John Tower folly in Bradgate Country Park

The Queen's Head

★★★★ ◉◉ ⌿ INN

Address: 2 Long Street, BELTON, Loughborough, LE12 9TP
Tel: 01530 222359
Fax: 01530 224860
Email: enquiries@thequeenshead.org
Website: www.thequeenshead.org
Map ref: 8 SK42
Directions: On B5324 between Coalville & Loughborough
Open: all day all week **Closed:** 25-26 Dec ▭ **L** all wk 12-2.30,
Sat all day **D** Mon-Fri 7-9.30, Sat all day ⊙ **L** all wk 12-2.30,
Sun 12-4 **D** Mon-Sat 7-9 **Rooms:** 6 en suite **S** £65 **D** £80-£100
Facilities: Parking Garden **Notes:** ⊕ FREE HOUSE ⋔ ⋔ ♈ 14

A stunning contemporary gastro-pub with bedrooms, located in the very heart of the East Midlands.
Whether you just want to enjoy a drink in the comfortable bar or try the culinary creations of head chef
David Ferguson in the bistro or the restaurant, The Queen's Head has something to offer for all. There's
a bar menu available nearly all week, and a set menu offers impressive dishes using local produce.
Recommended in the area
National Forest; Conkers; The Great Central Railway

The Staff of Life

Address: Main Street, MOWSLEY, LE17 6NT
Tel: 0116 240 2359
Website: www.staffoflifeinn.co.uk
Map ref: 3 SP68
Directions: M1 junct 20, A4304 to Market
Harborough. Left in Husbands Bosworth onto A5199.
In 3m turn right to pub
Closed: Mon L (ex BH)
Facilities: Parking Garden
Notes: ⊕ FREE HOUSE ♀ 19

An integral part of the rich heritage of the beautiful village in which it stands, the Staff of Life captures the true essence of a good country pub while delivering the standards and qualities of a fine restaurant. The atmosphere is warm and convivial, with traditional features such as high-backed settles, a wood-panelled ceiling and flagstone floors, warmed by a roaring open fire in winter. In the warmer seasons you can enjoy the inviting front patio, surrounded by herbs and flowers, or the garden at the rear.
In the dining area overlooking the garden, the interesting menu includes a good mix of British pub classics and dishes with more of an international influence. Recent examples from the daily-changing blackboard lunch menu have included Joseph Morris faggots on mash with rich gravy, and Aberdeen Angus cottage pie with Black Bomber cheddar topping. The evening carte might include starters such as seared king scallops on tarragon-scented black pudding, followed perhaps by roast chicken breast stuffed with chargrilled red peppers on thyme courgettes. The wine list is extensive, with many offered by the glass. Sunday lunch here is a great favourite – and great value – featuring roasts of meat sourced from local farms.

Recommended in the area

Stanford Hall; Mallory Park; Wicksteed Park

The Bradgate

Address: 37 Main Street, NEWTOWN LINFORD, LE6 0AE
Tel: 01530 242239
Fax: 01530 249391
Email: john@thebradgate.co.uk
Website: www.thebradgate.co.uk
Map ref: 3 SK50
Directions: M1 junct 22, A50 towards Leicester 1.5m. At 1st rdbt left towards Newton Linford 1.5m, at end of road turn right 0.25m. Pub on right

Open: all week winter: 11.30-3 5.30-11 (Sun 12-9) summer: all day, every day 🍺 **L** Mon-Thu 12-2.30, Fri-Sun all day **D** Mon-Thu 6-9, Fri-Sun all day 🍽 **L** Mon-Thu 12-2.30, Fri-Sun all day **D** Mon-Thu 6-9, Fri-Sun all day **Facilities:** Parking Garden **Notes:** ⊕ EVERARDS ♦♦ ♀ 10

This village pub has long been a favourite with locals and walkers, both as a watering hole and for its widely recognised good food. It's run by husband and wife team John and Eve Bowtell, daughter Joanne and her partner Craig, who was brought up in the licensed trade, so he also knows his stuff. When brewery Everards refurbished it a little while back, it worked closely with John and Eve to create today's light, airy atmosphere and modern décor with a light wood bar, flooring and furniture, and off-white walls. Dinner here might start with tiger prawns wrapped in filo pastry served with chilli dipping sauce; followed with pork medallions and black pudding on mashed potato in brandy cream and peppercorn sauce; then finished with warm pear galette, and almond and Armagnac ice cream. At lunchtime enjoy fresh baked filled baguettes, triple-decker sandwiches, salad, snacks or main plates such as herb and lemon battered fish. There are often pie, steak and themed nights, plus regular live music. John and Eve welcome families, offering a dining area with highchairs and children's menus.

Recommended in the area

Calke Abbey; Donington Park; Great Central Railway

Griffin, City of Westminster

The Bleeding Heart Tavern

Address: 19 Greville Street, LONDON, EC1N 8SQ
Tel: 020 7242 8238
Fax: 020 7831 1402
Email: bookings@bleedingheart.co.uk
Website: www.bleedingheart.co.uk
Map ref: 3 TQ38
Directions: Close to Farringdon tube station,
at corner of Greville St & Bleeding Heart Yard
Open: all day 7am-11pm **Closed:** BH, 10 days at

Xmas, Sat-Sun ⊚ **L** Mon-Fri 12-2.30 **D** Mon-Fri 5.30-11 **Notes:** ⊕ FREE HOUSE ⏺ 17

The Tavern has guarded the entrance to Bleeding Heart Yard since 1746. Today it offers a traditional neighbourhood bar with Adnams real ales and a light lunchtime menu. Downstairs is the Dining Room, an open rotisserie and grill providing free-range, organic British meats, game and poultry. On the menu: braised mutton hotpot; and smoked haddock with poached egg. The Tavern also opens for breakfast.
Recommended in the area
St Paul's Cathedral; Tower of London; Museum of London

The Fire Station

Address: 150 Waterloo Road, LONDON, SE1 8SB
Tel: 020 7620 2226
Email: firestation.waterloo@pathfinderpubs.co.uk
Website: www.firestation.waterloo@marstons.co.uk
Map ref: 3 TQ38
Directions: Turn right at exit 2 of Waterloo Station
Open: all day all week 9am-mdnt (Sun 10am-mdnt)
Closed: 1 Jan ⊞ **L** Mon-Sat 9am-12am, Sun 10am-12am
D Mon-Sat 9am-12am, Sun 10am-12am ⊚ **L** all wk 12-3
D all wk 5-10.45 **Notes:** ⊕ PATHFINDER PUBS ⏺⏺ ⏺ 8

Built in 1910, this former Fire Brigade Station is especially
popular with travellers, given that Waterloo Station is next door.
Inside is a big room with shiny red brick walls and an assortment of old domestic dining tables, with views of the open-plan kitchen. Expect traditional British/European dishes, such as calves' liver with bacon and mustard mash, and lemon sole with Jerusalem artichokes. Drinks include a wide range of draught beers, cask ales and New and Old World wines.
Recommended in the area
London Eye; Royal Festival Hall; London Aquarium

North Pole Bar & Restaurant

Address: 131 Greenwich High Road, Greenwich,
LONDON, SE10 8JA
Tel: 020 8853 3020
Fax: 020 8853 3501
Email: natalie@northpolegreenwich.com
Website: www.northpolegreenwich.com
Map ref: 3 TQ38
Directions: From Greenwich rail station turn right,
pass Novotel. Pub on right (2 min walk)
Open: all day all week noon-2am ⓑ **L** all wk 12-10
D all wk 12-10 ⓘ **L** Sat-Sun 12-5 **D** all wk 6-10.30
Facilities: Garden **Notes:** ⊕ FREE HOUSE ⁆ 20

Drinking, dining, dancing – you can do it all at this grand old corner pub, which offers a complete night out under one roof. Start with a cocktail in the bar, then, if you're there on a Thursday to Sunday evening, head upstairs to the stylish Piano Restaurant, where the resident pianist will entertain you. Look up and you'll see goldfish swimming around in the chandeliers, but don't worry, they're for real and nothing to do with that earlier cocktail. An extensive bar menu is available all day, with choices including chorizo risotto; swordfish steak; and oriental platter. The cooking style in the Piano Restaurant's grand green room and elegant red room is modern European, typified by prosciutto salad; Asian-style crab and noodle salad; lamb shank tagine; pan-fried sea bream; twice cooked Asian pork belly; veal escalopes; and roasted spicy squash risotto. Desserts include ice peach soufflé with mixed berries; and chocolate nemesis with crème fraîche and strawberries. In the basement is the South Pole club, where you can dance until 2am. Sunday is the day for live jazz, funk and Latin music. To complete the picture there's a terrace, an ideal spot for a Pimms on a summer evening.

Recommended in the area

Maritime Greenwich; Royal Observatory; Eltham Palace

The Bountiful Cow

Address: 51 Eagle Street, Holborn, LONDON, WC1R 4AP
Tel: 020 7404 0200
Email: manager@roxybeaujolais.com
Website: www.thebountifulcow.co.uk
Map ref: 3 TQ38 **Directions:** 230mtrs NE from Holborn tube station, via Procter St. Walk through 2 arches into Eagle St. Pub between High Holborn & Red Lion Square **Open:** all day Mon-Sat 11-11 **Closed:** Sun, BH ℔ **L** 12-5 **D** 5-10.30 **Notes:** ⅰ⅟ ℗ 6

Roxy Beaujolais, proprietor of the ancient Seven Stars in WC2, found a 1960s pub between Red Lion Square and High Holborn and turned it into The Bountiful Cow, 'a public house devoted to beef'. You enter below green waterfalls of periwinkles to find two floor levels that feel neatly halfway between a funky bistro and a stylish saloon. Walls are bedecked with pictures of cows, bullfights, cowgirls, meat cuts diagrams and cow-themed films, presided over by a colourful poster for Cattle Queen of Montana starring Barbara Stanwyck and a former president of the United States. The house seats 70 diners; the music is jazzy but discreet. Head Cook Roxy is author of the pub cookbook *Home From the Inn Contented* and was a presenter of the BBC's *Full On Food*. Her menu, based on beef sourced at Smithfield Market and aged in-house, features exceptionally large and well-made hamburgers and big steaks (rib-eye, sirloin, T-bone, filet, onglet) destined to be accurately cooked by the grill chef, alongside cask-conditioned ales and wines. Lunches are of particularly notable value: the pub pays homage to the Free Lunch tradition of US pre-prohibition days with an Almost Free Lunch. Memorable choices, including vegetarian ones, are offered at 'nugatory', i.e. low, prices, with the customer requested to also buy a drink (it could be a soft drink). The sights and tourist destinations of central London are an improving short walk away.

Recommended in the area

British Museum; Dr Johnson's House; Dickens House Museum; Sir John Soame's Museum

The Seven Stars

Address: 53 Carey Street, LONDON, WC2A 2JB
Tel: 020 7242 8521
Email: roxy@roxybeaujolais.com
Map ref: 3 TQ38 **Directions:** From Temple N via The Strand &
Bell Yard to Carey St. From Holborn SE via Lincoln's Inn Fields &
Searle St to Carey St **Open:** all day all week 11-11 (Sat noon-11,
Sun noon-10.30) **Closed:** 25-26 Dec, 1 Jan, Good Fri, Etr Sun
L Mon-Fri 12-3, Sat-Sun 12-9 **D** Mon-Fri 5.30-9, Sat-Sun
12-9 **Notes:** FREE HOUSE

Built in 1602, this charming little pub at the back of the Royal
Courts of Justice is presided over by the celebrated 'alewife'
(as she calls herself) Roxy Beaujolais, cookbook author and TV
food show presenter. Since she took it over it has had a subtle freshening and has expanded into the
former legal wig shop next door—wigs are still displayed—to now provide 28 covers at green chequed
oilcloth-covered tables, in case you are diffident about sitting at the bar on Lloyd Loom stools. The
improvements were managed with such Grade II discretion by Roxy's architect husband that some
think his glazed, mahogany-mullioned dumbwaiter is ancient. Roxy and her assistants cook simple
dishes seven days a week that are, famously, slightly revisionist. A blackboard reveals what the market
provides, which might include a meat, fowl or game pie; cockle bisque; paella with mixed sausages;
linguine with chestnuts and truffle oil. Real ales from Adnams, Dark Star, Fullers and others are served,
and a few good wines. The venerable pub cat Tom Paine wears a chorister's ruff, to the delight of
customers - many of them barristers from across the road. The chalkboard outside lists frequently
changing rules such as 'no querulousness', 'no apostrophe mistakes' and 'no dogs except Archie'.
Even if you don't need the loo, try the narrow and ridiculously steep Elizabethan stairs.

Recommended in the area

The Soane Museum; The Hunterian Museum; Lincoln's Inn

The London Eye, South Bank

NORFOLK

Horsey Gap

Happisburgh lighthouse

Kings Head

Address: Harts Lane, BAWBURGH, NR9 3LS
Tel: 01603 744977
Email: anton@kingshead-bawburgh.co.uk
Website: www.kingshead-bawburgh.co.uk
Map ref: 4 TG10
Directions: From A47 W of Norwich take B1108 W
Open: all week **Closed:** 25-27 Dec eve, 1 Jan eve
🛏 🍽 **L** Mon-Sat 12-2, Sun 12-4 **D** Mon-Sat
5.30-9, Sun 5.30-8.30 **Facilities:** Parking Garden
Notes: ⊕ FREE HOUSE ♥ 18

A peaceful setting by the banks of the River Yare is perfect for visitors who want to head out of Norwich and enjoy the relaxing atmosphere of a genuine village pub, complete with heavy timbers and bulging walls. Standing opposite the village green, the pub is big on traditional charm, with wooden floors, log fires and comfy leather seating. The monthly changing carte menu and daily changing specials board include pub classics with imaginative and local twists. Fresh bread is hand-made every day and the range of puddings is based on locally grown seasonal fruits, hand-made ice creams and local cheeses.
Recommended in the area
Norwich Cathedral; Norfolk Broads; Norwich Theatre Royal

White Horse Hotel

Address: 4 High Street, BLAKENEY, NR25 7AL
Tel: 01263 740574
Fax: 01263 741303
Email: info@blakeneywhitehorse.co.uk
Website: www.blakeneywhitehorse.co.uk
Map ref: 4 TG04
Directions: From A148 (Cromer to King's Lynn road) onto A149 signed to Blakeney **Open:** all week 10.30am-11pm **Closed:** 25 Dec ⅬL all wk 12-2.15 **D** Thu-Sun 6-9, Fri-Sat 6-9.30
Facilities: Parking Garden **Notes:** ⊕ FREE HOUSE ♦♦ ♥ 30

Blakeney is a gem of a coastal village. Narrow streets of flint-built fishermen's cottages wind their way to a small tidal harbour, beyond which vast marshes surround the creeks and estuary. Dominating the horizon is the shingle ridge of Blakeney Point. Norfolk doesn't often do steep, but it does here, at least from the quayside to the 17th-century White Horse, formerly a coaching inn, and run by the same team for many years. There are three eating areas – the bar, the conservatory, and the Dining Room. Lobster, crab and mussels come from local fishermen as the seasons dictate; butchers, graziers and Norfolk estates supply meat and game; soft fruit, salads, asparagus and free-range eggs come from local smallholders. Lunchtime snacks include granary bread sandwiches, ciabattas, and smoked haddock and crayfish kedgeree. A daily changing main menu offers confit duck leg with lyonnaise potatoes, savoy cabbage, chestnuts and bacon; pan-fried halibut, saffron potatoes, roast squash, wild mushrooms and mushroom stock; and warm tart of beetroot, Cashel Blue cheese, chives, buttered Anya potatoes and salad. A blackboard of daily specials, with the accent on fish, adds further choice. A 75-bin wine list, 30 available by the glass, and four regional real ales complete the picture.

Recommended in the area

North Norfolk Heritage Coast; Wells & Walsingham Light Railway; Holkham Hall

The Hoste Arms

★★★ 87% ◉◉ HOTEL
Address: The Green, BURNHAM MARKET, PE31 8HD
Tel: 01328 738777
Fax: 01328 730103
Email: reception@hostearms.co.uk
Website: www.hostearms.co.uk
Map ref: 4 TF84 **Directions:** Signed off B1155, 5m
W of Wells-next-the-Sea **Open:** all week ⓑ ⓣ L all
wk 12-2 **D** all wk 6-9 **Rooms:** 35 en suite (7 GF)
S £104-£190 **D** £128-£225 **Facilities:** Parking
Garden **Notes:** ⊕ FREE HOUSE ⌁ ♞ 11

Paul Whittome's 17th-century coaching inn is very much the social hub of Burnham Market, famed
for its fabulous shops and galleries. The traditional front bar, with its log fire and great atmosphere,
is popular with locals and visitors alike. The stylish eating areas, include a panelled dining room, a
conservatory, and the canopied Moroccan Garden. The chefs pride themselves on serving imaginative
food, and source local and seasonal ingredients. The 35 bedrooms are individually styled.
Recommended in the area
Titchwell Bird Reserve; Holkham Hall; The Sandringham Estate

The Lord Nelson

Address: Walsingham Road, BURNHAM THORPE,
King's Lynn, PE31 8HN
Tel/Fax: 01328 738241
Email: simon@nelsonslocal.co.uk
Website: www.nelsonslocal.co.uk
Map ref: 4 TF84
Directions: B1355, 1.75m from Burnham Market
Open: all day noon-11 **Closed:** Mon eve ex school
hols ⓑ **L** all wk 12-2.30 **D** Tue-Sun 6-9
ⓣ **L** all wk 12-2.30 **D** Tue-Sun 6-9
Facilities: Parking Garden **Notes:** ⊕ GREENE KING ⓫ ⌁ ♞ 15

Dating back 400 years, this pub is in the village where Lord Nelson was born, and the great Admiral
used to eat and drink here, hosting a farewell meal for the whole village here in 1793. There is no
bar – all drinks are served from the tap room, and the pub is famous for its real ales, direct from the
cask. It also has a popular menu of freshly prepared food. Outside, the massive garden has seating, a
barbecue, and wooden play equipment. Dogs are allowed, except in the restaurant.
Recommended in the area
Holkham Hall; Titchwell Nature Reserve; Sandringham House

The George Hotel

Address: High Street, CLEY NEXT THE SEA,
Holt, NR25 7RN
Tel: 01263 740652
Fax: 01263 741275
Email: info@thegeorgehotelatcley.co.uk
Website: www.thegeorgehotelatcley.co.uk
Map ref: 4 TG04
Directions: On A149 through Cley next the Sea,
approx 4m from Holt
Open: all day all week 11-11 ⓺ L all wk 12-2.30
D all wk 6.30-9 **Facilities:** Parking Garden **Notes:** ⊕ FREE HOUSE ⅋ ⅋ ⅋ 8

Set within the pretty and historic village of Cley next the Sea, not far from Cley's famous old windmill, the George Hotel is a classic Edwardian Norfolk inn. This is walking and birdwatching country par excellence, and the wonderful sunsets are also renowned. The first naturalist trust was formed here, and the area's wildlife reserves boast abundant birdlife and local seal colonies. Across the road are the atmospheric marshes, with the sea beyond. The inn has been modernised to create tasteful seating and decor where visitors can mingle comfortably with locals. It has an excellent reputation for its wide selection of real ales and for freshly prepared food made from finest ingredients, supplied from the local area. Locally caught fish and shellfish are a highlight, including smoked salmon and prawns from the Cley Smoke House. The dinner menu includes starters such as pastrami-style smoked salmon with citrus oil; and oysters served with lemon and tarragon olive oil. Main dishes include grilled fillet of red snapper with roasted fennel; Dijon peppered chicken with tagliatelle; and pan-fried strips of lambs' liver served with crispy bacon and Madeira. Desserts might be sticky toffee pudding; lemon and lime posset; or honey and lavender crème brûlée. There are vegetarian options and a kids' menu.

Recommended in the area

Henry Blogg Museum; Felbrigg Hall (NT); North Norfolk Railway

The coast at Brancaster

Lifeboat Inn

★★ 78% ⊕ HOTEL

Address: Ship Lane, THORNHAM, PE36 6LT
Tel: 01485 512236
Fax: 01485 512323
Email: reception@lifeboatinn.co.uk
Website: www.maypolehotels.com
Map ref: 4 TF74
Directions: A149 from Hunstanton for approx 6m.
1st left after Thornham sign
Open: all week **Rooms:** 13 en suite (1 GF)
Facilities: Parking Garden **Notes:** ⊕ FREE HOUSE ⁀ ⊀ ♀ 10

Retaining many original features, this 16th-century inn overlooks the salt marshes and Thornham Harbour. Inside, the warm glow of paraffin lamps enhances the welcoming atmosphere, while the adjoining conservatory has an ancient vine. The best available fish and game feature on the frequently changing menus of traditional country fare. Bowls of steaming mussels are legendary, harvested daily by local fishermen. Popular bar meals include roast loin of pork and Lifeboat fish pie.

Recommended in the area

Peddars Way and Norfolk Coast Path; Sandringham; Norfolk Lavender

The Crown

Address: The Buttlands, WELLS-NEXT-THE-SEA,
NR23 1EX
Tel: 01328 710209
Fax: 01328 711432
Email: reception@crownhotelnorfolk.co.uk
Website: www.crownhotelnorfolk.co.uk
Map ref: 4 TF94
Directions: 10m from Fakenham on B1105
Open: all week ⅃ **L** all wk 12-2.30 **D** all wk
6.30-9.30 **D** all wk 7-9 **Facilities:** Parking Garden
Notes: ⊕ FREE HOUSE ☆ ⅃ ♀ 14

The Crown is a handsome former coaching inn overlooking the tree-lined green known as the Buttlands in Wells-next-the-Sea. This superb location is just a few minutes from the beach on the north Norfolk coast. Striking contemporary furnishings work well with the old-world charm of the 17th-century building, and the bar, with its open fire and ancient beams, is an appealing place for a drink – Adnams Ales, Woodforde's Wherry, wines by the glass – or light meal from the interesting bar menu. This might include marinated pork belly with stir-fried noodles and hot-and-sour sauce; smoked haddock chowder; or beef burger with Gruyère cheese, sweet onions and pepper relish. The Crown Restaurant offers dishes freshly prepared from the finest ingredients, in modern and traditional styles with a hint of Pacific Rim. A recent menu included such starters as flash-fried squid, bacon and black pudding; cream of curried parsnip soup; and grilled goat's cheese. Main courses featured Thai marinated duck breast with seared scallops and chilli jam; steamed North Sea cod with ginger, lemongrass and lime; and roast partridge breasts and confit legs. A private dining room is also available.

Recommended in the area

Holkham Hall; Wells and Walsingham Light Railway; Blakeney Point (NT)

Wiveton Bell

Address: Blakeney Road, WIVETON, Holt, NR25 7TL
Tel: 01263 740101
Email: enquiries@wivetonbell.co.uk
Website: www.wivetonbell.com
Map ref: 4 TG04
Directions: 1m from Blakeney. Wiveton Rd off A149
Open: all week ᴁ L all wk 12-2.15 D all wk 6-9
ᵢᴼᵢ L all wk 12-2.15 D all wk 6-9
Facilities: Parking Garden
Notes: ⬡ FREE HOUSE ⚑ ♟ 18

This pretty, 17th-century inn overlooks the village green just a mile from Blakeney on Norfolk's beautiful north coast. Inside, an inglenook fireplace, settles, scrubbed wooden tables and oil paintings create a relaxed atmosphere where customers are just as likely to be walkers with muddy boots (and muddy dogs) as members of the area's business community. The award-winning restaurant is strong on local produce such as mussels, crabs, oysters and lobster, as well as game from the Holkham Hall Estate. Other dishes might include slow-roast Norfolk pork belly or braised oxtail with venison faggots. At lunchtime, lighter dishes are on offer, including chicken and bacon bruschetta, omelette Arnold Bennett, or a fine steak sandwich. Some of the Norfolk beers come from neighbouring brewery Yetmans, whose owner regards the Bell as his brewery taproom. In summer, the sheltered gardens, with their fine views of the village church and countryside, come into their own. Nice touches are the wind-up torches and umbrellas left in the bus shelter on the green for customers to use on the way to and from their cars. For those who wish to stay in the area, the Bell has four well-equipped rooms and a tastefully restored fisherman's cottage.

Recommended in the area

Holkham Beach; seal-watching trips to Blakeney Point; Wells Beach

The Rushton Triangular Lodge

The Queen's Head

Address: Main Street, BULWICK, NN17 3DY
Tel: 01780 450272
Email: queenshead-bulwick@tiscali.co.uk
Map ref: 3 SP99
Directions: Just off A43, between Corby & Stamford
Closed: Mon ⓑ L Tue-Sun 12-2.30 D Tue-Sat
6-9.30 ⓘ L Tue-Sun 12-2.30 D Tue-Sat 6-9.30
Facilities: Parking Garden **Notes:** ⊕ FREE HOUSE
🛈 🚲 ♟ 9

The Queen's Head is believed to have been a pub since 1647, but its history goes back even further, with parts of the building dating back to 1400. It was named after Charles II's wife, Catherine of Braganza (known, apparently, for her very elaborate hair styles), and is the only pub in this charming village. Its cosy interior is a warren of small rooms, with low beamed ceilings, flagstone floors and four open fireplaces, and the lively local social life adds greatly to the atmosphere. The pub has a resident darts and dominos team, and a group of bellringers who each Wednesday show off their skills at the 12th-century church opposite the pub. Special events and themed nights are also organised, including the popular Hog Roast for Spring Bank Holiday. The landlord is very keen on real ale, and always keeps Shepherd Neame's Spitfire, Rockingham Ales and Newby Wyke on tap, plus guest ales. Hearty pub food includes some interesting and unusual dishes, such as chicken and goats' cheese wontons with lemon and mixed herb cous cous; vanilla roasted monkfish tail with spinach, fondant potato and spiced port jus; and noisettes of roasted lamb with red pepper and Savoy cabbage. All ingredients are fresh and locally sourced where possible, with an emphasis on fish and game when in season. Outside there is a very pretty patio, candlelit at night, which is a great place to enjoy lunch or dinner in the summer, when it echoes with the sounds of peacocks from Bulwick Hall.
Recommended in the area
Kirby Hall; Deene Park; Rockingham Raceway

Canons Ashby House

George and Dragon

Address: Silver St, CHACOMBE,
nr Banbury, OX17 2JR
Tel: 01295 711500
Fax: 01295 710516
Email: info@pubdiningbanbury.co.uk
Map ref: 3 SP44
Directions: From M40 junct 11 take A361 (Daventry road). Chacombe 1st right **Open:** all week noon-12
🍴 **L/D** Mon-Thu 12-9, Fri-Sat 12-9.30, Sun 12-7
🍴 **L/D** Mon-Thu 12-9, Fri-Sat 12-9.30, Sun 12-7
Facilities: Parking Garden **Notes:** ⊕ EVERARDS ♦♦

On the edge of a peaceful and picturesque village, this 17th-century stone pub features a copper-topped bar, stone-flagged floor, wood-burning stoves, sun terrace and a well. Freshly prepared food served from a seasonal menu throughout the day, every day, includes a range of starters and light mains – examples are corned beef hash cakes; bangers and mash; braised pork belly; seared duck breast; smoked haddock rarebit; and spaghetti carbonara.

Recommended in the area

Sulgrave Manor; Silverstone Circuit; Broughton Castle

The Red Lion

Address: 43 Welland Rise, SIBBERTOFT, Nr Market Harborough, Leicester, LE16 9UD
Tel: 01858 880011
Email: andrew@redlionwinepub.co.uk
Website: www.redlionwinepub.co.uk
Map ref: 3 SP68
Directions: From Market Harborough take A4304, through Lubenham, left through Marston Trussell to Sibbertoft
Open: 12-2 6.30-11 **Closed:** Mon & Tue lunch, Sun eve 🍽 L Wed-Sun 12-2 D Mon-Sat 6.30-9.30 ⭐ L Wed-Sun 12-2 D Mon-Sat 6.30-9.30
Facilities: Parking Garden **Notes:** ⊕ FREE HOUSE ⁑ ⚘ 20

A giant wine bottle outside proclaims: 'Top food, top wines, at pub prices!' Andrew and Sarah Banks have spent much time rejuvenating this 300-year-old, friendly, contemporary-style pub/restaurant; they call it 'A little bit of London in the sticks'. Certainly, it offers an appealing blend of contemporary and classic decor, with oak beams and leather upholstery inside and a quiet garden outside. In the buzzy bar, reliable real ales from Adnams and Timothy Taylor vie with European imports. In the smartly turned-out restaurant, enthusiastic and clued-up staff know about organic ingredients and things like when and where the asparagus was picked. The menu changes monthly to offer, for instance, roasted cod on a bed of leeks with bacon butter; trio of pork casserole slowly cooked in cider; roasted pheasant breast wrapped in bacon with cranberry mash; and wild mushroom risotto, while Monday night is curry night. The game is shot on the farm next door, and the beef cattle are reared in the surrounding area and prepared for the kitchen in the next village. More than 200 wine bins reflect Andrew's particular passion.

Recommended in the area

Coton Manor; Mallory Park; Rutland Water

The Crown

Address: Helmdon Road, WESTON, nr Towcester, NN12 8PX
Tel: 01295 760310
Fax: 01295 760310
Email: info@thecrownweston.co.uk
Website: www.thecrownweston.co.uk
Map ref: 3 SP54
Directions: Accessed from A43 or B4525
Open: 6-11.30 (Fri-Sat noon-3.30 6-11.30 Sun noon-3.30
7-11) **Closed:** 25 Dec ♨ **L** Fri-Sun 12-2.30 **D** Tue-Sat 6-9.30
Facilities: Parking Garden
Notes: ⊕ FREE HOUSE ⌗ ♀ 7

This is a place that's oozing with history: a hostelry since the
reign of Elizabeth I, the first documented evidence of The Crown pins the year down to 1593 and the
first recorded owner was All Souls College, Oxford. Current owner Robert Grover has more recently
completed a refurbishment of the building and brought renown to the pub for its excellent food, all
prepared from fresh ingredients. A typical menu might start with goats' cheese and sun-dried tomato
tart; or moules marinière and French bread. Mains range from the simple Charolais minute steak and
caramelised onion baguette; or shepherd's pie with steamed vegetables; to lamb casserole with mint
and apricots, vegetables and herb mash; wild mushroom risotto; or breast of duck with potato, Savoy
cabbage, bacon rösti and kumquat sauce. Desserts take in a selection of ice creams and sorbets, as
well as raspberry crème brûlée; lemon curd and ginger sponge pudding; and spiced apple pie with
custard. A 45-bin wine list has been carefully selected to complement the food, and beer drinkers are
rewarded with Greene King IPA, Hook Norton Best, Black Sheep, Landlord and other fine ales.

Recommended in the area

Sulgrave Manor; Silverstone; Canons Ashby House (NT)

The Wollaston Inn

Address: 87 London Road,
WOLLASTON, NN29 7QS
Tel: 01933 663161
Email: info@wollaston-inn.co.uk
Website: www.wollaston-inn.co.uk
Map ref: 3 SP96
Directions: From Wellingborough, onto A509
towards Wollaston. After 2m, over rdbt, then
immediately left. Inn at top of hill
Open: all day all week **Facilities:** Parking Garden
Notes: ⊞ MARSTONS ⬥ 12

Chris Spencer took over this historical pub, once the Sunday night venue of the late DJ John Peel, in 2003, reinventing it as a restaurant within a pub and giving it a new name. His loving restoration of the 350-year-old building's original features sits comfortably with the Italian leather sofas and casual tables and chairs. A commitment to please both formal and casual diners is reflected in the reasonably priced set lunch menus (available until 7pm), and an evening carte of seasonal dishes, with everything from the bread and infused oils to the ice creams and dark chocolate truffles made in the kitchen. Daily-changing selections, with ingredients coming from regional suppliers, might include venison haunch steak; Thai red chicken curry; slow roasted pork belly with pancetta and cannellini bean cassoulet; Mediterranean vegetable and buffalo mozzarella stack; and lots of fresh fish and seafood, such as lobster and monkfish thermidor; baked mackerel, sunblush tomato and courgette risotto; and organic sustainable cod, braised oxtail and caramelised apple. There is also a traditional Sunday roast. Service is attentive wherever you eat – choose from the bar, restaurant, patio or garden – and there is a good selection of real ales and an extensive wine list.

Recommended in the area

Summer Leys Nature Reserve; Santa Pod Raceway; Silverstone

NORTHUMBERLAND

Yeavering Bell in Northumberland National Park

The Pheasant Inn

★★★★ INN

Address: Stannersburn, FALSTONE, NE48 1DD
Tel: 01434 240382
Fax: 01434 240382
Email: enquiries@thepheasantinn.com
Website: www.thepheasantinn.com
Map ref: 6 NY78
Directions: A69, B6079, B6320, follow signs for Kielder Water
Open: 12-3 6.30-11 **Closed:** 25-26 Dec, Mon-Tue (Nov-Mar) ⚏ L Mon-Sat 12-2.30 ⚏ L Mon-Sat 12-2.30 D Mon-Sat 6.30-8.30 **Rooms:** 8 en suite (5 GF) **S** £50-£55 **D** £85-£90 **Facilities:** Parking Garden **Notes:** ⊕ FREE HOUSE ⊪ ⊣

Set close by the magnificent Kielder Water, this classic country inn, built in 1624, has exposed stone walls, original beams, low ceilings, open fires and a display of old farm implements in the bar. Run by the welcoming Kershaw family since 1985, the inn was originally a farmhouse and has been refurbished to a very high standard. The bright, modern en suite bedrooms, some with their own entrances, are all contained in stone buildings adjoining the inn and are set round a pretty courtyard. All the rooms, including one family room, are spotless, well equipped, and have tea- and coffee-making facilities, hairdryer, TV and radio alarm clock; all enjoy delightful country views. Delicious home-cooked breakfasts and evening meals are served in the bar or in the attractive dining room, or may be taken in the pretty garden courtyard if the weather permits. Irene and her son Robin are responsible for the traditional home cooking using local produce and featuring delights such as game pie and roast Northumbrian lamb, as well as imaginative vegetarian choices. Drying and laundry facilities are available and, for energetic guests, cycle hire can be arranged.

Recommended in the area

Hadrian's Wall; Scottish Borders; Northumbrian castles and stately homes

Battlesteads Hotel & Restaurant

Address: Wark, HEXHAM, NE48 3LS
Tel: 01434 230209
Fax: 01434 230039
Email: info@battlesteads.com
Website: www.battlesteads.com
Map ref: 7 NY96
Directions: 10m N of Hexham on B6320
(Kielder road)
Open: all week **Facilities:** Parking Garden
Notes: ⊕ FREE HOUSE 🍴 🐾

Originally built in 1747, this traditional Northumbrian inn and restaurant features a cosy bar with wood-burning stove, sunny conservatory and secret walled garden, excellent bar meals and à la carte menus (including vegetarian) using fresh, local produce, and a choice of 20 wines and five cask ales. Taken over some five years ago by Richard and Dee Slade, Battlesteads has quickly gained a reputation for its character and warm welcome as a friendly, family run establishment. Chefs source the best of local ingredients (within a 30 mile radius) to ensure freshness and flavour – including top quality Northumbrian lamb, prime Cumbrian beef and seasonal game. Fish and seafood is sourced from North Shields Fish Quay, and smoked fish and game from Bywell Smokery. Fresh vegetables and herbs are grown in the hotel garden, and vegetarian choices are always available. A range of traditional roast dinners featuring locally reared beef, lamb and pork are available at the popular Sunday Carvery, all at set prices. Battlesteads has 17 en suite rooms; four ground floor rooms have facilities for the disabled. Broadband access is available in all rooms.

Recommended in the Area

Hadrian's Wall; Kielder Forest and Lake; Alnwick Castle

The Anglers Arms

Address: Weldon Bridge, LONGFRAMLINGTON, Morpeth, NE65 8AX
Tel: 01665 570271 & 570655
Email: johnyoung@anglersarms.fsnet.co.uk
Website: www.anglersarms.com
Map ref: 10 NU10
Directions: From N, 9m S of Alnwick right Weldon Bridge sign. From S, A1 to by-pass Morpeth, left onto A697 for Wooler & Coldstream. 7m, left to Weldon Bridge

Open: all week 11-11 (Sun 12-11) **Facilities:** Parking Garden **Notes:** ⊕ FREE HOUSE ♦♦

A 1760s coaching inn, now traditional pub and restaurant, overlooking the picturesque Weldon Bridge across the River Coquet. Your hosts here are John and Julie Young, who have created a bar that derives some of its warmth and friendliness from a collection of nice little touches - ornaments, antiques, quaint pieces of bric-a-brac, including some interesting hand-painted wall tiles, and fishing memorabilia. Meals in here are typified by mixed grill; home-made steak and ale pie; grilled salmon; oriental sizzling platter; and vegetable stew. As an unusual experience, dine in style in the Pullman railway carriage, where your choice might be a starter of garlic king prawns; scallop and bacon salad; or twice-cooked belly pork with honey-spiced apples, followed by a main course of tournedos Flodden, a prime fillet stuffed with Applewood cheese in bacon with garlic sauce; Borders rack of lamb; pan-fried breast of duck with honey-roasted parsnips, sweet potatoes and Cumberland glaze; or oven-baked peppers. Lighter meals include sandwiches and fresh garden leaf salads. The desserts board changes daily. Children will probably head outside for the playground.

Recommended in the Area

Bamburgh Castle; Brinkburn Priory; Hadrian's Wall

The Olde Ship Inn

★★★★ INN

Address: 9 Main Street, SEAHOUSES, NE68 7RD
Tel: 01665 720200
Fax: 01665 721383
Email: theoldeship@seahouses.co.uk
Website: www.seahouses.co.uk
Map ref: 10 NU23
Directions: Lower end of main street above harbour
Open: all day all week 11-11 (Sun noon-11) ⓛ **L** all wk 12-2.30 **D** all wk 7-8.30 (no **D** late Nov-late Jan) ⓘ **L** Sun 12-2 **D** all wk 7-8.30 (no **D** late Nov-late Jan) **Rooms:** 18 en suite (3 GF) **S** £50-£60 **D** £100-£116 **Facilities:** Parking Garden **Notes:** ⓓ FREE HOUSE ⓕ 10

A former farmhouse dating from 1745, the inn stands overlooking the harbour in the tiny port of Seahouses, from where grain was once exported. The Olde Ship was first licensed in 1812 and has been in the same family for over 100 years, and these days it is a fully residential inn. The corridors, the boat gallery and the bars of the hotel are bulging at the seams with nautical memorabilia, creating a wonderful atmosphere, full of character, and the main saloon bar is warmed by an open fire and lit by stained glass windows. The overnight accommodation ranges through a self-catering fisherman's house, an all ground-floor self-catering cottage, adjoining executive suites and bedrooms in the hotel itself, including two four-poster rooms. They are all en suite, offering TVs, refreshment facilities and direct-dial telephones. Some have marvellous views over to the bird and sea sanctuary on the nearby Farne Islands. Good home cooking features locally caught seafood and majors on soups, pastries, puddings and pies. Meals are served in the Restaurant, the Cabin Bar and the Locker Room. Boat trips run from the pier and there are wonderful coastal walks and attractive villages in the vicinity.

Recommended in the area

Farne Islands; Bamburgh Castle; Lindisfarne

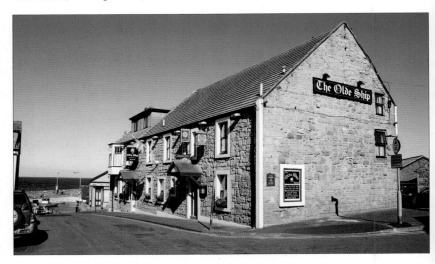

Newstead Abbey

The Martin's Arms

Address: School Lane, COLSTON BASSETT,
NG12 3FD
Tel: 01949 81361
Fax: 01949 81039
Email: martins_arms@hotmail.co.uk
Website: www.themartinsarmsinn.co.uk
Map ref: 8 SK73
Directions: Off A46 between Leicester & Newark
Open: all week noon-3.30 6-11 **Closed:** 25 Dec eve
L Mon-Sat 12-2, Sun 12-2.30 **D** Mon-Sat 7-9.30
L all wk 12-2 **D** Mon-Sat 7-9.30 **Facilities:** Parking Garden **Notes:** FREE HOUSE 7

So popular is this award-winning inn that it has made appearances on both regional and national television. It is a listed 18th-century building, set close to the old market cross in this stunning village in the Vale of Belvoir, an area that is renowned for its Stilton cheese. The interior has a real country house feel to it, with period furnishings, traditional hunting prints and seasonal fires in the Jacobean fireplace. Outside there is an acre of landscaped grounds, which includes a herb garden and well established lawns, backing on to National Trust land. The inn is a free house, serving a good range of real ales – Marston's Pedigree, Interbrew Bass, Greene King Abbot Ale, Timothy Taylor Landlord – from hand pumps. The wine list also offers seven wines by the glass. Good regional ingredients are a feature of the menu. Take, for example, the classic ploughman's lunch comprising Melton Mowbray pork pie, Colston Bassett Stilton or Cheddar, home-cured ham, pickles and bread. Alternatives in the bar include game pie, or fresh gnocchi with oven roasted tomatoes, peppers, spinach and parmesan cream. Typical restaurant dishes are cod fillet with lobster ravioli, potato rösti and creamed leek sauce; and bacon-wrapped rump of lamb with potato fondant and Puy lentils. Dogs are allowed in the garden only.

Recommended in the area

Belvoir Castle; Belton House; The National Water Sports Centre at Holme Pierrepoint

The Farndon Boathouse

Address: Riverside, FARNDON, Newark, NG24 3SX
Tel: 01636 676578
Fax: 01636 673911
Email: info@farndonboathouse.co.uk
Website: www.farndonboathouse.co.uk
Map ref: 8 SK75
Directions: From Newark follow A46 to Farndon x-rds, turn right and follow rd to river. Boathouse on riverside
Open: all day all week 10am-11pm ⓑ L Mon- Fri 12-2.30, Sat-Sun 12-3 D all wk 6-9.30 ⓞ L Mon-Fri 12-2.30, Sat-Sun 12-3 D all wk 6-9.30
Facilities: Parking Garden **Notes:** ⊕ FREE HOUSE ⧫ ♏ 16

Some visitors might recall the New Ferry Restaurant that stood on this verdant riverside site until 2008; that's when it was comprehensively redeveloped as this stylish dining pub. Observe how its wood-clad exterior evokes an old Victorian boathouse; inside, look up at its hefty exposed roof beams and trusses, down at its stone floors and finally all around at the cutting-edge fixtures and fittings. Then gaze through the extensively glazed frontage of the bar and restaurant at the Trent as it meanders slowly towards Newark. Monthly changing menus are clearly planned, typically listing fresh, locally sourced modern dishes of smoked duck breast on walnut, orange and endive salad; poached cod loin with parsley sauce, creamy leeks and watercress; home-grown beetroot and mascarpone risotto with crumbled Wensleydale cheese; steaks, ham and eggs, and a variety of burgers. Many of the meats, fish, spices and cheeses come from the in-house smokery, and herbs, roots, leaves and peppers grow in profusion in the rear garden. With ever-changing cask-conditioned beers, and with live music every Sunday evening, this buzzing venue has fast become the fashionable place to be.

Recommended in the area

Belvoir Castle; Lincoln Cathedral; Newark Antiques Warehouse

OXFORDSHIRE

High Street, Oxford, from the Carfax Tower

The Vines

Address: Burford Road, Bampton,
BLACK BOURTON, OX18 2PF
Tel: 01993 843559
Fax: 01993 840080
Email: info@vineshotel.com
Website: www.vinesblackbourton.co.uk
Map ref: 3 SP20
Directions: From A40 Witney, take A4095 to
Faringdon, then 1st right after Bampton to Black
Bourton **Closed:** lunch Mon-Fri 🍴 🍽️ **L** Sat & Sun

from 12 **D** Mon-Fri 6-9 **Facilities:** Parking Garden **Notes:** ⊕ FREE HOUSE 🍴 🍷 7

Situated in a picturesque village setting, The Vines is a traditional stone-built inn with an elegant, contemporary feel and surrounded by delightful gardens. The restaurant and bar were designed by the BBC *Real Rooms* team. Food is offered from the carte menu, with dishes prepared from fresh local produce, especially fish. An alternative venue for a drink or a snack is the comfortable lounge with its leather sofas and cosy winter fire. On sunny days dine on the patio or play a game of Aunt Sally.
Recommended in the area
Cogges Manor Farm Museum; Cotswold Wildlife Park; Blenheim Palace

The Lord Nelson Inn

Address: BRIGHTWELL BALDWIN,
nr Watlington, OX49 5NP
Tel: 01491 612497
Email: ladyhamilton1@hotmail.co.uk
Website: www.lordnelson-inn.co.uk
Map ref: 3 SU69
Directions: Off B4009 between Watlington & Benson
Open: all week 12-3 6-11 (Sun 12-10.30)
🍴 **L** all wk 12-2.30 **D** all wk 6-10 🍽️ **L** all wk

12-2.30 **D** all wk 6-10 **Facilities:** Parking Garden
Notes: ⊕ FREE HOUSE 🍷 20

This traditional 300-year-old inn, furnished with beautiful antiques, is set in an unspoilt village, opposite the church, and its exterior will be familiar to *Midsomer Murders* fans. In 1905 it was forced to close by the local lord who was trying to stop his workers from drinking, and did not reopen until 1971. There is a comprehensive wine list, and all the dishes are freshly cooked to order by the inn's experienced chefs. There are also some good hearty bar snacks and a varied Sunday lunch menu.
Recommended in the area
Stonor Park; The Rideway; Wallingford Museum

The Lamb Inn

★★★ 81% ◉◉ SMALL HOTEL
Address: Sheep Street, BURFORD, OX18 4LR
Tel: 01993 823155
Fax: 01993 822228
Email: info@lambinn-burford.co.uk
Website: www.cotswold-inns-hotels.co.uk/lamb
Map ref: 3 SP21
Directions: M40 junct 8, follow A40 & Burford signs, 1st turn, down hill into Sheep St
Open: all week 11-11 🍴 **L** all wk 12-2.30 **D** all wk 6.30-9.30 🍴 **L** all wk 12-2.30 **D** all wk 7-9.30 **Rooms:** 17 en suite (4 GF) **Facilities:** Garden
Notes: ⊕ FREE HOUSE ♦♦ 🐾 🍷 9

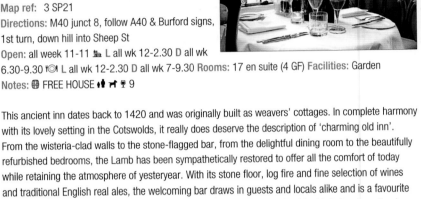

This ancient inn dates back to 1420 and was originally built as weavers' cottages. In complete harmony with its lovely setting in the Cotswolds, it really does deserve the description of 'charming old inn'. From the wisteria-clad walls to the stone-flagged bar, from the delightful dining room to the beautifully refurbished bedrooms, the Lamb has been sympathetically restored to offer all the comfort of today while retaining the atmosphere of yesteryear. With its stone floor, log fire and fine selection of wines and traditional English real ales, the welcoming bar draws in guests and locals alike and is a favourite spot to exchange news and views. There is an extensive menu if you should wish to lunch or dine in these relaxed surroundings. The finest fresh ingredients, many produced locally, are used to create a cuisine that is contemporary English with strong traditional influences. A daily fish board is also available. Alternatively enjoy a drink or lunch in the walled patio garden, a veritable sun-trap which leads down to a beautiful traditional English cottage garden, a lovely area in which to relax, read or take an afternoon nap.

Recommended in the area

Blenheim Palace; Cotswold Wildlife Park; Burford Garden Company

The Red Lion Inn

Address: The High Street, CHALGROVE, OX44 7SS
Tel: 01865 890625
Email: raymondsexton@btinternet.com
Website: www.redlionchalgrove.co.uk
Map ref: 3 SU69
Directions: B480 from Oxford ring road, through Stadhampton, left then right at mini-rdbt. At Chalgrove Airfield right into village **Open:** all week 11.30-3 6-mdnt (Sat 11.30-3 6-1am Sat 11.30am-1am Sun 11.30am-mdnt in summer) ⓫ ⦿ L Mon-Sat 12-2, Sun 12-3 **D** Mon-Sat 6-9 **Facilities:** Garden **Notes:** ⊕ FREE HOUSE ⦿ ⌁ ♀ 8

Rather unusually, the local parish church owns the 15th-century Red Lion. How appropriate then, that the surname of the landlords, Suzanne and Raymond, is Sexton. Food is served in the bar and the restaurant from 'a menu that tries to please everyone'. Starters include spicy lamb samosas with mixed leaf salad; and that old favourite, prawn cocktail. Expect main courses such as braised shank of lamb with root vegetables, and pan-fried fillet of halibut on risotto rice with chorizo and baby peas.
Recommended in the area
City of Oxford; Courthouse, Ridgeway Path; Long Crendon (NT)

The Sir Charles Napier

◉◉

Address: Spriggs Alley, CHINNOR, OX39 4BX
Tel: 01494 483011 **Fax:** 01494 485311
Website: www.sircharlesnapier.co.uk
Map ref: 3 SP70
Directions: M40 junct 6 to Chinnor. Turn right at rdbt, up hill to Spriggs Alley
Open: noon-4 6-mdnt (Sun noon-6) **Closed:** 25-26 Dec, Mon, Sun eve ⓫ L Tue-Fri 12-2.30 **D** Tue-Fri 6.30-9 ⦿ L Tue-Sat 12-2.30, Sun 12-3.30 **D** Tue-Sat 6.30-10 **Facilities:** Parking Garden **Notes:** ⊕ FREE HOUSE ⦿ ⌁ ♀ 15

The Sir Charles Napier is in the scenic Chiltern Hills surrounded by beech woods and fields. The furnishings are eclectic, and wonderful sculptures are exhibited throughout the year. In summer, lunch is served on the terrace beneath vines and wisteria, overlooking the herb gardens and lawns. The wine list complements blackboard dishes and imaginative seasonal menus. Typical dishes are halibut with pea purée, and sea bream with saffron and crayfish tails.
Recommended in the area
The Chiltern Hills; West Wycombe Park; Garsington Opera

Broughton Castle, Banbury

Coach & Horses Inn

★★★ 🍺 INN

Address: Watlington Road, CHISELHAMPTON,
OX44 7UX

Tel: 01865 890255 **Fax:** 01865 891995

Email: enquiries@coachhorsesinn.co.uk

Website: www.coachhorsesinn.co.uk

Map ref: 3 SU59 **Directions:** From Oxford on B480
towards Watlington, 5m **Open:** all week 11-11 (Sun
11-10.30) 🍴 **L** Mon-Sat 12-2 🍽 **L** all wk 12-2 **D**
Mon-Sat 7-9.30 **Rooms:** 9 en suite **S** £59-£68 **D**
£68-£78 **Facilities:** Parking Garden **Notes:** 🍺 FREE HOUSE 🍷 8

A charming, family-run 16th-century inn, just 200 yards from the River Thame. When it's chilly
someone lights the huge log fire in the bar, while in the summer it's hard to beat the courtyard or lawn
for a pleasant drink. You may eat outside, or in the oak-beamed, candlelit restaurant, from a seasonal
menu featuring Angus steaks, game and fresh seafood, while at lunchtimes bar meals and snacks are
available. The bedrooms are ranged around the courtyard, with most looking out over the countryside.

Recommended in the area

City of Oxford; Ridgeway Path; Hughenden Manor

The White Lion

Address: Goring Road, Goring Heath, CRAY'S POND, Reading, RG8 7SH
Tel: 01491 680471
Fax: 01491 684254
Email: reservations@thewhitelioncrayspond.com
Website: www.thewhitelioncrayspond.com
Map ref: 3 SU68
Directions: From M4 junct 11 follow signs to Pangbourne, through toll bridge to Whitchurch. N for 3m into Cray's Pond

Closed: 25-26 Dec, 1 Jan, Sun eve, Mon **Facilities:** Parking Garden
Notes: ⊕ GREENE KING ♨ ⚑ ♟ 11

Up in the Chilterns' hamlet of Cray's Pond stands this popular, 250-year-old pub. Looking as though it was originally a cottage, it acts once a year as the unofficial headquarters of the Woodcote Rally, one of the country's largest veteran and vintage transport fairs, which is held in a nearby field. Photographs taken of steam engines during the last four decades line the deep red walls, while also worth a browse is the fascinating collection of old and new menus from famous restaurants around the world. The beamed ceilings are low, so watch your head; the dining room charms with its open fires, oak floors and candles; and the conservatory overlooks the garden through large bay windows. In the kitchen there is a real emphasis on quality, freshness and attention to detail before the frequently changing modern British menu sees the light of day. Usually offered are eight starters and main courses, among the latter possibly a whole Dover sole, grilled to perfection with a caper sauce, or dry aged beef from Macey's Organics in Cookham. Sticky toffee pudding, butterscotch sauce and Jersey clotted cream is but one of the tempting desserts. The wine list is compact, but well chosen.

Recommended in the area

Basildon House; Beale Park; Ridgeway Path

Blenheim Palace, Woodstock

The Trout at Tadpole Bridge

★★★★ 🍺 INN

Address: Buckland Marsh, FARINGDON, SN7 8RF
Tel: 01367 870382
Email: info@troutinn.co.uk
Website: www.troutinn.co.uk
Map ref: 3 SU29
Directions: Halfway between Oxford & Swindon on A420 take road signed Bampton, pub approx 2m
Open: 11.30-3 6-11 **Closed:** 25-26 Dec, Sun eve (1 Nov-30 Apr) 🍴 L all wk 12-2 D all wk 7-9 🍽 L all wk 12-2 D all wk 7-9 **Rooms:** 6 en suite **Facilities:** Parking Garden **Notes:** 🛢 FREE HOUSE 🍴 🐾 🍷 10

Right by the Thames Path, with six bedrooms and berthing for six boats, the historic Trout is a destination in its own right, as so many drinkers, diners and overnight guests would undoubtedly testify. Standing proud among its many awards - AA Pub of the Year for England 2009/2010. The kitchen makes expert use of the best ingredients and from a recent menu come Cornish crab, avocado and home-cured gravadlax with toasted brioche, or free-range Great Farm guinea fowl cooked three ways.

Recommended in the area

Kelmscott Manor; Badbury Hill; Kingston Lisle Park

The White Hart

Address: Main Road, FYFIELD, Nr Abingdon, OX13 5LW
Tel: 01865 390585
Email: info@whitehart-fyfield.com
Website: www.whitehart-fyfield.com
Map ref: 3 SU49
Directions: 7m S of Oxford just off A420 (Oxford to Swindon road) **Open:** noon-3 5.30-11 (Sat noon-11 Sun noon-10.30) **Closed:** Mon ex BH ⅃ ⑇ L Tue-Sat 12-2.30, Sun 12-4 **D** Tue-Sat 7-9.30 **Facilities:** Parking Garden
Notes: ⊕ FREE HOUSE ⅋⅌ ⚲ 14

An historic, 15th-century chantry house, the White Hart retains many original features, including a tunnel to Fyfield Manor (possibly used as an escape route for priests during the Dissolution of the Monasteries). The setting is breathtaking, from soaring eaves in the great hall and minstrels' gallery, to the terrace full of aromatic herb gardens. Given that owners, Mark and Kay Chandler, are self-confessed 'foodies' it is no surprise that the White Hart is renowned for superb locally sourced food, including their own kitchen garden where fruit, vegetables and herbs are grown for the restaurant. Menus change daily depending on what is fresh and seasonal and everything is made in-house, including bread, pasta and ice creams. Starters may include home-cured salmon gravadlax with marinated cucumber salad. For main courses, there might be wild sea bass fillet with samphire and crab bisque, or slow roasted pork belly with celeriac purée, crackling and cider jus. Puddings are just as tempting, especially hot chocolate fondant with pistachio ice cream. Although standards of food and service are high, the pub is still very much a village local, with a cosy bar and inglenook fireplace. Two beer festivals are held annually (May Day and August bank holidays) with real ales, live jazz and a hog roast.

Recommended in the area

Ashmolean Museum, Oxford; White Horse, Uffington; Blenheim Palace, Woodstock

Miller of Mansfield

★★★★★ ® RESTAURANT WITH ROOMS

Address: High Street, GORING ON THAMES,
nr Reading, RG8 9AW
Tel: 01491 872829
Fax: 01491 873100
Email: reservations@millerofmansfield.com
Website: www.millerofmansfield.com
Map ref: 3 SU68
Directions: From Pangbourne take A329 to Streatley.
Right on B4009, 0.5m to Goring
Open: 8am-11pm ⓑ L 12-10 D 12-10 ⓘ L 12-4.30 D 6.30-10 **Rooms:** 13 en suite S £100-£125
D £125-£225 **Facilities:** Parking Garden **Notes:** ⊕ FREE HOUSE ⸻ 15

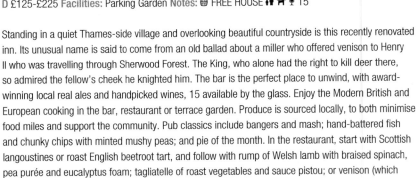

Standing in a quiet Thames-side village and overlooking beautiful countryside is this recently renovated inn. Its unusual name is said to come from an old ballad about a miller who offered venison to Henry II who was travelling through Sherwood Forest. The King, who alone had the right to kill deer there, so admired the fellow's cheek he knighted him. The bar is the perfect place to unwind, with award-winning local real ales and handpicked wines, 15 available by the glass. Enjoy the Modern British and European cooking in the bar, restaurant or terrace garden. Produce is sourced locally, to both minimise food miles and support the community. Pub classics include bangers and mash; hand-battered fish and chunky chips with minted mushy peas; and pie of the month. In the restaurant, start with Scottish langoustines or roast English beetroot tart, and follow with rump of Welsh lamb with braised spinach, pea purée and eucalyptus foam; tagliatelle of roast vegetables and sauce pistou; or venison (which comes from the nearby Yattendon Estate) with baby carrots, confit garlic purée and jus de Cassis. Rooms and suites come with marble bathrooms and flat-screen TVs.

Recommended in the area

Basildon House (NT); The Ridgeway Path; Beale Park

Henley-on-Thames

The Five Horseshoes

Address: Maidensgrove, HENLEY-ON-THAMES, RG9 6EX
Tel: 01491 641282
Fax: 01491 641086
Email: admin@thefivehorseshoes.co.uk
Website: www.thefivehorseshoes.co.uk
Map ref: 3 SU78
Directions: Take A4130, in 1m take B480 to right, signed Stonor. In Stonor left, through woods, over common, pub on left. **Open:** noon-3.30 6-11 (Sat noon-11 Sun noon-6) **Closed:** Sun eve ⓓ ⓘⓄⓘ **L** Mon-Fri 12-2.30, Sat 12-3, Sun 12-4 **D** Mon-Sat 6.30-9.30 **Facilities:** Parking Garden **Notes:** ⊕ BRAKSPEAR ⓘⓘ ⓘ ⓘ 11

The Five Horseshoes is in an Area of Outstanding Natural Beauty with amazing views over the Chilterns. This 17th-century pub exudes old world character with its wooden beams and open fires; there are two snug bar areas and a large restaurant. Dishes, created from locally sourced produce, include game terrine with fig chutney, roasted crayfish, haunch of wild Oxfordshire venison or home-made pork pie.

Recommended in the area

River & Rowing Museum; Mapledurham House & Watermill; Warburg Nature Reserve

The Black Boy Inn

Address: MILTON, Banbury, OX15 4HH
Tel: 01295 722111
Fax: 01295 722978
Email: info@blackboyinn.com
Website: www.blackboyinn.com
Map ref: 3 SP43
Directions: From Banbury take A4260 to Adderbury. After Adderbury turn right signed Bloxham. Onto Milton Road to Milton. Pub on right
Open: all week 🏠 🍽 **L** Mon-Sat 12-2.30, Sun 12-3 **D** Mon-Thu 6.30-9, Fri-Sat 6.30-9.30
Facilities: Parking Garden

Although this 16th-century coaching inn has been completely refurbished, its stylish interior and solid pine furniture are entirely in keeping with such an old building. Located in picturesque Milton, the pub is thought to take its name from the dark-skinned Charles II, although other theories point to the slave trade. The long room has a real wood stove at one end and a comfortable dining room at the other; in between is the bar, with conservatory-style dining. Outside there is plenty of seating in the patio and garden, the latter providing a half-acre of space for children to run around. A rotating list of guest ales and a selection of wines by the glass ensure that drinkers can enjoy the informal atmosphere of this quintessentially English inn. Food is important here, with modern British dishes based on fresh seasonal ingredients at sensible prices. There are plenty of pub classics, including beer-battered cod and home-made chips with crushed peas, as well as up-market mains such as roasted fillet of sea trout with crab tagliatelle and fennel. Excellent desserts, vegetarian options and a wide range of fresh salads and tasty sandwiches are also on offer.

Recommended in the area

Broughton Castle; Blenheim Palace; Waterperry Gardens

The Crown Inn

Address: PISHILL, Henley-on-Thames, RG9 6HH
Tel: 01491 638364
Email: enquiries@thecrowninnpishill.co.uk
Website: www.thecrowninnpishill.co.uk
Map ref: 3 SU78
Directions: On B480 off A4130, 8m NW of Henley-on-Thames
Open: all week 11.30-3 6-11 (Sun noon-3 7-10)
Closed: 25-26 Dec 🍴 **L** all wk 12-2.30 **D** all wk 7-9.30 🍽 **L** all wk 12-2.30 **D** all wk 7-9.30
Facilities: Parking Garden **Notes:** 🍺 FREE HOUSE 🚻 🐾 🍷 8

A pretty 15th-century brick and flint former coaching inn, The Crown has enjoyed a colourful history. It began life in medieval times, serving ale to members of the thriving local monastic community, and in later years served as a refuge for Catholic priests escaping Henry VIII's draconian rule. It contains possibility the largest priest hole in the country, complete with a sad story about one Father Dominique, who met his end here. Moving forward to the 'swinging 60s', the barn housed a nightclub hosting the likes of George Harrison and Dusty Springfield. Today, the barn is licensed for civil ceremonies as well as serving as a function room. In the pub itself, the menu changes frequently and features local produce cooked fresh to order. Lunch and dinner are served every day and can be enjoyed in the picturesque garden or inside where there are three log fires lit when the weather is cooler. Bed and breakfast accommodation is available.

Recommended in the area

Stonor Park; Greys Court, (NT); River and Rowing Museum

The Royal Oak

Address: High Street, RAMSDEN, OX7 3AU
Tel: 01993 868213
Fax: 01993 868864
Map ref: 3 SP31
Directions: From Witney take B4022 towards Charlbury, then right before Hailey, through Poffley End
Open: all week 11.30-3 6.30-11 (Sun 12-3 7-10.30) **Closed:** 25 Dec ⓑ L all wk 11.30-2 D all wk 7-10 ⓘ L all wk 11.30-2 D all wk 7-10
Facilities: Parking Garden **Notes:** ⊕ FREE HOUSE ⌁ ♚ 30

Once upon a time, stagecoaches between London and Hereford stopped at this 17th-century inn standing opposite the church in the pretty Cotswold village of Ramsden. These days it is popular with walkers exploring the lovely countryside, but whether you feel like walking or not, stop here for its old beams, warm fires, stone walls and, of course, refreshment. As a free house it offers beers for which real ale aficionados would willingly join the rambling fraternity, while the 200-bin wine list would particularly appeal to those appreciating their Bordeaux, with many of them available by the glass. The bar menu regularly features a pie of the week, and there are also favourites such as real Italian meatballs; home-made beef burgers; and wild mushroom pasta with shiitake and porcini mushrooms. The main menu features the very best of fresh, local, seasonal food, with regular fish deliveries. To start your meal, expect moules marinière (with Hebridean mussels); chicken liver parfait with cognac and raisins; and baked avocado, cheese and prawn gratin. Main courses include smoked haddock cooked with whisky, cream and cheese; confit of duck leg with quince sauce and Puy lentils; and pan-fried calf's liver with wild mushroom sauce.

Recommended in the area

Blenheim Palace; Minster Lovell Hall; Rollright Stones

Crooked Billet

Address: STOKE ROW, Henley-on-Thames, RG9 5PU
Tel: 01491 681048
Fax: 01491 682231
Website: www.thecrookedbillet.co.uk
Map ref: 3 SU68
Directions: Henley towards Oxford, A4130. Left at Nettlebed
Open: noon-3 7-mdnt (Sat-Sun noon-mdnt) ⓑ L Mon-Fri
12-3, Sat-Sun all day D Mon-Fri 7-10, Sat-Sun all day ⓘ L
Mon-Fri 12-3, Sat-Sun all day D Mon-Fri 7-10, Sat-Sun all day
Facilities: Parking Garden **Notes:** ⓦ BRAKSPEAR ⓘ♥ 12

The remote location of this charming pub was a boon to
highwayman Dick Turpin, who avoided the law and courted
the landlord's daughter here. Later, it became a favourite watering hole of George Harrison, who lived
nearby. But you don't have to be a celebrity to appreciate its pretty farmland setting and its fascinating
history, dating back to 1642. Chef/proprietor Paul Clerehugh is so keen to use local produce that he's
even been known to swap meals for produce. Seafood is a speciality, with Sevruga caviar served with
oysters, sour cream and smoked salmon blinis as a starter, and fillets of Dover sole with grilled king
prawns and Puy lentils to follow. For game choices try hare braised with lardons, mushrooms, baby
onions and thyme, served with herb dumplings. Other dishes include starters such as a selection of
Italian salami, served with artichoke, mozzarella, olives and sun-blushed tomato; or crispy-fried salt
and pepper squid with warm chick pea and roast vegetable salad; or main courses such as breast of
chicken stuffed with goats' cheese and baked in pancetta, served with warm chorizo salad and Puy
lentils. Vegetarians may find sage and pecorino polenta with asparagus and artichoke heart salad, or
leek and Oxford Blue pancakes with roast winter roots.

Recommended in the area

Mapledurham House; Greys Court (NT); Beale Park

The Mason's Arms

Address: Banbury Road, SWERFORD,
Chipping Norton, OX7 4AP
Tel: 01608 683212
Fax: 01608 683105
Email: admin@masons-arms.com
Website: www.masons-arms.com
Map ref: 3 SP33
Directions: Between Banbury & Chipping Norton
on A361
Closed: 25-26 Dec, Sun eve 🍽 L Mon-Sat 12-2 **D** Mon-Sat 7-9 🍽 L Mon-Sat 12-2, Sun 12-3.30
D Mon-Sat 7-9 **Facilities:** Parking Garden **Notes:** ⊕ FREE HOUSE 🍴 ♟ 14

A former Masonic lodge built of local honey-coloured stone, this free house is situated in beautiful surroundings just a stone's throw from the Hook Norton Brewery. Traditional charm is balanced by plenty of modern comforts under the enthusiastic ownership of Bill and Charmaine Leadbeater. The chef/proprietor trained with Gordon Ramsay and Marco Pierre White, so expect something special. All the meat is from rare breeds; poultry is free range; fish is delivered daily. The menu, boldly entitled Bill's Food, has a distinctly continental outlook, featuring unusual and frequently changing dishes. Starters might include smoked halibut with avocado parfait and cider and apple dressing, while main course options of chargrilled marlin loin; steamed vegetable pancake wrap; and Gloucester Old Spot pork done three ways might feature. A treat for four to share, given 48 hours' notice, is whole roast leg of Oxford Down lamb with rosemary and garlic, dauphinoise potatoes, haricot verts and rosemary jus. Bar snacks take include a range of pub favourites, beers are well-kept, and there's also a good choice of malt whiskies.

Recommended in the area

Burford Wildlife Park; Hook Norton Brewery and Pottery; Wiggington Waterfowl Sanctuary

The Bridge of Sighs in Oxford

The Crown Inn

Address: Sydenham Road, SYDENHAM,
Nr Chinnor, OX39 4NB
Tel: 01844 351634
Website: www.crownsydenham.co.uk
Map ref: 3 SP70
Directions: M40 junct 6 north & 1st left A40. At
Postcombe, right to Sydenham **Open:** Tue-Fri 12-3,
5.30-11, Sat 12-11, Sun 12-3 **Closed:** Mon, Sun
eve ⧆ **L** Tue-Sun 12-2.30 **D** Tue-Sat 6.30-9.30
Facilities: Parking Garden
Notes: ⊕ FREE HOUSE ⁑ ⌂ ⚐ 6

Good news travelled fast in 2008 when Max, the chef/landlord, and his wife Louise arrived in this
village just under the scarp slope of the Chilterns to take over its 16th-century pub. The real fires create
an atmosphere both warm and welcoming, and the seasonal menus, real ales and worldly wines rapidly
earned a fine reputation. Food from local suppliers is freshly prepared so the menu is short but sweet,
barely a dozen lines long. There is a large garden with Aunt Sally pub game. Booking is advisable.
Recommended in the area
Hell Fire Caves; Stonor Park; City of Oxford

Tudor architecture, Ludlow

The Boyne Arms

Address: Bridgnorth Road, BURWARTON,
WV16 6QH
Tel: 01746 787214
Email: theboynearms@btconnect.com
Website: www.theboynearms.co.uk
Map ref: 2 SO68
Directions: On B4364 between Ludlow & Bridgnorth
Open: all week all day (wknds only) 🍴 **L** Mon-Sat
12-2 **D** Tue-Sat 6.30-9 🍴 **L** Fri-Sun 12-2
D Tue-Sat 6.30-9 **Facilities:** Parking Garden
Notes: ⊕ FREE HOUSE 🕇 ♟ 8

Located in an Area of Outstanding Natural Beauty, the Boyne Arms is a striking example of a rural, Georgian coaching inn. Boasting an impressive frontage and beautiful mature walled garden with a children's play area, the pub, which is part of the Boyne Estate and has been part of Lord Boyne's family for generations, has been drawing visitors and locals alike for some time. The food is a real draw, and husband and wife Jamie and Nere Yardley and their team offer a high quality dining experience either in one of the comfortable bars – where four real ales plus a real cider are always on the hand pumps – or in the elegant dining room, with its crisp white napery and attentive friendly service. Well-presented dishes combine fresh regional produce with classic French flavours, as in assiette of new season lamb with confit potatoes and vegetable jardinière or seared scallops with boudin noir, followed by simple lemon tart. More simple fare, such as an unbeatable pork pie ploughman's bar lunch, is also available. The extensive wine list to suit all tastes and pockets sits comfortably alongside a range of excellent local award-winning real ales from the likes of Hobsons and Wood's breweries.

Recommended in the area

Historic towns of Ludlow and Bridgnorth; Shropshire Hills; Ludlow Castle

The Crown Inn

Address: Hopton Wafers, CLEOBURY MORTIMER, DY14 0NB
Tel: 01299 270372
Fax: 01299 271127
Website: www.crownathopton.co.uk
Map ref: 2 SO67
Directions: On A4117 8m E of Ludlow, 2m W of Cleobury Mortimer
Open: all week **Facilities:** Parking Garden
Notes: FREE HOUSE 10

Surrounded by streams, farmland, wooded valleys and immaculately kept gardens with a duck pond, this 16th-century, one-time coaching inn appears to be constructed from Virginia creeper, so densely does its foliage cover the façade. It was once estate property and local tenants paid whatever they owed in the Rent Room, now one of the three restaurants, and offering traditional pine kitchen-style seating. The second area is Poachers, with exposed beams, bare stonework and a large inglenook fireplace, while number three is the Shropshire Restaurant extension, overlooking the Crown's rural surroundings. Locally born chef Kevin Clark, who achieved two AA Rosettes here in an earlier spell, has returned to work his magic again. A believer in using regional produce, he goes for such dishes as grilled asparagus wrapped in Parma ham with mixed cress, rocket and hollandaise sauce; medallions of monkfish with tiger prawns and couscous and dill cream; fillet of beef on beetroot risotto with port reduction; and Mediterranean vegetable and goat's cheese Wellington with roasted tomato sauce. Typically, specials are seared king scallops, asparagus and radish salad with lemon dressing; and chargrilled chicken and vegetable kebab with basil aioli.

Recommended in the area

Clee Hill; Severn Valley Railway; Ironbridge

Ironbridge

SOMERSET

Nether Stowey in the Quantock Hills

Exmoor National Park from Tivington Kowle

King William

Address: 36 Thomas Street, BATH, BA1 5NN
Tel: 01225 428096
Email: info@kingwilliampub.com
Website: www.kingwilliampub.com
Map ref: 2 ST76
Directions: At junct of Thomas St & A4 (London Rd), on left from Bath towards London. 15 mins walk from Bath Spa main line station
Open: noon-3 5-close (Sat-Sun noon-close)
Closed: Mon L ⓑ available ⓘ L Sat-Sun 12-3 D Wed-Sat 6-10 **Notes:** ⊕ FREE HOUSE ⁑ ⚲ ♟ 21

A traditional corner free house with a cosy snug in the cellar and a chic restaurant upstairs. The wine list is excellent, the real ales come from local microbreweries, the cider from Somerset. Meat and poultry are free range or organic, and seafood arrives daily from Cornwall; in fact everything except bread, butter and cheese is home made. For burgers and beer-battered hake with chips head for the bar, while the dining room's weekly menus feature roast grouse for two or plaice with leek and mussel broth.
Recommended in the area
Roman Baths; Bath Abbey; Claverton Pumping Station

The Hunters Rest

★★★★ INN

Address: King Lane, Clutton Hill,
CLUTTON, BS39 5QL
Tel: 01761 452303
Fax: 01761 453308
Email: info@huntersrest.co.uk
Website: www.huntersrest.co.uk
Map ref: 2 ST65
Directions: On A37 follow signs for Wells through

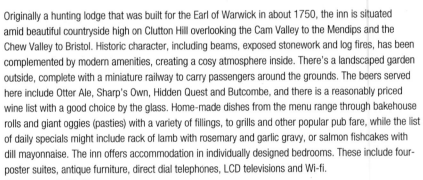

Pensford, at large rdbt left towards Bath, 100mtrs
right into country lane, pub 1m up hill **Open:** all week noon-3 6-11 (Fri-Sun noon-11)
 L Mon-Thu 12-3, Fri-Sun 12-10 **D** Mon-Thu 6-10, Fri-Sun 12-10 **Rooms:** 5 en suite
S £62.50-£79.50 **D** £87.50-£125 **Facilities:** Parking Garden **Notes:** ⊞ FREE HOUSE ♦♦ ♦ ♀ 14

Originally a hunting lodge that was built for the Earl of Warwick in about 1750, the inn is situated amid beautiful countryside high on Clutton Hill overlooking the Cam Valley to the Mendips and the Chew Valley to Bristol. Historic character, including beams, exposed stonework and log fires, has been complemented by modern amenities, creating a cosy atmosphere inside. There's a landscaped garden outside, complete with a miniature railway to carry passengers around the grounds. The beers served here include Otter Ale, Sharp's Own, Hidden Quest and Butcombe, and there is a reasonably priced wine list with a good choice by the glass. Home-made dishes from the menu range through bakehouse rolls and giant oggies (pasties) with a variety of fillings, to grills and other popular pub fare, while the list of daily specials might include rack of lamb with rosemary and garlic gravy, or salmon fishcakes with dill mayonnaise. The inn offers accommodation in individually designed bedrooms. These include four-poster suites, antique furniture, direct dial telephones, LCD televisions and Wi-fi.

Recommended in the area

Bath; Cheddar Caves; Wells Cathedral

The Luttrell Arms

★★★ 73% HOTEL
Address: High Street, DUNSTER, TA24 6SG
Tel: 01643 821555
Fax: 01643 821567
Email: info@luttrellarms.fsnet.co.uk
Map ref: 1 SS94
Directions: From A39 (Bridgewater to Minehead), left
onto A396 to Dunster (2m from Minehead)
Open: all week 8am-11pm ⓑ L 11.30-3, all day
summer D 7-10 ⓘ L Sun 12-3 D 7-10 **Rooms:** 28
en suite S £70-£102 D £104-£140 **Facilities:** Garden **Notes:** ⊕ FREE HOUSE ⓘ ⓘ

Set in the only street in the medieval village of Dunster, within Exmoor National Park, this 15th-century hotel was once a guest house for the Abbots of Cleeve. Inside, it is certainly rich in atmosphere and history and is a good spot to escape the pace of modern life. The open fires and oak beams make the bar a welcoming place in winter, with locally brewed beers on offer, while the murmuring of ghostly monks is rumoured to cure even the most stubborn insomniacs, should you choose to stay the night in one of the stylish bedrooms. All of the rooms boast high ceilings and leather armchairs, and some have four-posters. The hotel has two eating places to choose from: the bar, which spills out onto the garden in summer months and serves such warming delights as rib-sticking wild venison casserole, or the more formal restaurant. Diners can enjoy meals such as smoked haddock fishcakes, followed by wild pigeon and mushroom parcels with cider jus in the latter. Desserts include sticky ginger parkin with vanilla-steeped pineapple and ginger ice cream in the restaurant, and clotted cream rice pudding in the bar. Locally brewed beers and a good-value wine list complete the picture.

Recommended in the area

Dunster Castle (NT); Exmoor National Park; Dunster Station Steam Railway

Glastonbury Tor

The Helyar Arms

★★★★ ◉ INN

Address:	Moor Lane, EAST COKER, BA22 9JR
Tel:	01935 862332
Fax:	01935 864129
Email:	info@helyar-arms.co.uk
Website:	www.helyar-arms.co.uk
Map ref:	2 ST51

Directions: 3m from Yeovil. Take A57 or A30, follow East Coker signs **Open:** all week ⓑ **L** 12-2.30 **D** 6.30-9.30 ⓞ **L** 12-2.30 **D** all wk 6.30-9.30

Rooms: 6 en suite **S** £65 **D** £89 **Facilities:** Parking Garden **Notes:** ⊕ PUNCH TAVERNS ♔ ⚘

Parts of this traditional village inn date back to 1468. Forget the TV and games machines; instead enjoy the rustic charm of a beamed bar, open log fire, horse brasses, copper pots and a traditional skittle alley. Virtually all the food is prepared to order by whoever's name is on the notice board by the bar. Stocks, sauces, ice creams and chutneys are all home made, and what the pub can't grow or produce itself is sourced mostly from Somerset and Dorset. Character en suite rooms offer good amenities.

Recommended in the area

Glastonbury Tor; Barrington Court; Somerset Levels

The Crown Hotel

★★★ 75% ◉ HOTEL

Address: EXFORD, Exmoor National Park, TA24 7PP
Tel: 01643 831554
Fax: 01643 831665
Email: info@crownhotelexmoor.co.uk
Website: www.crownhotelexmoor.co.uk
Map ref: 2 SS83
Directions: From M5 junct 25 follow Taunton signs.
Take A358 then B3224 via Wheddon Cross to Exford
Open: all week noon-11pm ☚ **L** all wk 12-2.30
winter, 12-5.30 summer **D** all wk 6-9.30 **D** all wk 7-9 **Rooms:** 17 en suite **S** £72.50 **D** £125-£145
Facilities: Parking Garden **Notes:** ⊕ FREE HOUSE ♦♦ ⚞ ⚑ 12

A family-run, 17th-century coaching inn, the Crown Hotel is set in its own three acres of gardens at the heart of the Exmoor National Park. The surrounding countryside is renowned for its Exmoor ponies, red deer and birds of prey. In summer dine outside, in either the water garden or the terrace patio as an alternative to the elegant restaurant, you might prefer the cosy country bar, with its log fire and range of real ales. All meals are home made and freshly cooked to order using the freshest produce, locally sourced and organic where possible; the well-balanced menus have seasonal emphasis and a local twist. Smoked haddock, chilli and coriander fishcake with brie and cranberry wonton and roasted fillet of sea bass with basil crushed potatoes and vegetable Provençal can be found alongside organic pork loin with chorizo potatoes, apple compote and port sauce. Extensive vegetarian options are also available. Mouth-watering desserts include treacle tart with clotted cream ice cream and vanilla pavlova with crème Chantilly and summer fruits, or finish with the highly regarded Somerset and Devon cheese plate. Dogs and horses are also made most welcome.

Recommended in the area

Tarr Steps; Dunster Castle; Lynmouth

The Globe

★★★ 🛏 INN

Address: Fore Street, MILVERTON, TA4 1JX
Tel: 01823 400534
Email: info@theglobemilverton.co.uk
Website: www.theglobemilverton.co.uk
Map ref: 2 ST12
Directions: On B3187 **Open:** noon-3 6-11 (Fri-Sat
12-3 6-11.30) **Closed:** Sun eve, Mon L 🛏 **L** Tue-
Sun 12-2 **D** Mon-Sat 6.30-9 🍽 **L** Tue-Sun 12-2
D Mon-Sat 6.30-9 **Rooms:** 2 en suite **S** £45-£50
D £55-£60 **Facilities:** Parking **Notes:** ⊕ FREE HOUSE ♦♥ ♟ 8

Originally a coaching inn, The Globe is a village free house with a difference. A Grade II listed building, it has been refurbished in a clean-looking, contemporary style that creates both its distinctive character, which follows through to the three en suite bedrooms, and its warm, friendly atmosphere. In addition, husband-and-wife team Mark and Adele Tarry are building an excellent reputation for their quality home-cooked food. As a result, the community has taken them to their hearts, and the walls of the restaurant and bar are adorned with the work of local artists. All of the food here is home made, including the bread, and the menus, which draw heavily on West Country sources, change frequently to offer attractions such as broccoli and gorgonzola soup; River Fowey mussels; traditional steak and kidney pie; grilled pollack with kale; slow-roasted Gloucester Old Spot belly pork; Mark's mum's faggots; and baked parsnip and onion tart with roasted root vegetables. The children's menu is also thoughtfully compiled, while a real taste of the west comes in the form of the cheese board. Local ales from Exmoor and Cotleigh sit alongside guest ales from brewers such as Otter and Quantock. Local cider and English wines are also available.

Recommended in the area

Exmoor National Park; Hestercombe Gardens; Dunster Castle (NT)

The Notley Arms

Address: MONKSILVER, Taunton, TA4 4JB
Tel: 01984 656217
Website: www.thenotleyarms.co.uk
Map ref: 2 ST03
Directions: Village on B3227 N of Wiveliscombe towards Watchet & Minehead
Open: all week **Closed:** Mon lunch in summer
Facilities: Parking Garden
Notes: ⊕ ENTERPRISE INNS 🐾 ♟ 10

This English country drinking and dining pub, built in the 1860s and named after a prominent local family, is located in a hamlet on the edge of Exmoor. The village name comes from the Latin word silva, meaning 'wooded area'. When monks from Monmouthshire arrived at nearby Cleeve Abbey, it became known as Silva Monachorum or Monksilver. The cuisine offers a distinct bias towards traditional but imaginative British food, using fresh produce from the south west of England. Look forward also, to southern African influences (the owners come from Zimbabwe), which show through in the form of ostrich steaks and bobotie. Menus change often so you may not always find pork and three mustard Stroganoff; Exmoor shin of beef and Seville orange casserole; Deerstalker venison pie; bacon-wrapped chicken breast stuffed with pepperoni and apricots; or Thai-style butternut and pineapple curry. Depending on catches landed at St Mawes in Cornwall, fresh fish on the plate may be lightly breaded whitebait with tartare sauce; chunky cod fillet with lemon sauce on parsley mash; or smoked Cornish haddock rarebit with sauteéd spinach. Smaller portions are available for children. Puddings include Somerset apple and hazelnut cake with toffee sauce and clotted cream, and raspberry coulis and toasted almonds. The pretty garden is bordered by an Exmoor stream called the Silver, and there is also a selection of toys to keep children happy.

Recommended in the area

Exmoor National Park; Combe Sydenham Country Park; Cleeve Abbey

Woods on the Quantock Hills

The Carpenters Arms

Address: STANTON WICK, Nr Pensford, BS39 4BX
Tel: 01761 490202
Fax: 01761 490763
Email: carpenters@buccaneer.co.uk
Website: www.the-carpenters-arms.co.uk
Map ref: 2 ST66
Directions: A37 to Chelwood rdbt, then A368.
Pub 8m S of Bath
Open: all day all week 11-11 (Sun 12-10.30)
Closed: 25-26 Dec ⓑ L Mon-Sat 12-2, Sun 12-9
D Mon-Sat 6-9.30, Sun 12-9 ⓘ◯ⓘ L Mon-Sat 12-2, Sun 12-9
Facilities: Parking Garden
Notes: ⊕ BUCCANEER HOLDINGS ⓘⓘ ⓣ 12

Just 20 minutes from either Bath or Bristol, this charming stone-built pub is set in the tranquil hamlet of Stanton Wick, overlooking the Chew Valley. It began life as a row of miners' cottages and retains its cottagey style, with a spacious terrace, perfect for summer drinks. Behind the pretty flower bedecked façade, you'll find a low-beamed bar with a convivial atmosphere and no intrusive music. A choice of real beers is served, including Butcombe, Sharp's Doom Bar, and an extensive wine list combining New and Old World favourites. The menu changes regularly to offer the best seasonal produce, including fish from Cornwall, West Country beef and local game in season. Typical dishes include a starter of trio of smoked halibut, salmon and trout with light horseradish cream, and a main course of pork chop on mashed potato with braised savoy cabbage and an onion and thyme sauce. A function room is available for use by groups of 20–36.

Recommended in the area

Cheddar Gorge; Longleat; Wookey Hole Caves

The Monkton Inn

Address: Blundells Lane,
WEST MONKTON, TA2 8NP
Tel: 01823 412414
Website: www.themonkton.co.uk
Map ref: 2 ST22
Directions: M5 junct 25 to Taunton, right at Creech
Castle for 1m, left into West Monkton
Open: noon-3 6-11 (Sat-Sun noon-11)
Closed: Sun eve, Mon L ▙ L Tue-Sun 12-2
🍽 L Tue-Sun 12-2 **D** Mon-Sat 6.30-9.30
Facilities: Parking Garden
Notes: 🛢 ENTERPRISE INNS ♦♦ ♟ 7

Hidden away, but well worth finding, say the owners, Eddie Street and Guy Arnold, and indeed it is. The duo have invested significantly in a wholesale refurbishment of the interior, kitchen and patio to create an appealing village pub, with lots of wood, stylish dining furniture, leather sofas and warm-coloured walls. They live by a mission statement that requires staff to greet customers within 30 seconds of their arrival, a simple obligation that surely scores highly on the Brownie points scale. The tally is boosted by Eddie and Guy's provision of local real ales and fresh, locally sourced, home-made food at sensible prices; but please note that it is not served in the bar. With menus (try the two-course lunch for £9, or the £15 two-course dinner) that change daily, a great many possibilities are opened up, including starters of beef tomato, red onion and goat's cheese salad, and 'really creamy' fresh mushroom soup; main courses of flash-fried liver and bacon on colcannon; and savoury pancake. Desserts could be strawberry and white chocolate cheesecake; and blueberry and Drambuie crème brûlée. That you ought to book for Sunday lunch may partly be explained by Eddie's 'legendary' Yorkshire puddings.

Recommended in the area

Hestercombe Gardens; Sheppy's Cider Farm & Museum; West Somerset Railway

White Hart

★★★★ INN

Address: West Street, WIVELISCOMBE, TA4 2JP
Tel: 01984 623344
Fax: 01984 624748
Email: reservations@whitehartwiveliscombe.co.uk
Website: www.whitehartwiveliscombe.co.uk
Map ref: 2 ST02
Directions: M5 junct 26. Pub in town centre
Open: all day all week 10.30am-11pm (Fri-Sat 10am-mdnt)
🥂 L Tue-Sun 12-2 **D** all wk 6.30-9 ⏹ L Tue-Sun 12-2
D all wk 6.30-9 **Rooms:** 16 en suite **S** £55-£65 **D** £70-£90
Facilities: Parking Garden **Notes:** ⊕ FREE HOUSE 🕴 🏄 🍷 10

Dating back some 350 years, this former coaching inn stands in the square of 'Wivey', an old market town that, as home to both Cotleigh and Exmoor breweries, is often referred to as Somerset's brewing capital. The ales from both are normally served alongside other regional beers, as well as award-winning brews from further afield. Under the stewardship of head chef Barry Comley, the kitchen has built up a fine reputation for its Somerset-sourced, home-cooked food. Possibilities include steak and Cotleigh Tawny ale pie with crushed new potatoes and seasonal vegetables; fresh battered Brixham cod and home-made chips; and roasted vegetable lasagne. Other recent favourites have included River Exe mussels in white wine and cream; and free-range West Country duck breast on confit garlic mash with orange and rosemary sauce. On Sundays, 21-day roast beef is served with a fresh thyme Yorkshire pudding, roasted potatoes and vegetables. Sandwiches, baguettes and omelettes are available at lunchtime. En suite rooms display a blend of original and contemporary features, and offer flat-screen TVs and other thoughful amenities.

Recommended in the area

Exmoor National Park; Quantock Hills; West Somerset Railway

Mow Cop (National Trust)

Thor's Cave, Manifold Valley

The Yorkshireman

Address: Colton Road, COLTON, WS15 3HB
Tel: 01889 583977
Email: theyorkshireman@btconnect.com
Website: www.wine-dine.co.uk
Map ref: 3 SE54
Directions: 10m from Stafford **Open:** all week
noon-2.30 5.30-11 (Sun noon-6) **L** Mon-Sat
12-2.30, Sun 12-6 **D** Mon-Sat 6-9.30 **L** Mon-Sat
12-2.30, Sun 12-6 **D** Mon-Sat 6-9.30 **Facilities:**
Parking Garden **Notes:** ⊕ FREE HOUSE ⁝ ⁝ ⁝ 9

When they bought the former Railway Tavern in 2007, John and Jo Ashmore gave it a complete makeover. The result is this chic and friendly dining pub, its character defined by antique furniture and old prints. One of the beers from nearby Blythe Brewery is Palmer's Poison, named after William, Rugeley's famous serial-murdering doctor. Locally sourced, home-made dishes may change daily, but typical are poached smoked haddock with mustard and white wine sauce; and vegetable and chickpea tandoori.

Recommended in the area

Cawarden Reclamation Centre; Cannock Chase; Lichfield Cathedral

The Holly Bush Inn

Address: Salt, STAFFORD, ST18 0BX
Tel: 01889 508234
Fax: 01889 508058
Email: geoff@hollybushinn.co.uk
Website: www.hollybushinn.co.uk
Map ref: 7 SJ92
Directions: Telephone for directions
Open: all week 12-11 (Sun 12-10.30)
Facilities: Parking Garden
Notes: 🛢 FREE HOUSE ♦♦ 🍷 12

In an area cut through by several major trunk roads, it's good to find such a peaceful spot, and then take time to discover the glorious Staffordshire countryside that lies hidden away from the highways. The Holly Bush Inn was licensed during the reign of Charles II (1660–85), although the building itself dates from around 1190, and heavy carved beams, open fires and cosy alcoves still characterise the comfortably old-fashioned interior. Like most other landlords, owner Geoff Holland aims to serve good quality real ales and wines. What helps to differentiate Geoff, though, is his insistence on providing non-processed, mostly organic, fully traceable food, and on minimising his hostelry's impact on the environment by setting up a worm farm. Traditional British dishes on the main menu include grilled pork chops with a honey and whole-grain mustard glaze; braised lamb and apples flavoured with nutmeg and allspice; and breaded wholetail scampi. Daily specials might be butternut squash and goats' cheese lasagne; fillet of beef Wellington; chargrilled red snapper with Jamaican spiced chutney; and baked perch with watercress sauce. Holly Bush mixed grill is a favourite plateful. At lunchtime tripledecker sandwiches, jacket potatoes and toasties are available. Beers include Adnams, Pedigree and guest ales.

Recommended in the area

Shugborough Hall (NT); Weston Park; Cannock Chase

The Crown Inn

Address: Den Lane, WRINEHILL, Crewe, CW3 9BT
Tel: 01270 820472
Fax: 01270 820547
Email: mark_condliffe@hotmail.com
Map ref: 6 SJ74
Directions: Village on A531, 1m S of Betley.
6m S of Crewe; 6m N of Newcastle-under-Lyme
Open: noon-3 6-11 (Sun noon-4 6-10.30)
Closed: 26 Dec ᨐ **L** Mon-Sat 12-2, Sun 12-3
D Mon-Fri 6.30-9.30, Sat 6-10, Sun 6-9
Facilities: Parking Garden **Notes:** ⊕ FREE HOUSE ☗ 9

A former coaching inn with a village setting, The Crown stands six miles equidistant from Crewe and Newcastle-under-Lyme. The interior is largely open plan but retains its oak beams and large inglenook fireplace, and the renovated garden has an attractive patio area for dining. A family-run free house for some 30 years, the pub has a great reputation for its real ales. There is always a choice of six traditional cask ales, including Marstons Pedigree, Adnams Bitter and Timothy Taylor Landlord, and there are two regularly changing guest beers; wine is an integral part of the inn's drinks portfolio. Food also plays a significant part and the inn is renowned for its generous portions and consistent good quality. The monthly changing menus reflect the time of year and the fresh produce available locally. The team here is well established – Charles and Sue Davenhill run the business with their daughter and son-in-law, Anna and Mark Condliffe. Mother and daughter are both vegetarians, so the food on offer always includes meat-free choices and a vegan dish. Meat-eaters are spoilt for choice, with such dishes as piri-piri chicken; Cumberland grill; and plaice roulade with a hazelnut and gruyère crust. Desserts include sticky toffee pudding, ice cream sundaes and home-made jam sponge and custard.

Recommended in the area

The Potteries; Bridgemere Garden World; Trentham Gardens and Monkey Forest

Hedingham Castle

The Swan Inn

Address: Swan Lane, BARNBY, NR34 7QF
Tel: 01502 476646
Fax: 01502 562513
Map ref: 4 TM49
Directions: Just off A146 between Lowestoft & Beccles
Open: all week **Facilities:** Parking Garden
Notes: ⊕ FREE HOUSE ⁑

Two windows upstairs, two down and a central door – the classic front elevation of buildings everywhere. Behind the distinctive pink-painted façade of this warm and friendly gem in the Suffolk countryside is one of the county's foremost fish restaurants – it is, after all, owned by Donald and Michael Cole, whose family have been fish wholesalers in Lowestoft since grandfather set up the business in 1936. With deep-sea trawling in deep decline by the mid-1980s, Donald thought it prudent to diversify and bought the run-down Swan. It was during the refurbishment that he had a dinghy installed up in the rafters (although he might try and kid you there's just been a particularly high tide!). The property dates from 1690, and in the rustic Fisherman's Cove restaurant you'll find the original low beams and a collection of nautical memorabilia, including trawlers' bells, wheels and a binnacle, all placed on show as 'a tribute to the brave people who bring ashore the fruits of the sea'. The menu, which lists some 80 different seafood dishes, is very much aimed at fish-lovers, with starters including smoked sprats, smoked trout pâté and Italian seafood salad, and main dishes such as whole grilled wild sea bass; whole grilled turbot; whole grilled Dover sole; monkfish tails in garlic butter; and crab gratin. The Swan has its own smokehouse, one of just three remaining out of 200 in what was once one of Britain's busiest fishing ports. Anyone preferring meat to fish has a choice of fillet, rump and gammon steaks.

Recommended in the area

Lowestoft; Suffolk Heritage Coast; Great Yarmouth

The Queen's Head

Address: The Street, Bramfield,
HALESWORTH, IP19 9HT
Tel: 01986 784214
Email: qhbfield@aol.com
Website: www.queensheadbramfield.co.uk
Map ref: 4 TM37
Directions: 2m from A12 on A144 towards
Halesworth **Open:** all week 11.45-2.30 6.30-11 (Sun
noon-3 7-10.30) **Closed:** 26 Dec **L** all wk 12-2
D Mon-Fri 6.30-9.15, Sat 6.30-10, Sun 7-9
Facilities: Parking Garden **Notes:** ⊕ ADNAMS ♦♦ ⊬ ⊉ 8

A lovely old building with a pretty garden by the village church with its unusual round bell tower. Inside, picture exposed beams, enormous fireplaces, scrubbed pine tables and a vaulted bar serving Adnams beers. During thirteen years here, Mark Corcoran has built a formidable reputation for high quality, home-made meals produced from local, often organic, produce. A typical meal might comprise carrot and ginger soup; local partridge braised in red wine with bacon; and warm Bakewell tart.

Recommended in the area

Suffolk Heritage Coast; Minsmere Nature Reserve; Snape Maltings

---

The Star Inn

Address: The Street, LIDGATE,
Newmarket, CB8 9PP
Tel/Fax: 01638 500275
Email: tonyaxon@aol.com
Map ref: 4 TL75
Directions: From Newmarket clocktower in High St
follow signs towards Clare on B1063. Lidgate 7m
Open: noon-3 6-mdnt **Closed:** 25-26 Dec, 1 Jan
⅃ **L** Tue-Sun 12-3 **D** Tue-Sun 7-10
⑩ **L** Tue-Sun 12-3 **D** Tue-Sat 7-10
Facilities: Parking Garden **Notes:** ⊕ GREENE KING ♦♦

This pretty Elizabethan building is made up of two cottages with gardens front and rear; inside, two traditionally furnished bars with heavy oak beams, log fires and pine furniture lead into the dining room. Yet The Star's quintessentially English appearance holds a surprise, for here you'll find a renowned Spanish restaurant offering authentic Mediterranean cuisine. The inn provides an important meeting place for local residents; it's also popular with Newmarket trainers on race days.

Recommended in the area

Newmarket Racecourse; National Horseracing Museum and Tours

The Crown Inn

Address: Bridge Road, SNAPE, Nr Saxmundham,
IP17 1SL
Tel: 01728 688324
Email: snapecrown@tiscali.co.uk
Website: www.snape-crown.co.uk
Map ref: 4 TM35 **Directions:** A12 N to Lowestoft,
right to Aldeburgh, then right again in Snape at x-rds
by church, pub at bottom of hill **Open:** all week 🏨
🍽 L all wk 12-2.30, Tue-Sun 12-2.30 (Nov-Apr)
D all wk 6-9.30, Tue-Sat 6-9.30 (Nov-Apr)
Facilities: Parking Garden **Notes:** ⊕ ADNAMS 🚶 🐕 🍷 18

Within walking distance of Snape Maltings, this atmospheric pub is the perfect place for a pre- or post
show meal. Inside, it is not too difficult to imagine its 15th-century incarnation as a haunt of smugglers.
The old beams and brick floors are still in place, but now you will find a warm welcome from landlord/
chef Garry Cook and his wife Teresa, top quality Adnams ales, and superb food. Garry offers modern
British cuisine using own home rear meats, vegetables from their allotment, plus other local produce.
Recommended in the area
Suffolk Coast National Nature Reserve; RSPB Mismere and Orford Ness reserves; Framlingham Castle

The Crown Hotel

★★ 85% ⊛ HOTEL
Address: The High Street, SOUTHWOLD, IP18 6DP
Tel: 01502 722275
Fax: 01502 727263
Email: crown.hotel@adnams.co.uk
Website: www.adnamshotels.co.uk
Map ref: 4 TM57
Directions: A12, A1095 to Southwold. Into town
centre **Open:** 8am-11pm (Sun 8am-10.30pm)
🏨 L Sun-Fri 12-2, Sat 12-2.30 D Sun-Fri 6-9, Sat
6-9.30 **Rooms:** 14 en suite **Facilities:** Parking Garden **Notes:** ⊕ ADNAMS 🚶 🍷 20

Combining the appeal of a pub, wine bar and restaurant, this small hotel is always buzzing with lively
informality. The Crown is one of two Adnams-owned hotels in the home of their renowned brewery, and
has an excellent reputation for it food, wine and, of course, beer. Originally a posting inn, the building
dates from 1750 and its central location is just two minutes from the beach. Visit the cellar and kitchen
store in the hotel's yard for a full selection of wines and bottled beers.
Recommended in the area
Minsmere RSPB Reserve; Suffolk Wildlife Park; Suffolk Heritage Coast

The Anchor

◉◉

Address: Main Street, WALBERSWICK,
Southwold, IP18 6UA
Tel: 01502 722112
Fax: 01502 724464
Email: info@anchoratwalberswick.com
Map ref: 4 TM47
Directions: Please telephone for directions
Open: all week 🍴 L all wk 12-3 D all wk 6-9
🍴 L all wk 12-3 D all wk 6-9
Facilities: Parking Garden **Notes:** ⊞ ♟ ⊁ ☘ 16

Sophie Dorber's long-standing connections with the Suffolk coast, include running the food franchise at Aldeburgh yacht club; in London, husband Mark ran what was twice voted the UK's top pub. Then one day in 2004, breakfasting with friends on a golden Walberswick beach, they decided to buy The Anchor's lease and create a family-friendly village local. And that's what they've done. They stock a good range of characterful real ales, twenty world-class bottled beers and 150 wines from some highly inspired winemakers, choosing to offer: "Only (what) we would actively seek to drink if the flood waters were to surround Walberswick and we became an island". Their approach to food is robust, following the seasons with produce from their own garden and villagers' allotments. Starter examples would be West Mersea oysters with red onion vinaigrette; main courses of mushroom and Stilton risotto; roast cod with brioche herb crust; and Suffolk rib-eye steak with horseradish and caper butters; and for dessert, Jamaican ginger bread with clotted cream ice cream. Curry nights are every second Friday. Plans are in hand to renovate the dining room, turn a corridor into a bar, and sow wild flowers to create a picnic meadow. There is a splendid rear terrace and garden.

Recommended in the area

Suffolk Heritage Coast; Snape Maltings; Minsmere

The Westleton Crown

★★★ 78% ◉◉ HOTEL

Address: The Street, WESTLETON, Nr Saxmundham, IP17 3AD
Tel: 01728 648777
Fax: 01728 648239
Email: info@westletoncrown.co.uk
Website: www.westletoncrown.co.uk
Map ref: 4 TM46
Directions: A12 N, turn right for Westleton just after Yoxford.
Hotel opposite on entering Westleton **Open:** all day all week
7am-11pm (Sun 7.30am-10.30pm) 🍴 **L** all wk 12-2.30
D all wk 7-9.30 🍽 **L** all wk 12-2.30 **D** all wk 7-9.30
Rooms: 25 en suite (8 GF) **S** £90-£115 **D** £115-£180
Facilities: Parking Garden **Notes:** ⊕ FREE HOUSE 👥 🐾 🍷 9

Nestled in a quiet village close to Suffolk's wild salt marshes, the coast and RSPB bird reserves, is this atmospheric and hospitable inn. Its origins go back to the 12th century, but the building itself dates from the 17th. The original buildings belonged to nearby Sibton Abbey, and the Crown has succeeded in combining the rustic charm of its heritage with the comforts of contemporary living. Inside you will find crackling log fires, real ales, good wines and an enticing menu. The team at the Crown are passionate about cooking. Impressive meals are made from fresh, locally-sourced ingredients, and can be taken in the parlour, the dining room or the conservatory. Start with baked goats' cheese with red onion crumble, or spicy pumpkin tart, before moving on to roast loin of venison with griottine cherries and root vegetable creamed potatoes; or the Crown's own cod and chips. Leave some space for dessert, which may take the form of pear tarte Tatin with blackberry ice cream, home-made Arctic roll, or marmalade and orange steamed sponge pudding with English egg custard sauce.

Recommended in the area

Ipswich; Aldeburgh; Suffolk Heritage Coast; Southwold; Minsmere RSPB; Dunwich

Ruins of Newark Priory in Pyrford

Hare and Hounds

Address: Common Road, LINGFIELD, RH7 6BZ
Tel/Fax: 01342 832351
Email: info@hareandhoundspublichouse.co.uk
Website: www.hareandhoundspublichouse.co.uk
Map ref: 3 TQ34
Directions: From A22 follow signs for Lingfield Racecourse into Common Rd
Closed: 1 Jan, Sun Eve 🍴 L Mon-Sat 12-3
D Mon-Sat 7-10 🍽 **L** Mon-Sat 12-3 **D** Mon-Sat 7-10 **Facilities:** Parking Garden
Notes: ⊕ PUNCH TAVERNS 🐕 🍷 8

The promise of this friendly establishment is that, despite a commitment to providing food of unusual excellence, it remains at heart a proper pub. This means there are plenty of real ales, including Greene King IPA, Flowers Original and Old Speckled Hen, and a friendly bunch of locals who enjoy nothing more than a convivial conversation at the bar. There's a peaceful atmosphere throughout because the pub is entirely free of the electronic interference that has ruined many good places, and the walls are decked with a changing display of original art works, all of which are for sale. There's also a lovely split level garden to enjoy when the weather is sunny. The food really is a highlight. The menu is eclectic, and everything – bread, pasta, ice cream – is made on the premises. You might begin with a dish of linguini, spinach, parmesan, poached egg and truffle oil, before choosing between enticing main courses that might include slow-roasted belly of pork with chorizo mash and Granny Smith, tomato and basil salsa; or baked stuffed aubergine, with crostini and basil dressing, rocket, pink grapefruit and parmesan salad. The equally unusual desserts take some classic ideas and give them a startling twist, resulting in mouthwatering delights.

Recommended in the area

Standen (NT); Godstone Farm; Hever Castle

Waverley Abbey ruins

Bryce's at The Old School House

Address: OCKLEY, Dorking, RH5 5TH
Tel: 01306 627430
Fax: 01306 628274
Email: bryces.fish@virgin.net
Website: www.bryces.co.uk
Map ref: 3 TQ14
Directions: 8m S of Dorking on A29
Open: noon-3 6-11 **Closed:** 25-26 Dec, 1 Jan,
(Sun pm Nov, Jan-Feb) **L** all wk 12-2.30 **D** all wk
6-9.30 **L** all wk 12-2.30 **D** all wk 7-9.30 **Facilities:** Parking **Notes:** FREE HOUSE 15

Formerly a boarding school, this Grade II listed building dates from 1750 and has been established for 18 years as Bryce's. The village is set amid lovely countryside offering some great downland walking. Its distance from the sea may come as a surprise, as Bill Bryce is passionate about fresh fish and offers seven starters and main courses of exclusively fish dishes in the restaurant, with non-fish daily specials and a vegetarian selection. The bar has its own tempting menu, and there are excellent house wines.

Recommended in the area

The Hannah Peschar Sculpture Garden; Leith Hill; Denbies Wine Estate, Dorking

The Inn @ West End

Address: 42 Guildford Road, WEST END, GU24 9PW
Tel: 01276 858652
Email: greatfood@the-inn.co.uk
Website: www.the-inn.co.uk
Map ref: 3 SU96
Directions: On A322 towards Guildford. 3m from M3 junct 3, just beyond Gordon Boys rdbt
Open: all week **Facilities:** Parking Garden
Notes: ⊕ FREE HOUSE ⇥ ⏻ 17

The name gives a hint that The Inn @ West End is a modern place. It is a restaurant pub run for the last nine years by owners (Gerry and Ann Price) who pride themselves on the great food, wine and atmosphere here. Indeed, its role as a focus for local social life has seen it being described as more of a community centre than a pub or restaurant, with special events such as quiz nights and wine tastings, and involvement in a variety of clubs and societies. In addition to the dining room, the bar and the garden room, there is a private gastronomic cellar, available for private hire, and the garden offers further facilities in the shape of a lovely dining patio and a boules terrain. An interesting wine list takes in wines from all over the world, but with a leaning towards Portugal and Spain; there is also an impressive Champagne section. Real ales include Fuller's London Pride and a changing selection of guests. Food is fresh and local, with fish and game dishes as a speciality on the modern British menu. Fish is acquired on weekly buying trips to Portsmouth Harbour and game comes directly from the farm for processing – they even have their own plucking machine here.

Recommended in the area

Windsor Great Park; Airborne Forces Museum; Thorpe Park; National Shooting Centre, Bisley

EAST SUSSEX

Battle Abbey

The Greys

Address: 105 Southover Street,
BRIGHTON, BN2 9UA
Tel: 01273 680734
Email: chris@greyspub.com
Website: www.greyspub.com
Map ref: 3 TQ30
Directions: 0.5m from St Peters Church in Hanover
area of Brighton **Open:** all week 4-11 (Sat noon-
mdnt Sun noon-11) **D** Tue-Thu & Sat 6-9 ⭐ **L** Sun
12-4.30 **D** Tue-Thu & Sat 6-9 **Facilities:** Parking
Notes: ⊕ ENTERPRISE INNS 🐕

Find Southover Street and you can't miss this great pub – it's painted deep turquoise! Acclaimed well beyond the city for its great cuisine, live music, real ales and extensive range of Belgian beers, you will feel very comfortable here. Chef Roz Batty, never forgetting customers want value for money, changes her menus monthly regularly to reflect seasonal produce, dishes like braised baby octopus in tomatoes and chilli; grilled Rye plaice with Burgundy potatoes; spiced pumpkin tart; and knickerbocker glory.
Recommended in the area
Devil's Dyke; Palace Pier; Beachy Head

The Coach and Horses

Address: DANEHILL, RH17 7JF
Tel/Fax: 01825 740369
Map ref: 3 TQ42 **Directions:** From East Grinstead,
S through Forest Row on A22 to junct with A275
(Lewes road), right on A275, after 2m, left onto
School Ln, 0.5m, pub on left **Open:** all week 11.30-3
6-11 (Sat-Sun 11.30-11) 🚲 ⭐ **L** all wk 12-2
D Mon-Sat 7-9 **Facilities:** Parking Garden
Notes: ⊕ FREE HOUSE 👫 🐕 🍷 10

Built in 1847 of local sandstone, the Coach and Horses is ideal for walkers and lovers of stunning scenery. Homely winter fires and neatly tended gardens add plenty of character, and half-panelled walls, highly polished wooden floorboards and vaulted beamed ceilings give the place a charming, timeless feel. Food plays a key role in the pub's success; locally sourced produce features heavily on the varied menu - lamb from the neighbouring farm, fish landed on the Sussex coast and delivered daily, plus vegetables, venison and game from nearby suppliers. Popular dishes include Moroccan spiced lamb, pan-roasted haunch of venison and steamed mussels with chorizo and sweet chilli.
Recommended in the area
The Ashdown Forest; Sheffield Park Gardens (NT);The Bluebell Railway

The Bull

★★★★ ⇔ INN

Address: 2 High Street, DITCHLING, BN6 8TA

Tel/Fax: 01273 843147

Email: info@thebullditchling.com

Website: www.thebullditchling.com

Map ref: 3 TQ31

Directions: S on M23/A23 5m. N of Brighton follow signs to Pyecombe/Hassocks then signs to Ditchling, 3m **Open:** all day all week 11-11 (Sun noon-10.30) ⓑ **L** Mon-Fri 12-2.30, Sat 12-9.30,

Sun 12-9 **D** Mon-Fri 6-9.30, Sat 12-9.30, Sun 12-9 **Rooms:** 4 en suite **Facilities:** Parking Garden **Notes:** ⊕ FREE HOUSE ᵢᵢ ᵣ ☻ 20

The Bull, a 16th-century former coaching inn, is the place to head for following a day on the South Downs. It's been restored with passion (and a contemporary touch), by Dominic Worrall, yet still exudes historic charm and character. In the bar you'll find feature fireplaces with glowing log fires, sagging ceiling timbers, bare boards and a mixture of simple benches, carved settles and farmhouse chairs at big scrubbed wooden tables. Quirky objets d'art, modern art and vases of lilies on the bar add a touch of class. There are four individually decorated bedrooms, each named after their principle colour. Ruby, for example, has bright red walls, white-painted wall timbers, Thai silk curtains, a plasma TV/DVD player, digital radio, a sleigh bed with Egyptian cotton sheets and a claw-foot bath in the tiled bathroom. Local is the watchword when it comes to food and drink, with top notch ales from Harvey's (Lewes) and Welton's (Horsham) breweries on hand pump and a quaffable fizz from Ridge View Vineyard up the road. Menus change daily and make good use of lamb from Foxhole Farm on the edge of the village, seasonal game, including venison from the Balcombe Estate and south coast fish.

Recommended in the area

Booth Museum of Natural History; Royal Pavilion, Brighton; Borde Hill Garden

The Hatch Inn

Address: Coleman's Hatch, HARTFIELD, TN7 4EJ
Tel/Fax: 01342 822363
Email: nickad@bigfoot.com
Website: www.hatchinn.co.uk
Map ref: 3 TQ43
Directions: A22, 14m, left at Forest Row rdbt, 3m to Colemans Hatch, right by church. Straight on at next junct, pub on right
Open: all week 11.30-3 5.30-11 (Sat-Sun all day)
Closed: 25 Dec 🍴 L all wk 12-2.30 D Mon-Thu 7-9, Fri-Sat 7-9.30 🍴 L all wk 12-2.30 D Mon-Thu 7-9, Fri-Sat 7-9.30
Facilities: Garden **Notes:** ⊕ FREE HOUSE 🐕 🍷 10

Reputedly dating back to 1430, The Hatch Inn was converted from three cottages thought to have housed workers at the local water-driven hammer mill, and it may also have been a smugglers' haunt. The pub is well placed for country walking, and features in a number of 'top ten pubs' lists, as well as serving as a filming location for television dramas and advertisements. There are two large beer gardens for alfresco summer dining, one of which enjoys views out over the forest, and is only minutes away from the restored Poohsticks Bridge, immortalised in A.A. Milne's *Winnie the Pooh* stories. Owner Nicholas Drillsma and his partner, Sandra Barton, have collected many accolades over the last 14 years. Quality ingredients and imaginative techniques make for exciting menus created by head chef Gregory Palmer and his team. Evening appetisers might include a red onion marmalade and goat's cheese tart Tatin with roast beetroot salad, Roquefort and walnuts, followed by roast rump of lamb with dauphinoise potatoes and rosemary and port reduction. All desserts are home made – highly recommended is the sticky toffee pudding, hot toffee sauce and locally made ice cream. No reservations are available at lunchtime and evening booking is essential.
Recommended in the area
Ashdown Forest; Standen (NT); Royal Tunbridge Wells

The Middle House

Address: High Street, MAYFIELD, TN20 6AB
Tel: 01435 872146
Fax: 01435 873423
Email: kirsty@middle-house.com
Website: www.middlehousehotel.co.uk
Map ref: 4 TQ52
Directions: E of A267, S of Tunbridge Wells
Open: all week **Facilities:** Parking Garden
Notes: ⊞ FREE HOUSE ⊪ ♀ 9

Built in 1575 for Sir Thomas Gresham, Elizabeth I's Keeper of the Privy Purse and founder of the London Stock Exchange, The Middle House is one of the finest timber-framed buildings in Sussex, with a wonderfully ornate wooden façade. Inside, the house retains many of its original features, including a Grinling Gibbons' fireplace and a splendid oak-panelled restaurant. This is a family-run business specialising in a very wide variety of food using all local, fresh produce. On offer are over 40 dishes, including a large fish selection and vegetarian options on an ever-changing menu. Among the choices that may be enjoyed in the cosy bar or the more formal restaurant, are chicken breast filled with leeks and gruyère cheese wrapped in filo pastry with a parsley, cream and white wine sauce; seared tuna loin steak on a bed of pak choi with a sweet and sour sauce; pan-fried local venison steak served with game crisps and a rich bacon lardon, port and prune sauce. An extensive wine list offers wines and champagne by the glass, and the pub's bar offers real ales including Harveys, the local brew and several guest beers. A great high street pub whether you're nipping in for a pint or stopping a little longer to enjoy both the food and the atmosphere. Ample parking is available.

Recommended in the area

Bateman's (NT); Spa Valley Railway; Royal Tunbridge Wells

The Ypres Castle Inn

Address: Gun Garden, RYE, TN31 7HH
Tel: 01797 223248
Email: info@yprescastleinn.co.uk
Website: www.yprescastleinn.co.uk
Map ref: 4 TQ92
Directions: Behind church & adjacent to Ypres Tower
Open: all week 🍺 L all wk 12-3 D Mon-Sat 6-9
🍽 L all wk 12-3 D Mon-Sat 6-9
Facilities: Garden **Notes:** 🍺 FREE HOUSE 🍴 🍷 11

'The Wipers', as locals call it, was once the haunt of smugglers.
Built in 1640 in weather-boarded style, and added to by the
Victorians, it's the only pub in the citadel area of the old Cinque
Port of Rye with a garden. The garden, with roses, shrubs and views of the 13th-century Ypres
Tower, once defensive, then became a prison before becoming a museum, and of the River Rother
with its working fishing fleet. Colourful art and furnishings help make the interior warm and friendly.
The seasonally changing menu is largely sourced locally, providing a good range of lunchtime snacks,
including ploughman's, and sandwiches, backed by half a dozen daily specials. The evening menu
may propose moules marinière, cracked Dungeness crab, grilled Rye Bay plaice and turbot, and
meaty options of grilled rack of Romney salt marsh lamb, organic Winchelsea beef and pork, and
home-made prime beefburger. There are usually four cask-conditioned ales and an extensive wine
list. On Friday nights the atmosphere hots up with live jazz, rock and blues. The pub has no
accommodation facilities, but there are plenty of possibilities nearby, including Rye Windmill, one
of the town's most famous landmarks.

Recommended in the area

Smallhythe Place; Romney, Hythe & Dymchurch Railway; Port Lympne Wild Animal Park

The Lamb Inn

Address: WARTLING, Herstmonceux, BN27 1RY
Tel: 01323 832116
Website: www.lambinnwartling.co.uk
Map ref: 4 TQ60
Directions: A259 from Polegate to Pevensey rdbt. Take 1st left to Wartling & Herstmonceux Castle. Pub 3m on right
Open: all week **Closed:** Sun eve, Mon in winter ⓑ **L** all wk 12-2.15 **D** Tue-Sat 7-9 ⓘⓞⓘ **L** all wk 12-2.15 **D** Tue-Sat 7-9
Facilities: Parking Garden **Notes:** ⓲ ⓱ ⓹ 8

A family-run inn with a long history, this white-painted building is a popular watering hole for locals and walkers enjoying the tiny hamlet and stunning East Sussex countryside. Inside, it provides comfortable cream sofas, which can be drawn up to the fire on chilly days, and a good selection of real ales and wines by the glass. The pub is well known for the quality of its food, and the ethos is to source the best of local produce, from meat and fish through to locally grown vegetables. Everything is home made including the bread. The inn makes good use of meat from nearby Chilley Farm, which specialises in raising stock without additives in unhurried fashion, and rears animals such as Gloucester Old Spot pigs and Kent Cross lamb. Fish from Hastings and Newhaven is a house speciality, offered daily on the specials board. As well as a comprehensive dinner menu, which might include braised shank of lamb on roasted smoked garlic mash and thoughtful vegetarian options such as Wellington of mushrooms with goats' cheese, lighter dishes, baps and ploughman's are served at lunchtime. Traditional desserts along the lines of lemon and sultana bread-and-butter pudding are not to be missed.

Recommended in the area

Rye; De La Warr Pavilion, Bexhill; Herstmonceux Castle

The Dorset Arms

Address: WITHYHAM, Nr Hartfield, TN7 4BD
Tel: 01892 770278
Fax: 01892 770195
Email: pete@dorset-arms.co.uk
Website: www.dorset-arms.co.uk
Map ref: 3 TQ43
Directions: 4m W of Tunbridge Wells on B2110
between Groombridge & Hartfield
Open: all week 11.30-3 6-11 **Closed:** Mon L
🍴 L Tue-Sun 12-2 **D** Tue-Sat 7.30-9 🍽 L Tue-Sun
12-2 **D** Tue-Sat 7.30-9 **Facilities:** Parking Garden **Notes:** ⊕ HARVEYS OF LEWES 🐕 🍷 8

Local records suggest that this tile-hung, family-run pub and restaurant at the edge of the Ashdown
Forest has been an inn since the 18th century. Its origins go much further back – to the 15th century
when it was an open-halled farmhouse. Today it retains its original flagstone floors, and among the
many interesting features that remain are the ice-house buried in the hillside behind the building,
the oak-floored bar, a magnificent open log fireplace, and the massive wall and ceiling beams in the
restaurant. There's seating on the lawn outside for fine summer days. As a focus of village life, the
Dorset Arms hosts periodic quiz nights and occasional live music. When it comes to the food on offer,
wherever possible owner Peter Randell sources ingredients locally, including what some say is the
best fillet steak in the area. Starters might include oak-smoked salmon with brown bread; deep-fried
tempura battered king prawns with chilli dip; or crispy whitebait. Continue with a fillet steak, wrapped
in bacon and in a port and redcurrant sauce; a halibut steak, poached in white wine; medallions of pork
fillet with mushrooms in a stilton, white wine and cream sauce; or perhaps seared scallops with bacon
and onions. For dessert, one of the favourites is warm chocolate fudge brownies with ice cream.
Recommended in the area
Tunbridge Wells; Groombridge Place; Spa Valley Railway

The Weald and Downland Open Air Museum, Singleton

George & Dragon

Address: BURPHAM, Arundel, BN18 9RR
Tel: 01903 883131
Email: sara.cheney@btinternet.com
Website: www.burphamgeorgeanddragoninn.com
Map ref: 3 TQ00
Directions: Off A27 1m E of Arundel, signed
Burpham, 2.5m pub on left
Open: all week 11.30-3 6-mdnt ⌷ L Mon-Fri 12-2,
Sat-Sun 12-3 **D** all wk 6-9 ⌷◎⌷ L Mon-Sat 12-2
D Mon-Sun 6-9 **Facilities:** Parking Garden
Notes: ⌷ FREE HOUSE ⌷⌷ ⌷⌷

In a tranquil village at the end of a long no-through road, this lovely old pub has the church and cricket pitch as its close neighbours. The interior is full of old-world character, with beams and worn flagstone floors providing a setting for the modern prints on the walls. Smaller rooms have been opened out to create space, but there are still some nooks and crannies for that quiet meal or drink. Real ales come from nearby Arundel Breweries, with guests from surrounding counties. The owners acknowledge that during the last 30 years the pub has developed from a village local serving mostly beer, into not so much a gastro-pub, but a 'traditional pub that serves excellent food'. It offers a seasonal, largely locally-sourced menu of British rustic cooking, but with clear international influences as seen in honey-roasted Scottish salmon on citrus couscous, pan-roasted vegetables and soy sauce dressing. From nearer home might come wild mushroom, garlic, leek and thyme crumble topped with Sussex Cheddar. Diners don't risk breaking the bank with the compact wine list. The area is well endowed with walks, especially over the South Downs and along the River Arun (dogs are welcome in the bar area).

Recommended in the area

Arundel Castle; Amberley Working Museum; Goodwood

Fulking Escarpment

The Fox Goes Free

Address: CHARLTON, nr Goodwood, PO18 0HU
Tel: 01243 811461
Fax: 01243 811712
Email: enquiries@thefoxgoesfree.com
Website: www.thefoxgoesfree.com
Map ref: 3 SU81
Directions: A286, 6m from Chichester towards Midhurst. 1m from Goodwood racecourse **Open:** 11-11 (Sun noon-11) **Closed:** 25 Dec eve 🍴 **L** Mon-Fri 12-2.30, Sat-Sun 12-10 **D** Mon-Fri 6.30-10, Sat-Sun 12-10 🍽 **L** 12-2.30 **D** 6.30-10 **Facilities:** Parking Garden **Notes:** ⌖ FREE HOUSE ♟ ➤ ♟ 8

In unspoilt countryside, this 16th-century, brick and flint building was William III's favourite hunting lodge. Now it's a charming and friendly free house, with inglenooks, old pews, brick floors and five dining areas. A locally sourced, daily-changing menu of pub classics is bolstered by crispy confit of duck; pan-fried chicken breast in Parma ham; and roast shoulder of lamb. There are four local real ales and an own brew named after the pub. In the summer, gaze over the South Downs from the large garden.
Recommended in the area
Weald and Downland Open Air Museum; Goodwood Racecourse; West Dean Gardens

Royal Oak Inn

★★★★★ @ INN

Address: Pook Lane, East Lavant, CHICHESTER, PO18 0AX
Tel: 01243 527434
Fax: 01243 775062
Email: enquiries@royaloakeastlavant.co.uk
Website: www.royaloakeastlavant.co.uk
Map ref: 3 SU80
Directions: A286 from Chichester signed Midhurst, 2m then right at mini-rdbt, pub over bridge on left **Open:** all week 7am-11.30pm **Closed:** 25 Dec ⑩ **L** 12-3 **D** 6.30-11 **Rooms:** 8 en suite **Facilities:** Parking Garden **Notes:** ⊕ FREE HOUSE ⅰⅰ ⌖ 20

In a quiet village two miles north of Chichester stands this archetypal country pub and restaurant, offering stylish en-suite rooms and two self-catering cottages. The interior is characterised by beams, bare brick walls, fireplaces and an intimate bar area with highly slumpworthy sofas and armchairs. The restaurant itself is furnished with pine tables and tall, modern leather chairs, and serves French, Mediterranean and New English cuisine backed by daily blackboard specials, all crying out to be accompanied by one of the many world-sourced wines. Extensively used local ingredients include crab and scallops from the English Channel. Try a starter of tian of smoked salmon, fresh salmon and salmon roe; or West Sussex pork and rabbit terrine with fig chutney, warm toast and salad leaves, then follow with duck, duck and duck (breast, ballantine and Charlotte), pan-fried skate with confit of pork belly; or Scotch quails' eggs made with rolled ham hock and pineapple jelly; or smoked garlic polenta cake, chargrilled haloumi and harissa-spiced aubergine provençale. Among the inviting desserts are spiced plum and oat crumble with home-made custard; and glazed lemon tart with a hedgerow compote and mascarpone.

Recommended in the area

Chichester Cathedral; Goodwood House; South Downs Way

The Star & Garter

Address: EAST DEAN, nr Chichester, PO18 0JG
Tel: 01243 811318
Email: thestarandgarter@hotmail.com
Website: www.thestarandgarter.co.uk
Map ref: 4 SU91
Directions: On A286 between Chichester & Midhurst. Exit A286 at Singleton. Village in 2m
Open: all week 🍴 ❍ Mon-Fri L and D, Sat-Sun all day
Facilities: Parking Garden
Notes: ⊞ FREE HOUSE ♦♦ ⅲ ⅻ 10

Close to the attractions of Goodwood, this downland free house stands just above the village pond. Built in 1740 from traditional Sussex knapped flint, it has an opened-out, light and airy interior that looks great, thanks to original brickwork, oak flooring, antique panelling, scrubbed tables and a wood-burning stove. Any of the three locally brewed real ales served straight from the barrel go well with a lunchtime baguette; or there's the main menu, changing almost daily, and well known for its fresh and local fish and wide choice of quality meats and game. Typical starters are the salad of fresh diver caught scallops with pancetta; and tapas comprising prosciutto, chorizo, feta cheese, anchovies in oil, balsamic vinegar and bread. Seafood platter features fresh local Selsey crab and lobster, smoked salmon, crevettes and other shellfish. Two people can share a Star platter, four should ask for a Garter. Game grill, comprising pheasant and pigeon breasts, a whole roasted partridge, and venison sausage with red wine jus, is popular too. Among the vegetarian options you may find wild mushroom and butternut squash risotto. Enjoy the afternoon sun on the patio or in the garden.

There are six en suite bedrooms available.

Recommended in the area

Goodwood; Arundel Castle; Weald & Downland Open Air Museum; Cowdray Park, Midhurst

The Lickfold Inn

Address: LICKFOLD, Nr Petworth, GU28 9EY
Tel: 01798 861285
Email: lickfold@evanspubs.co.uk
Website: www.evanspubs.co.uk
Map ref: 3 SU92
Directions: From A3 take A283, through Chiddingfold, 2m on right signed 'Lurgashall Winery', pub in 1m **Open:** all day all week noon-11 (Sun noon-5) **Closed:** 25 Dec **Facilities:** Parking Garden
Notes: ⊕ FREE HOUSE ⋔ ⋔ ☻ 12

Someone once told Radio 2 DJ Chris Evans never to buy his local pub, so he bought this one nine miles away. Later, having bought a house round the corner, he ended up owning his local (and two others) anyway. It dates from 1460, as its herringbone-brick exterior and beamed interior easily affirm. Cousin Mark Evans offers Irish sausages on champ with Guinness and onion gravy; beer-battered haddock, hand-cut chips and minted mushy peas; and wild mushroom risotto with rocket, Parmesan and truffle oil. Outside is a large courtyard and terraced gardens. A local children's hospice receives half the pub's profits.

Recommended in the area

Petworth House (NT); Amberley Museum & Heritage Centre; Bignor Roman Villa

---

Black Horse Inn

Address: Nuthurst Street, NUTHURST,
Horsham, RH13 6LH
Tel: 01403 891272
Email: clive.henwood@btinternet.com
Website: www.theblackhorseinn.com
Map ref: 3 TQ12
Directions: 4m S of Horsham, off A281, A24 & A272
Open: all week ⓑ L all wk 12-2.30 D all wk 6-9.30
⑩ L all wk 12-2.30 D all wk 6-9.30
Facilities: Parking Garden
Notes: ⊕ FREE HOUSE ⋔ ⋔ ☻ 7

Once on the main route from Brighton to Horsham, this used to be a smugglers' hideout, with a secret passage from the pub to the church which can still be seen. Quietly hidden away, it retains plenty of original features: stone-flagged floors, an inglenook fireplace and an exposed wattle and daub wall. The pub has a reputation for good ales and home-made, freshly prepared food, with universal appeal and menus that specify gluten-free and vegetarian options. There are also some very tempting desserts.

Recommended in the area

Four local pub walks; Wakehurst Place; Pulborough Brooks Nature Reserve; Leonardslee Gardens

The Grove Inn

Address: Grove Lane, PETWORTH, GU28 0HY
Tel: 01798 343659
Email: steveandvaleria@tiscali.co.uk
Website: www.groveinnpetworth.co.uk
Map ref: 3 SU92
Directions: On outskirts of town, just off A283 between Pullborough & Petworth. 0.5m from Petworth Park
Closed: Sun eve & Mon 🍽 L Tue-Sun 12-2.30
D Tue-Sat 6-9.15 🍽 L Tue-Sun 12-2.30
D Tue-Sat 6-9.15 **Facilities:** Parking Garden **Notes:** 🍺 FREE HOUSE 👬 🐾

The Grove Inn is a 17th-century free house in the heart of the South Downs. It sits on the outskirts of historic Petworth, a town much visited for its many and varied antique shops. Inside, the inn provides a cosy bar with oak-beamed ceilings and a large stone inglenook fireplace, as well as the Conservatory Restaurant, where diners can look out over the garden and enjoy good views of the South Downs. There is also a patio area with a pergola. Dishes are chosen from a seasonal menu, which is completely rewritten every six to eight weeks, with some daily changes for good measure. Typical starters include smoked salmon, chive and cream cheese roulade; home-made parsnip soup; and duck liver and mushroom terrine. Among the main courses are natural smoked haddock topped with Welsh rarebit; well-matured chargrilled fillet steak with truffle mash and cracked black peppercorn sauce; and wild mushroom risotto with parmesan and truffle oil. To follow there could be banana pancake with honey rum toffee sauce or lemon posset, as well as a choice of cheeseboards. Three whites, three reds and a rosé are available by the glass, with many more available on the main wine list.

Recommended in the area

Cowdray Park; Lurgashall Winery; Petworth House and Park

Chichester Cathedral

Royal Oak Inn

Address: The Street, POYNINGS, BN45 7AQ
Tel: 01273 857389
Fax: 01273 857202
Email: ropoynings@aol.com
Website: www.royaloakpoynings.biz
Map ref: 3 TQ21
Directions: N on A23 just outside Brighton, take A281 signed Henfield & Poynings, then follow signs into Poynings
Open: all day all week 11-11 (Sun 11.30-10.30)
Facilities: Parking Garden **Notes:** ⊕ FREE HOUSE ♦♦ ⌕ ♟ 12

Built as a small hotel and tea gardens during the 1880s, the inn has undergone a comprehensive refurbishment. It has a smart cream-painted exterior, and inside you'll find solid oak floors, old beams and crackling log fires along with more contemporary decor and comfy sofas. For summer enjoyment there is a large garden with splendid views of the Downs. This popular free house, has, for more than a decade, maintained a commitment to good quality pub food featuring locally sourced produce.

Recommended in the area

Brighton; South Downs Way; Bramber Castle (NT)

The Countryman Inn

Address: Countryman Lane, SHIPLEY, RH13 8PZ
Tel: 01403 741383
Fax: 01403 741115
Email: countrymaninn@btinternet.com
Website: www.countrymanshipley.co.uk
Map ref: 3 TQ12
Directions: From A272 at Coolham into Smithers Hill Ln. 1m to junct with Countryman Ln
Open: 10-4 6-11 **Closed:** Sun eve (Jan) ⓑ L all wk 11.30-3.30 D all wk 6-10 ⓘ L all wk 11.30-3.30
D all wk 6-10 **Facilities:** Parking Garden **Notes:** ⓦ FREE HOUSE ⚇ 20

A rural hostelry in the traditional style, The Countryman is set in open countryside close to the small village of Shipley, surrounded by 3,500 acres of farmland owned by the Knepp Castle Estate. The area is in the process of being turned back to a more natural state, with the introduction of fallow deer, free-roaming Tamworth pigs, Exmoor ponies and English Longhorn cattle. Many wild birds have also been encouraged to return to the area, as the new growth of wild grasses and plant life provide a welcoming habitat. You can even do a bit of bird watching from the inn's garden in fine weather. During the winter you'll find warming log fires, Harvey's and organic Horsham ales in the cosy bar, together with over 30 wines from around the world, and freshly ground coffee. Free-range meat and vegetables from local farms make their appearance on the restaurant menu alongside fresh fish from Shoreham and Newhaven and local game in season. Menus change frequently, and as well as the carte there is also a range of ploughman's lunches, bar snacks and daily specials. Shipley's historic eight-sided smock mill (so-called because of its likeness to a traditional farm labourer's smock) is worth a visit.

Recommended in the area

Leonardslee Lakes & Gardens; Parham House & Gardens; Amberley Working Museum

River Avon, Stratford-upon-Avon

The Baraset Barn

Address: 1 Pimlico Lane, ALVESTON,
Stratford-upon-Avon, CV37 7RF
Tel: 01789 295510
Fax: 01789 292961
Email: barasetbarn@lovelypubs.co.uk
Website: www.barasetbarn.co.uk
Map ref: 3 SP25

Open: all day 11am-mdnt **Closed:** 25 Dec & 1 Jan,
Sun eve, Mon (Jan-Feb) 🍴 **L** all wk 12-2.30 **D** Mon-
Sat 6.30-9.30 ⭐ **L** Mon-Sat 12-2.30, Sun 12-3.30
D Mon-Sat 6.30-9.30 **Facilities:** Parking Garden **Notes:** ♥ 🐾 ♔ 12

Surrounded by glorious Warwickshire countryside, the hugely impressive Baraset Barn is one of those country gastro-pubs you won't want to forget. Converted from an old barn, the interior's original flagstones and other historic features sit harmoniously alongside new granite, pewter and oak, and a glass-fronted kitchen. From the bar, stone steps lead to the main dining area with high oak beams and brick walls, an open mezzanine level, and a luxurious lounge area with sumptuous sofas for a relaxing morning coffee with the papers. The menu successfully blends classic British dishes with an interesting Mediterranean choice; typically, starters of Dolcelatte and shallot Tatin with roasted vine tomatoes; fennel and chilli-crusted squid with mango and spring onion salsa; and crispy Asian beef salad. Then, from the rotisserie, you could choose spit-roast chicken peri peri; from the stove, herbed rack of lamb with asparagus, button onions and chorizo; and from the sharing plate selection, Greek meze of taramasalata, hummous, tzatziki, feta, olives and flatbreads. A chalkboard lists daily fish dishes. Allow too for baked plum cheesecake and black pepper mascarpone. Among the wines are "forgotten" Old World classics. The continental-style patio garden is perfect for alfresco dining and drinking.

Recommended in the area

Stratford-upon-Avon; Charlecote Park (NT); Anne Hathaway's Cottage

The Granville @ Barford

Address: 52 Wellesbourne Road,
BARFORD, CV35 8DS
Tel: 01926 624236
Fax: 01926 624806
Email: info@granvillebarford.co.uk
Website: www.granvillebarford.co.uk
Map ref: 3 SP24
Directions: 1m from M40 junct 15. Take A429 for
Stow. Pub at end of village **Open:** 12-3 5.30-11 (Fri-
Sat 12-11.30 Sun 12-11) **Facilities:** Parking Garden
Notes: ⊕ ENTERPRISE INNS PLC ♦♦ ♦ ♥ 18

This friendly and stylish village dining pub in the heart of Shakespeare country is owned and run by Val Kersey. Relax on the leather sofas in the lounge with a pint or glass of wine. Everything on your plate here is home made from local produce delivered daily, except for the local, rustic bread. At lunchtime, try smoked salmon, dill and cucumber crème fraîche doorstop sandwich, and in the evening, perhaps butternut squash and herb risotto with Parmesan crisps. Enjoy alfresco dining in the patio garden.
Recommended in the area
Warwick castle; Stoneleigh Abbey, Kenilworth; Baddesly Clinton Hall

The Howard Arms

Address: Lower Green, ILMINGTON,
nr Shipston on Stour, CV36 4LT
Tel/Fax: 01608 682226
Email: info@howardarms.com
Website: www.howardarms.com
Map ref: 3 SP24
Directions: Off A429 or A3400, 7m from
Stratford-upon-Avon **Open:** 11-11 (Sun 11-10.30)
🍴 L 12-2.30 D 6-9.30 ◎ L 12-2.30 D 6-10
Facilities: Parking Garden
Notes: ⊕ FREE HOUSE ♥ 24

The village of Ilmington is set in a crook of the Cotswold Hills – the perfect spot for a leisurely stroll – and on the picturesque village green you'll find The Howard Arms, a 400-year-old Cotswold stone inn. The flagstoned bar and open-plan dining room create an informal atmosphere with period charm. The imaginative menu offers plenty of variety, and changes two or three times a week; check out the blackboard above the inglenook fireplace. The garden is delightful in summer.
Recommended in the area
Batsford Arboretum; Shakespeare's Birthplace; Anne Hathaway's Cottage

Warwick Castle mill

The Red Lion

★★★★ ◉ INN

Address: Main Street, Long Compton,
SHIPSTON ON STOUR, CV36 5JS
Tel: 01608 684221
Fax: 01608 684968
Email: info@redlion-longcompton.co.uk
Website: www.redlion-longcompton.co.uk
Map ref: 3 SP24
Directions: On A3400 between Shipston on Stour & Chipping
Norton **Open:** 11-11 ☒ **L** Mon-Thu 12-2.30 (Fri-Sun all meals
12-9:30) **D** Mon-Thu 6-9 ☒ **L** Mon-Thu 12-2.30 **D** Mon-Thu
6-9 **Rooms:** 5 en suite **Facilities:** Parking Garden
Notes: ⊕ FREE HOUSE ☒ ☒ ☒ 7

Built as a coaching inn in 1748, this Grade II listed, stone free house is located in an Area of
Outstanding Natural Beauty. Though with tales of witches in the village and a nearby prehistoric stone
circle, there is as a much to interest the historian as there is the tourist. If you're tempted to stay, five
elegant en suite bedrooms offer tea- and coffee-making facilities and flat-screen TVs. The inn's interior
retains its old world atmosphere with oak beams, log fires and gleaming wood, but has a contemporary
vibe with comfy leather armchairs. Eat in the character bar, with its settles and inglenook fireplace, or
the smart restaurant area, choosing from one long menu or daily blackboard specials. Options range
from a sandwich of crayfish, rocket and lemon mayonnaise on ciabatta to rack of lamb with crushed
black olive and herb crust, grilled aubergine and provençal sauce. Favourites include cod and chips
served on the Red Lion Times and a steak and Hook Norton pie, washed down with real ale or your
choice from a carefully selected wine list. Live music on the first Wednesday of the month.
Recommended in the area
Shakespeare's Birthplace; Warwick Castle; Cotswold Wildlife Park

Town Hall and Christmas market, Birmingham

The Malt Shovel at Barston

Address: Barston Lane, BARSTON, Solihull, B92 0JP
Tel/Fax: 01675 443223
Website: www.themaltshovelatbarston.com
Map ref: 3 SP27
Directions: M42 junct 5, take turn towards Knowle.
1st left on Jacobean Ln, right at T-junct. Sharp left
into Barston Ln. Restaurant 0.5m **Open:** all day all
week ▤ **L** Mon-Sat 12-2.30, Sun 12-4 **D** Mon-Sat
6-9.30 ▢ **L** Sun 12-4 **D** Mon-Sat 7-9.30
Facilities: Parking Garden **Notes:** ⊕ FREE HOUSE ▮ 8

Converted from an early 20th-century mill where malt was ground, this delightful country pub and
restaurant features log fires, stripped wooden floors, heavy fabrics and a beautiful garden. Cask-
conditioned ales are served in the bar, where you can lunch on faggots, chilli chicken, or a fresh fish
special. In a converted barn is the stylish restaurant, offering a seasonally-changing menu of dishes
such as baby pork ribs with home-made marinade; or corn-fed duck breast, celeriac and potato rösti.
Recommended in the area
National Exhibition Centre (NEC); Birmingham city centre; Solihull countryside

The Orange Tree

Address: Warwick Road, CHADWICK END, B93 0BN
Tel: 01564 785364
Fax: 01564 782988
Email: theorangetree@lovelypubs.co.uk
Website: www.theorangetreepub.co.uk
Map ref: 3 SP27
Directions: 3m from Knowle towards Warwick
Open: 11-11 **Closed:** 25 Dec ▤ ▢ **L** all wk
12-2.30 **D** all wk 6-9.30 **Facilities:** Parking Garden
Notes: ⊕ FREE HOUSE ▮▮ ▮ ▮ 8

Despite its peaceful countryside setting, this pub/restaurant is just minutes from the National Exhibition
Centre, Solihull and Warwick. A relaxed Italian influence is reflected in the furnishings and the food.
The bar has comfortable seating and ambient music and is a great place to meet, and the sunny
lounge area, all sumptuous leather sofas and rustic decor, opens out onto the patio. The deli counter
dispenses breads, cheeses and olive oils, and there are several pasta dishes, pizzas, and a choice of
stove-cooked, grilled or spit-roasted meats and fish.
Recommended in the area
Baddesley Clinton Hall; Kenilworth Castle; National Motorcycle Museum

ISLE OF WIGHT

Cowes harbour

The Seaview Hotel & Restaurant

★★★ 82% ◉◉ HOTEL

Address: High Street, SEAVIEW, PO34 5EX
Tel: 01983 612711
Fax: 01983 613729
Email: reception@seaviewhotel.co.uk
Website: www.seaviewhotel.co.uk
Map ref: 3 SZ69
Directions: B3330 (Ryde to Seaview road), left via Puckpool along seafront road, hotel on left
Open: all week 🛏 **L** all wk 12-2.30 **D** 6.30-9.30 ⭐
L 12-2 (summer), Sat-Sun 12-2 (winter) **D** 6.30-9.30
Rooms: 28 en suite (4 GF) **D** £120-£199 **Notes:** ⊕ FREE HOUSE ♙ ⌁

In a sailing-mad Victorian village, this smart, sea-facing hotel is crammed with nautical associations. There are ships' wheels, oars, model ships, and lots of polished wood and brass. The Front Bar & Lounge resembles a naval wardroom and is home to a collection of naval artefacts, while the Pump Bar at the back is like a traditional pub, but with a more fish-focused menu than you'd find in most. You may also eat in the small Victorian dining room, or the Sunshine restaurant and conservatory, both of which share a modern European (with a hint of British) menu that offers the very best of the season, caught or grown around the island – fish straight from the sea; pork and beef from its lush grazing land; venison from the hotel's own farm; and tomatoes, garlic and herbs from its garden. If the menu offers it, consider spider crab risotto with fennel sauce as a starter; Wight lamb shepherd's pie, carrot purée and beef sauce; or lightly curried cod, spiced lentils, buttered spring greens, and herb crème fraîche sauce as a main course; and pineapple parfait, black pepper ice cream, and sweet red pepper and chilli syrup for dessert.

Recommended in the area

Seaview Wildlife Encounter (Flamingo Park); Osborne House; Isle of Wight Steam Railway

The Needles

The New Inn

Address: Mill Lane, SHALFLEET, PO30 4NS
Tel/Fax: 01983 531314
Email: info@thenew-inn.co.uk
Website: www.thenew-inn.co.uk
Map ref: 3 SZ48
Directions: 6m from Newport to Yarmouth on A3054
Open: all week 🍴 L 12-2.30 D 6-9.30 🍽 L 12-2.30 D 6-9.30
Facilities: Parking Garden **Notes:** ⊕ ENTERPRISE INNS 🍴 🍷 6

Built in 1743 to replace its fire-razed predecessor, this well-regarded dining pub is at the head of the Newtown estuary, putting it in pole position for nautical types. Inglenooks, flagstones and low beams provide bags of character, while its waterside location gives it enviable access to the best fish and seafood, such as specials of cracked crab, fillets of pollock and grilled mackerel. On the same board are slow-roasted pork belly and pan-fried chicken breast, while the standard menu offers steaks, prawn specialities, baguettes and salads. Island-brewed beers are on tap and more than 60 wines are always available.

Recommended in the area

The Needles; Blackgang Chine; Isle of Wight Steam Railway

WILTSHIRE

Wilton Windmill

Streets of Castle Combe

The Tollgate Inn

★★★★ ◉◉ INN

Address: Holt, BRADFORD-ON-AVON, BA14 6PX
Tel: 01225 782326
Fax: 01225 782805
Email: alison@tollgateholt.co.uk
Website: www.tollgateholt.co.uk
Map ref: 2 ST86
Directions: M4 junct 18, A46 towards Bath, then
A363 to Bradford-on-Avon, then B3107 towards
Melksham **Open:** 11.30-3 5.30-11 (Sun 11.30-3)

Closed: Mon ⬚ **L** Tue-Sun 12-2 **D** Tue-Sat 7-9 ⍥ **L** Tue-Sun 12-2 **D** Tue-Sat 7-9 **Rooms:** 4 en suite
S £55-£100 **D** £80-£100 **Facilities:** Parking Garden **Notes:** ⬚ FREE HOUSE ⬚ ⬚ ⬚ 9

A handsome country inn offering attractively presented bedrooms, with oak beams and antiques. There is a
dining terrace, gardens and a paddock with goats and sheep. Impressive modern English and Mediterranean
food is prepared from fresh local produce and served in a cosy downstairs room and the first-floor former
chapel. Daily changing guest beers are sourced. An onsite farm shop opens in Spring 2010.
Recommended in the area
Lacock National Trust Village; Georgian town of Bradford-on-Avon; Bath

The Three Crowns

Address: BRINKWORTH, Chippenham, SN15 5AF
Tel: 01666 510366
Website: www.threecrowns.co.uk
Map ref: 3 SU08
Directions: From Swindon take A3102 to Wootton
Bassett, then B4042, 5m to Brinkworth
Open: all day Mon-Sat 10am-11pm, Sun noon-11pm
Closed: 25-26 Dec 🍴 ◎ L Mon-Sat 12-2, Sun
12-9 **D** Mon-Sat 6-9.30, Sun 12-9
Facilities: Parking Garden
Notes: ⊕ ENTERPRISE INNS 🍴 🐾 🍷 20

The current licensees, Anthony and Allyson Windle, have been here over 20 years and are now well into researching this quiet little pub's history. They know that it opened with its current name in 1801, but suspect that in the 18th century it traded under a different name. In 1927 Kelly's directory lists it as a hotel, serving teas and light refreshments; today it is one of the area's most popular eating venues. Menus are written on large blackboards, which make it easy to keep up with the daily, market-driven changes. Everything is home made using top quality ingredients, main dishes being typified by aged West Country beef, lamb and mint pie, supreme of halibut and vegetarian tagliatelle, all cooked to order and served with a generous selection of fresh vegetables. Lighter lunches range from caesar salad to slow-roast belly pork and beef chilli. The bar stocks a wide range of well-kept cask ales, keg beers and lagers, and Anthony and his wine merchant have carefully chosen (and tasted, over a period, naturally!) an 80-bin wine list. In winter there is an open log fire, while in summer the doors are flung open to the peaceful patio and garden.

Recommended in the area

Westonbirt Arboretum; Cotswold Water Park; Lydiard Park

The Fox and Hounds

Address: The Green, EAST KNOYLE,
Salisbury, SP3 6BN
Tel: 01747 830573
Fax: 01747 830865
Email: pub@foxandhounds-eastknoyle.co.uk
Website: www.foxandhounds-eastknoyle.co.uk
Map ref: 2 ST83
Directions: 1.5m off A303 at the A350 turn off,
follow brown signs
Open: all week 11.30-3 5.30-11 🍺 L all wk

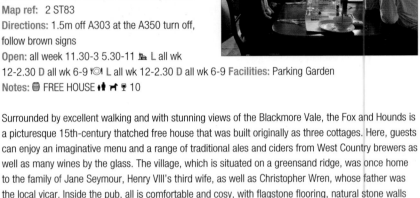

12-2.30 D all wk 6-9 🍽 L all wk 12-2.30 D all wk 6-9 **Facilities:** Parking Garden
Notes: ⊕ FREE HOUSE 👬 🐕 ☗ 10

Surrounded by excellent walking and with stunning views of the Blackmore Vale, the Fox and Hounds is a picturesque 15th-century thatched free house that was built originally as three cottages. Here, guests can enjoy an imaginative menu and a range of traditional ales and ciders from West Country brewers as well as many wines by the glass. The village, which is situated on a greensand ridge, was once home to the family of Jane Seymour, Henry VIII's third wife, as well as Christopher Wren, whose father was the local vicar. Inside the pub, all is comfortable and cosy, with flagstone flooring, natural stone walls and sofas positioned next to wood-burning fires in winter. Diners can enjoy a meal in the light, airy conservatory or in the patio area. A varied menu, based on local produce, contains a range of snacks and main meals. These might include ploughman's or pizzas (from the clay oven), as well as lamb chump on mash, venison, 21-day-old fillet or sirloin steak with a choice of sauces, Thai green curry or Moroccan vegetable tagine. For those with room to spare, Pavlova with passion fruit coulis and warm chocolate fudge cake are among the desserts.

Recommended in the area

Stonehenge (EH); Stourhead House and Gardens (NT); Longleat

The Angel Coaching Inn

Address: High Street, HEYTESBURY, BA12 0ED
Tel: 01985 840330
Fax: 01985 840931
Email: admin@theangelheytesbury.co.uk
Website: www.theangelheytesbury.co.uk
Map ref: 2 ST94
Directions: From A303 take A36 towards Bath, 8m, Heytesbury on left
Closed: Mon (ex BH) **Facilities:** Parking Garden
Notes: ⊕ GREENE KING ♦ ➚ ♀ 10

A 16th-century inn surrounded by countryside best appreciated on foot, so why not embark on one of the walks that start and end here. The Angel's interior is a blend of its original features and the contemporary; the beamed bar, for instance, has scrubbed pine tables, warmly decorated walls and an attractive fireplace with a wood-burning stove. As it's very much a dining pub you may eat in the restaurant, the bar, or in the secluded courtyard garden. Head chef Mark Ward, an emigré from Yorkshire, and his team pride themselves on offering value for money. Steaks, one of their specialities, come either from nearby Pensworth Farm or Scotland, and are then hung for 35 days, ready to be served with chunky chips, salad and sauce béarnaise. A satisfying choice at dinner may involve a starter of warm smoked salmon quiche with new potato salad; or chorizo and broad bean salad with sherry and shallot dressing. The main course might be free-range chicken breast with bubble and squeak, and oyster mushroom sauce; crab, chilli and coriander linguine; or pan-fried sea bass with ratatouille. Vegetarian options can always be found too. An extensive and carefully selected wine list offers several by the glass.

Recommended in the area

Stonehenge; Old Sarum; Longleat

The Lamb at Hindon

★★★★ ❀ INN

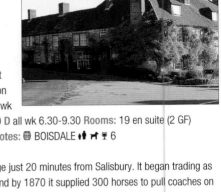

Address: High Street, HINDON, Salisbury, SP3 6DP
Tel: 01747 820573
Fax: 01747 820605
Email: info@lambathindon.co.uk
Website: www.lambathindon.co.uk
Map ref: 2 ST93
Directions: From A303 follow signs to Hindon. At
Fonthill Bishop right onto B3089 to Hindon. Pub on
left **Open:** all day all week 7.30am-mdnt ♨ **L** all wk

12-2.30 **D** all wk 6.30-9.30 ℄ **L** all wk 12-2.30 **D** all wk 6.30-9.30 **Rooms:** 19 en suite (2 GF)
S £70 **D** £90-£190 **Facilities:** Parking Garden **Notes:** ⊕ BOISDALE ♦♦ ♥ ♟ 6

The Lamb is set in the centre of a charming village just 20 minutes from Salisbury. It began trading as
a public house as long ago as the 12th century and by 1870 it supplied 300 horses to pull coaches on
the London–West Country route. The inn is part of the Boisdale group, with two other establishments
in London (Belgravia and Bishopsgate), and this is reflected in the distinctive interior design and in the
quality of the food and wine. The building still has plenty of historic character, with beams, inglenook
fireplaces, and wood and flagstone floors, all set off by fine antique furniture, old paintings and open
fires. Food is served from breakfast to dinner in the dining room or the intimate Whisky and Cigar Bar.
Dishes are prepared from carefully sourced ingredients, including fresh fish and game in season. A
dinner menu might feature main courses such as Macsween haggis; Gloucester Old Spot sausages
with Beaune mustard mash and gravy; and the 'famous Boisdale' burger, plus a fish of the day and pie
of the day. The Meeting Room, in a sunken area just off the main dining room, is available for private
dining or meetings. Each bedroom is richly decorated and has LCD screens.

Recommended in the area

Longleat; Stonehenge; Stourhead House & Gardens

Compasses Inn

★★★★ ⊛ INN

Address: LOWER CHICKSGROVE,
Nr Tisbury, SP3 6NB
Tel: 01722 714318
Email: thecompasses@aol.com
Website: www.thecompassesinn.com
Map ref: 2 ST92
Directions: On A30 (1.5m W of Fovant) take 3rd right to Lower Chicksgrove. In 1.5m turn left onto Lagpond Lane, pub 1m on left **Open:** all week noon-3 6-11 (Sun noon-3 7-10.30) **Closed:** 25-26 Dec ⅃ **L** all wk 12-2 **D** all wk 6.30-9
Rooms: 5 en suite **S** £65-£90 **D** £85-£90 **Facilities:** Parking Garden **Notes:** ⊕ FREE HOUSE ⅋ ⅏ ⅁ 8

You'll find this thatched inn tucked away down a single track lane in a tiny hamlet amid beautiful rolling countryside, which in turn forms part of a designated Area of Outstanding Natural Beauty. The Compasses is a 14th-century building of great character, and beyond the latched door there's a long, low beamed bar with high-backed stools, stone walls, worn flagstone floors and a large inglenook fireplace, where a large open fire is lit in the colder months. Adjacent to the bar is a dining room, ideal for private parties. There is a regularly changing blackboard menu of dishes freshly prepared from seasonal produce, and a choice of ales including Keystone Solar Brew, Hidden Potential, Bass and Keystone Large One. Extra seating is set out in the big garden, which has a grassed area and some wonderful views. If you want to make the most of the lovely location and stay over, there are lovely double bedrooms and a detached cottage accessed separately from the inn. All the bedrooms have hospitality trays and LCD Freeview TVs, one room is perfect for families, with an additional single bed, and z-beds for children.

Recommended in the area

Longleat; Stonehenge; Farmer Giles Farmstead

The Horse & Groom Inn

Address: The Street, Charlton,
MALMESBURY, SN16 9DL
Tel: 01666 823904
Email: info@horseandgroominn.com
Website: www.horseandgroominn.com
Map ref: 2 ST98
Directions: M4 junct 17, A429 follow Cirencester signs. Through Corston & Malmesbury. On at Priory rdbt, at next rdbt to Cricklade, then to Charlton
Open: all week ☙ ⚑ L Mon-Thu 12-2, Fri-Sat 12-2.30, Sun 12-3 **D** Mon-Thu 6.30-9, Fri-Sat 6.30-9.30, Sun 6.30-9 **Facilities:** Parking Garden
Notes: ⸮⸮ ⚑ ♟ 8

The Horse & Groom Inn is a proper English country hostelry offering great food and drink in glorious surroundings. Situated in the small village of Charlton, just east of Malmesbury, this solidly elegant 16th-century Cotswold stone house boasts a stunning interior full of original stone flags and fireplaces, roaring log fires and classic country inn charm. The dining room furnishings include solid oak tables and a rug-strewn wooden floor. Outside, extensive grounds include a gorgeous walled garden and a separate children's play area. In the dog-friendly bar the house beer is Archer's, along with weekly-changing guest beers. The inn is renowned for good quality, sensibly priced food, presented in relaxed, informal surroundings making it equally suitable for a casual lunch or a special occasion meal. Local produce sourced from within a 40-mile radius is a priority for the kitchen. Aside from the carte, there is a bar menu and a selection of classic pub dishes. Showcase dishes include home-made crab cakes with dill mayonnaise and baby salad leaves; double cooked Cotswold shoulder of lamb with whole grain mustard mash, sautéed curly kale and red wine sauce; and warm chocolate fondant with stem ginger ice cream.

Recommended in the area

Malmesbury Abbey; The Abbey House Gardens; The Cotswold Water Park, Cirencester

The George & Dragon

★★★★ ◉◉ RESTAURANT WITH ROOMS
Address: High Street, ROWDE, SN10 2PN
Tel: 01380 723053
Email: thegandd@tiscali.co.uk
Website: www.thegeorgeanddragonrowde.co.uk
Map ref: 2 ST96
Directions: 1m from Devizes, take A342 towards
Chippenham **Closed:** Sun eve ▣ ▯ **L** Mon-Fri 12-3,
Sat-Sun 12-4 **D** Mon-Fri 7-11, Sat 6.30-10
Rooms: 3 (2 en suite) (1 pri fac) £55-£85
Facilities: Parking Garden **Notes:** ⊕ FREE HOUSE ♦♦ ⌗ ♈ 11

Successfully combining the charm of a 16th-century inn with the relaxed atmosphere of a modern gastro-pub, the George and Dragon is located on Rowde High Street, a stone's throw from the Kennet and Avon Canal and the dramatic Caen Hill flight of locks. In summer the garden is a delight, with its lawned area and cottage-style flower borders, and there's seating for an alfresco meal or a quiet drink. During winter there are welcoming log fires in the panelled bars and dining room, and an interesting original feature is a carved Tudor rose on one of the old beams in the restaurant. Seafood delivered directly from Cornwall is the speciality of the house, so diners can take their pick from the latest catch. The choice is huge, and may comprise sea bass, lobster, lemon sole, John Dory, mackerel, scallops, turbot and mussels. Blackboards above the bar list the fish dishes of the day, while the carte offers a range of local meat and game options. The emphasis of the award-winning food is on home-made delicacies, and this extends from the bread served at the start of the meal, to the delicious desserts and ice creams, and the chocolate fudge served with coffee. Draught beers include Butcombe Bitter, Milk Street Brewery ales and Bath Ales Gem. There are three bedrooms available, each full of character.

Recommended in the area

Bowood House and Gardens; Lacock Abbey, Fox Talbot Museum & Village; Avebury

The West Kennet Long Barrow

The Bridge Inn

Address: 26 Church Street, WEST LAVINGTON, Devizes, SN10 4LD
Tel: 01380 813213
Fax: 01380 813213
Email: portier@btopenworld.com
Website: www.the-bridge-inn.co.uk
Map ref: 3 SU05
Directions: Approx 7m S of Devizes on A360 towards Salisbury. On edge of village, beyond church
Open: 12-3 6.30-11 **Closed:** 2wks Feb, Sun eve & Mon L 12-2 D 7-9 L 12-2 D 7-9 **Facilities:** Parking Garden **Notes:** ENTERPRISE INNS 12

Located on the outskirts of a village on the edge of Salisbury Plain, the well known Bridge Inn is a small but perfectly formed pub and restaurant with a beamed bar and log fire, and local paintings adorning the walls. The food-led establishment caters for all appetites, with light lunches, a regular carte and a specials board, and the kitchen produces English food with a French twist. In the large garden there is a boules pitch.

Recommended in the area

Longleat; Stonehenge; Lacock Abbey, Fox Talbot Museum & Village

The Pear Tree Inn

★★★★★ ◉◉ RESTAURANT WITH ROOMS

Address: Top Lane, WHITLEY, Melksham, SN12 8QX
Tel: 01225 709131
Fax: 01225 702276
Email: peartreeinn@maypolehotels.com
Website: www.maypolehotels.com
Map ref: 2 ST86
Directions: A365 from Melksham towards Bath, at Shaw right onto B3353 into Whitley, 1st left in lane, pub at end
Open: all week 11-11 ⮐ **L** 12-2.30 **D** 6.30-9.30
⬟ **L** 12-2.30 **D** 6.30-9.30 **Rooms:** 8 en suite (4 GF) **S** £95
D £125 **Facilities:** Parking Garden **Notes:** ⬟ ⬟ ⬟ 12

Here you'll find a delightful, stone-built country pub and restaurant that also offers cosy accommodation in beautifully designed bedrooms. Flagstone floors and two log fires help to give it a comfortable, lived-in feel, with pitchforks, old scythes and other agricultural antiques reminding one of its past as a farm. Indeed, the surrounding acres of wooded farmland prepare you for the possible imminent arrival of Farmer Giles for his pint of Sharp's Doom Bar, or one of the regularly changing guest beers.

The food, prepared from locally supplied produce, has been much praised and awarded two AA Rosettes. The menu, served throughout the pub, including in the terracotta and mustard barn-conversion restaurant, offers an updated approach to traditional British food. A typical three-course meal comprising Middle White pork and apricot pâté with home-made piccalilli followed by braised and rolled lamb shoulder, pea mousse, courgette and mint chutney, and sticky peach pudding. There is a healthy menu for children. Outside, in addition to the lovely cottage garden, there is also a patio area.

Recommended in the area

Lacock Abbey; Avebury; Silbury Hill

WORCESTERSHIRE

Worcester Cathedral

Iron Age hill fort, Malvern Hills

The Fleece Inn

Address: The Cross, BRETFORTON, WR11 7JE
Tel: 01386 831173
Email: nigel@thefleeceinn.co.uk
Website: www.thefleeceinn.co.uk
Map ref: 3 SP04
Directions: From Evesham follow signs for B4035 towards Chipping Campden. Through Badsey into Bretforton. Right at village hall, past church
Open: all week 11-3 6-11 (11-11 in summer)
L Mon-Sat 12-2.30, Sun 12-4 **D** Mon-Sat 6.30-9, Sun 6.30-8.30 **Facilities:** Garden **Notes:** ⊕ FREE HOUSE ♦♦ ♀ 12

The Fleece was built as a longhouse 600 years ago and its last private owner, Lola Taplin, – who died in the snug in 1977, bequeathing it to the National Trust, – was a direct descendant of the man who built it. Restorations after a fire in 2004 ensured that the Fleece looks as good as ever. Home-made dishes include local sausage of the day with mash, pork belly marinated in plum cider brewed on the premises and a fresh fish dish of the day. Look out for Morris dancers, folk singing and asparagus!
Recommended in the area
Chipping Campden; Hidcote Manor (NT); Cotswold Way; Abbey Park, Evesham

Whitby old town

The Black Bull Inn

Address: 6 St James Square, BOROUGHBRIDGE,
Nr York, YO51 9AR
Tel: 01423 322413
Fax: 01423 323915
Map ref: 8 SE36
Directions: From A1(M) junct 48 take B6265 E for
1m **Open:** 11-11 (Fri-Sat 11am-mdnt, Sun noon-11)
🍺 🍽 L all wk 12-2 D all wk 6-9 **Facilities:** Parking
Notes: ⊕ FREE HOUSE ♦♦ 🐕 🍷 10

Built in 1258, The Black Bull was one of the main watering holes for coaches travelling what is now the A1, and Dick Turpin allegedly stayed here. Back then it had stables and a blacksmith's shop attached; and these days, it still retains plenty of original features, including old beams, low ceilings and roaring open fires, not to mention the supposed ghost of a monk. Traditional pub fare is the order of the day here, with extensive menus covering all the options. Starters such as chicken liver pâté with Cumberland sauce; king prawn tails and queen scallops; and Scottish smoked salmon are sure to whet the appetite. The main courses that follow might include rump of English lamb with rosemary and olive mashed potato; chicken breast wrapped in Parma ham with pan-fried wild mushroom; and a selection of very substantial steak dishes. Several fish options are also available, including the likes of salmon, halibut, sea bass, tuna and Dover sole. Desserts include banoffee meringue roulade with toffee sauce; dark chocolate truffle torte; apple pie with custard; and mixed ice creams encased in brandy snap with fruit purées. Sizeable bar snacks range from pork and chive sausage with onion gravy, and deep-fried prawns, to Thai beef strips with egg noodles and stir fry vegetables. Among the array of sandwiches are hot roast pork and apple sauce; and cold smoked salmon with dill mayonnaise. Yorkshire beers are available, and there is a selection of 17 malts.

Recommended in the area

Newby Hall and Gardens; Mother Shipton's Cave; Ripon city and cathedral

Malt Shovel Inn

Address: BREARTON, Harrogate, HG3 3BX
Tel: 01423 862929
Email: bleikers@themaltshovelbrearton.co.uk
Website: www.themaltshovelbrearton.co.uk
Map ref: 8 SE36
Directions: From A61 (Ripon/Harrogate) onto B6165 towards Knaresborough. Left & follow Brearton signs. In 1m right into village
Open: 12-3 6-11 (Sun 12-4) **Closed:** Mon-Tue & Sun eve ▥ L 12-2 D 6-9 ▐◎▌ L 12-2 D 6-9
Facilities: Parking Garden **Notes:** ⊕ FREE HOUSE ▮♦ ♟ 21

At the heart of the picturesque village of Brearton lies the Malt Shovel, a fine family-run 16th-century inn. Although the pub is surrounded by rolling farmland, it is just 15 minutes from Harrogate and within easy reach of both Knaresborough and Ripon. One of the oldest buildings in an ancient village, it was taken over by the Bleiker family in 2006 and has been transformed into an atmospheric venue for eating and drinking, with open fires in winter, flagstoned floors and pianos in the bar and conservatory. Swiss-born Jürg's innovative cooking specialises in fresh fish – there's an on-site smoking kiln – classic sauces and well-sourced local produce, and diners can choose from the lunchtime and early-evening bistro menu or opt to eat à la carte. He and wife Jane bring their wealth of experience in food, hospitality and entertainment to create an ambience that combines elegance and theatricality – his son and daughter-in-law are international opera soloists, and it's not unheard of for the odd aria to be served up at dinner. However it's their commitment to great food, fine wine (over twenty are served by the glass), impeccable cask ales and the warmest of welcomes that bring customers back again and again.

Recommended in the area

Ripley Castle; Fountains Abbey (NT); Yorkshire Dales

The Bull

Address: BROUGHTON, nr Skipton, BD23 3AE
Tel: 01756 792065
Email: enquiries@thebullatbroughton.com
Website: www.thebullatbroughton.com
Map ref: 7 SD95
Directions: 3m from Skipton on A59
Open: all week Mon-Sat noon-11pm, Sun noon-10.30pm
⏱ **L** Mon-Sat noon-2, Sun noon-8.30 (Afternoon bites Mon-Sat 2-5.30) **D** Mon-Fri 6-9, Sat 5.30-9, Sun noon-8.30
Facilities: Parking Garden **Notes:** ⊕ FREE HOUSE ⋔ ⋔ ☻ 12

Long one of the county's landmark pubs, the Bull takes its name from the surrounding 3,000-acre Broughton Hall estate's famous herd of Shorthorns. Summer offers alfresco dining on the patios overlooking this parkland, which is often used for location filming; winter means eating and drinking warmed by blazing log fires. Real ales include Timothy Taylor Landlord and the unusual Saltaire Raspberry Blonde. The restaurant is acclaimed chef Nigel Haworth's first venture into Yorkshire (he honed his skills in Lancashire!). Star of BBC2's Great British Menu 2009, he loves working with the region's farmers, growers and fine food suppliers to create dishes strong on local tradition, thus it should be no surprise to find a menu offering Yorkshire pudding, gravy and slow-cooked oxtail bits; Wakefield rabbit pan-fried in butter; and Bolton Abbey lamb. Nor should you raise a quizzical eyebrow at Whitby scampi in beer batter, Limestone Country beef rib-eye, or any of the several dishes containing Wensleydale cheese, such as ploughman's platter. An option among the hot and cold sandwich fillings is 'real' chips cooked in dripping – your waistline has been warned! Desserts include sticky Parkin with treacle toffee sauce; traditional English pancakes; and home-made organic ice creams and milkshakes.

Recommended in the area

Yorkshire Dales National Park; Malham Cove; Haworth

Robin Hood's Bay

The Fox & Hounds

Address: CARTHORPE, Bedale, DL8 2LG
Tel: 01845 567433
Website: www.foxandhoundscarthorpe.co.uk
Map ref: 7 SE38
Directions: Off A1, signed on both N'bound & S'bound carriageways
Open: 12-3 7-11 **Closed:** 25-26 Dec eve & 1st wk Jan, Mon 🏠 **L** Tue-Sat 12-2 **D** Tue-Sat 7-9.30
Facilities: Parking **Notes:** ⊕ FREE HOUSE ⁂

Near the Great North Road, but in rural surrounds, The Fox and Hounds has been serving travellers for the past 200 years, and for the last 26, the same family have been making a thoroughly good job of continuing the tradition. The restaurant, once the village smithy, serves up imaginative dishes, and the midweek set-price menu is particularly good value, with dishes such as pan-fried lambs' liver with bacon and onion gravy; or, from the specials board, grilled whole Dover sole with parsley butter. Home-made desserts might include chocolate fondue and almond raspberry tart with vanilla ice cream.

Recommended in the area

Ariel Extreme; Snape Arboretum; Black Sheep Brewery Visitor Centre

The Durham Ox

Address: Westway, CRAYKE, York, YO61 4TE
Tel: 01347 821506
Fax: 01347 823326
Email: enquiries@thedurhamox.com
Website: www.thedurhamox.com
Map ref: 8 SE57
Directions: Off A19 from York to Thirsk, then Easingwold. Onto Crayke, left up hill, pub on right **Open:** 12-2.30 6-11 (Times may vary on Sun) **Closed:** 25 Dec ▥ **L** 12-2.30, Sun 12-3 **D** 6-9, Sun 6-8.30 ◉ **L** 12-2.30, Sun 12-3 **D** 6-9, Sun 6-8.30 **Rooms:** 4 en suite (2 GF) **S** £60-£100 **D** £80-£140 **Facilities:** Parking Garden **Notes:** ⊕ FREE HOUSE ⌁ ♟ 9 ▣

Three hundred years old, and family-owned for the last ten, the Durham Ox is an award-winning traditional pub with flagstone floors, exposed beams, oak panelling and roaring fires. Situated in historic Crayke, with breathtaking views over the Vale of York on three sides, and a charming view up the hill (reputedly the one the Grand Old Duke of York's men marched up and down) to the church. A print of the eponymous ox – and a hefty beast it was too – hangs in the bottom bar. The Ox prides itself on serving good pub food, using the best locally sourced ingredients when possible for seasonal menus, complemented by blackboard specials. Dishes likely to be found are braised lamb shank and clapshot mash; grilled plaice, new potatoes, spinach and brown shrimp butter sauce; and root vegetable casserole with 'wartime' herb dumplings. On Sundays, traditional rib of beef and Yorkshire puddings, fresh fish and other dishes are complemented by delicious desserts. Snacks include eggs Benedict, or Florentine, with cured bacon; chargrilled Ox burger with cheese, bacon, chips and onion rings; and a variety of open sandwiches. Four converted farm cottages provide overnight accommodation.

Recommended in the area

Castle Howard; Scampston; Byland Abbey

Wharncliffe Woods, Wortley

The Blue Lion

Address: EAST WITTON, Nr Leyburn, DL8 4SN
Tel: 01969 624273
Fax: 01969 624189
Email: enquiries@thebluelion.co.uk
Website: www.thebluelion.co.uk
Map ref: 7 SE18 **Directions:** From Ripon take A6108 towards Leyburn **Open:** 11-11
Closed: 25 Dec ⓑ **L** 12-2.15 **D** 7-9.30 ⑩ **L** Sun 12-2.15 **D** all wk 7-9.30 **Facilities:** Parking Garden
Notes: ⊕ FREE HOUSE ⅈ ⅎ ♟ 12

A sympathetically renovated country inn, built towards the end of the 18th century for coach travellers and cattle drovers journeying through Wensleydale. The bar, with an open fire and flagstone floor, is a beer drinker's heaven, while the freshly prepared food in the highly praised candlelit restaurant uses mainly Yorkshire ingredients. A meal might be salad of black pudding, smoked bacon, shallots and poached egg; chargrilled fillet of beef with shiraz sauce, lardons and mushrooms; and pineapple Tatin with home-made pineapple sorbet. Bar meals are listed on a blackboard.

Recommended in the area

Yorkshire Dales National Park; Jervaulx Abbey; Hardraw Force Waterfall

The Plough Inn

Address: Main Street, FADMOOR, York, YO62 7HY
Tel: 01751 431515
Fax: 01751 432492
Email: enquiries@theploughfadmoor.co.uk
Website: www.ploughrestaurant.co.uk
Map ref: 8 SE68
Directions: 1m N of Kirkbymoorside on A170
Open: 12-2.30 6.30-11 **Closed:** 25-26 Dec,
1 Jan, Mon-Tue (ex BH), Sun eve ▣ L 12-2,
12-2.30 D 6.30-8.45 ⦿ L 12-2 D 6.30-8.45
Facilities: Parking Garden **Notes:** ⊕ FREE HOUSE ♦♦ ♟ 8

Ramblers sampling the delights of the North Yorkshire Moors National Park will be pleased to find
this stylishly well-appointed country pub and restaurant in the pretty village of Fadmoor. The setting
overlooking the village green could not be more idyllic, and the inn boasts dramatic views over the Vale
of Pickering and the Wolds. Inside it is cosy, snug and welcoming, with log fires, beams and brasses
in the bar: the ideal spot to enjoy a pint of Black Sheep Best. The food is an undoubted attraction,
with meals available in the bar or in the attractively furnished rustic-style restaurant. A good value,
two-course meal is available at lunchtime and early evening. Options include smoked salmon and
asparagus terrine, followed by medallions of pork tenderloin with blue Stilton and white wine sauce; or
home-made steak and ale pie. The carte menu features such dishes as deep-fried duck and mango
spring rolls; seafood paella with Italian sausage; and pan-seared king scallops with a fricassée of spring
onion, garlic and bacon as starters, followed by, for example, basil and parmesan crusted cod; slow
roasted boneless half Gressingham duckling with orange and brandy sauce; or fillet of beef Wellington
topped with liver paté and Madeira sauce. There is a dedicated menu for vegetarians.

Recommended in the area

North Yorkshire Moors National Park; Rievaulx Terrace and Temples

The Bridge Inn

Address: GRINTON, Richmond, DL11 6HH
Tel: 01748 884224
Email: atkinbridge@btinternet.com
Website: www.bridgeinngrinton.co.uk
Map ref: 7 SE09
Directions: Exit A1 at Scotch Corner towards
Richmond. In Richmond take A6108 towards
Reeth, 10m
Open: all week **Facilities:** Parking Garden
Notes: ⊕ JENNINGS BROTHERS PLC ♠ ♟ 7

With a host of activities such as walking, fishing, horse riding and mountain biking all on the doorstep, and a range of en suite rooms available to stay in, The Bridge Inn makes a good base for those in search of country pursuits. Situated on the banks of the River Swale in the heart of the Yorkshire Dales National Park this fine former coaching inn dates from the 13th century. Now with its beamed ceilings and open fires tastefully restored, the inn is fast becoming known for its great food and ales. Customers are invited to sample Jennings award-winning cask ales, or try something a little different from a micro-brewery; there is also an extensive wine cellar. Menus are based on seasonal local produce under the experienced eye of resident chef John Scott, and flavoured with herbs from the pub's own garden. Light snacks such as hot or cold baguettes and jacket potatoes are served in the bar, while in the à la carte restaurant, typical main courses range from lamb shank in red wine and rosemary to spiced parsnip pie with herby pastry. For those with room to spare, the dessert menu includes a daily choice of old-fashioned traditional puddings.

Recommended in the area

Yorkshire Dales; Reeth; St Andrew's Church

The River Nidd from the castle at Knaresborough

The Boars Head Hotel

★★★ 83% ◉◉ HOTEL

Address: Ripley Castle Estate, HARROGATE, HG3 3AY
Tel: 01423 771888
Fax: 01423 771509
Email: reservations@boarsheadripley.co.uk
Website: www.boarsheadripley.co.uk
Map ref: 7 SE35 **Directions:** On A61 (Harrogate/
Ripon road). Hotel in village centre **Open:** all week
🍴 L all wk 12-2 D all wk 6-9.30 ⏹ L all wk 12-2
D all wk 7-9 **Rooms:** 25 en suite S £105-£125
D £125-£150 **Facilities:** Parking Garden **Notes:** ⊞ FREE HOUSE ♨ ⚘ ♟ 10

The original coaching inn was built in 1830, when Lord Ingilby rebuilt the village next to his castle.
Today's impressive hotel came about in a 1990 makeover, with oil paintings and furniture from the castle
helping to create the country-house feel. Handpumps dispense cracking Yorkshire ales, and the optics
some splendid Highland and Islay malts. Seasonal menus might feature loin of Kirby Malzeard lamb with
sea spinach and tomato fondant; and fillets of lemon sole, chervil, courgette and seared scallop.
Recommended in the area
Ripley Castle & Gardens; Fountains Abbey (NT); Ripon Cathedral

The General Tarleton Inn

★★★★★ ◉◉ RESTAURANT WITH ROOMS

Address: Boroughbridge Road, Ferrensby,
KNARESBOROUGH, HG5 0PZ
Tel: 01423 340284
Fax: 01423 340288
Email: gti@generaltarleton.co.uk
Website: www.generaltarleton.co.uk
Map ref: 8 SE35
Directions: A1(M) junct 48 at Boroughbridge, take
A6055 to Knaresborough. Inn 4m on right

Open: 12-3 6-11 🍺 **L** 12-2 **D** 6-9.15 🍴 **L** Sun 12-1.45 **D** Mon-Sat 6-9.15 **Rooms:** 14 en suite
(7 GF) **S** £75-£137 **D** £129-£150 **Facilities:** Parking Garden **Notes:** 🛢 FREE HOUSE 🚻 ⚲ 8

A tastefully redesigned old coaching inn owned and run by John and Claire Topham. Sir Banastre
Tarleton, after whom it was named, allegedly fired on surrendering troops during the American War
of Independence and became known as "Bloody Ban"; he later became a Liverpool MP. The inn's
low-beamed ceilings, rustic walls, log fires, cosy corners and modern black-and-white still lifes create
an inviting atmosphere. With two AA Rosettes, the GT's reputation for fresh seafood partly depends
on daily calls from fishing boat skippers with details of their catch; within hours perhaps mussel
chowder, or John's signature dish of seafood parcels in lobster sauce, will be on diners' plates in the
bar brasserie or restaurant. In the latter you might well find Nidderdale oak-roast hot smoked salmon
with fennel and pear salad, tapenade and Bloody Mary dressing; slow-braised Yorkshire beef and Black
Sheep ale suet pudding; and trio of rhubarb - brûlée, crumble and compôte. Home-made dishes on
the children's menu have been road-tested by the Topham offspring. Dine outdoors in the garden or
covered courtyard. An impressive selection of fine wines includes some great house wines.

Recommended in the area

Fountains Abbey; City of York; Yorkshire Dales National Park

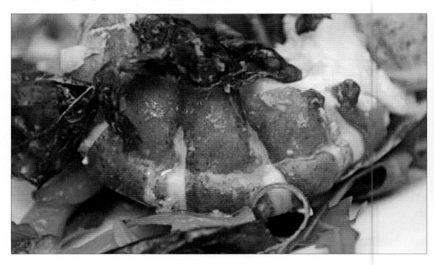

Sandpiper Inn

Address: Market Place, LEYBURN, DL8 5AT
Tel: 01969 622206
Fax: 01969 625367
Email: hsandpiper99@aol.com
Website: www.sandpiperinn.co.uk
Map ref: 7 SE19
Directions: From A1 take A684 to Leyburn
Open: 11.30-3 6.30-11 (Sun noon-2.30 7-10.30)
Closed: Mon & occasionally Tue ⓑ **L** all wk 12-2.30
¶⊚¶ **L** all wk 12-2.30 **D** all wk 6.30-9.30
Facilities: Garden Notes: ⊕ FREE HOUSE ⫙ ⌁ ⚑ 8

Although the Sandpiper Inn has been a pub for only 30 years, the building is the oldest in Leyburn, dating back to around 1640. It has a beautiful terrace, a bar, snug and dining room, and the menu offers a varied mix of traditional (fish in real ale batter and chips; steaks) and more unusual dishes, which might include apple-smoked black pudding on a garlic mash with a port wine jus; warm goats' cheese on rocket and beetroot salad; and crispy duck leg with fried potatoes and oriental dressing.
Recommended in the area
Wensleydale Railway; Forbidden Corner

The Sportsmans Arms Hotel

Address: Wath-in-Nidderdale, PATELEY BRIDGE,
 Harrogate, HG3 5PP
Tel: 01423 711306
Fax: 01423 712524
Map ref: 7 SE16
Directions: A59/B6451, hotel 2m N of Pateley
Bridge **Open:** all week noon-2.30 6.30-11
Closed: 25 Dec ⓑ **L** all wk 12-2 **D** all wk 7-9
¶⊚¶ **L** Sun 12-2 **D** Mon-Sat 7-9 **Facilities:** Parking
Garden Notes: ⊕ FREE HOUSE ⚑ 12

This very special pub is in one of the loveliest areas of the Yorkshire Dales. A custom-built kitchen, run by chef/patron Ray Carter for nearly 25 years (now assisted by his son), is the heart of the operation. True to the best pub traditions, real ales and wines accompany dishes served in an informal bar, while daily restaurant menus tempt all comers. Delights include loin of pork with mustard and mushroom sauce; and roast Scottish salmon with spring onions and stem ginger. Round off the meal in style with double chocolate roulade or the ever-popular Sportsmans summer pudding.
Recommended in the area
Fountains Abbey and Studley Royal; Stump Cross Caverns; Brimham Rocks

Fox & Hounds Country Inn

★★ 78% ◉ HOTEL

Address: Sinnington, PICKERING, YO62 6SQ
Tel: 01751 431577
Fax: 01751 432791
Email: fox.houndsinn@btconnect.com
Website: www.thefoxandhoundsinn.co.uk
Map ref: 7 SE78
Directions: 3m W of town, off A170
Open: noon-2 6.30-9 **Closed:** 25-26 Dec ⓑ **L** 12-2
D 6.30-9 ⓘ **L** 12-2 **D** 6.30-9 **Rooms:** 10 en suite
(4 GF) **S** £49-£69 **D** £70-£160 **Facilities:** Parking Garden **Notes:** ⊕ FREE HOUSE ⑂ ⌁ ♟ 7

Set in a pretty village with a river running by, and a large green with a small pack-horse bridge, this
18th-century inn offers good drinking, imaginative modern cooking, and well-designed rooms. In the
bar, oak beams, wood panelling and an open fire make ideal surroundings for a pint of Black Sheep
Special or a glass of wine. The menus range from sandwiches and light lunches to dishes like pan-fried
calves' liver with spring onion mashed potato. The rooms are equipped with TV and drinks trays.
Recommended in the area
North Yorkshire Moors Railway; Rievaulx Abbey; Nunnington Hall

Nags Head Country Inn

★★ 75% ◉ HOTEL

Address: PICKHILL, nr Thirsk, YO7 4JG
Tel: 01845 567391
Fax: 01845 567212
Email: enquiries@nagsheadpickhill.co.uk
Website: www.nagsheadpickhill.co.uk
Map ref: 8 SE38
Directions: 1m E of A1. 4m N of A1/A61 junct
Open: 11-11 (Times may vary Sun) **Closed:** 25 Dec
ⓑ **L** 12-2 **D** 6-9.30 ⓘ **L** 12-2 **D** 6-9.30 **Rooms:** 14
en suite (3 GF) **S** £60-£75 **D** £80-£102.50 **Facilities:** Parking Garden **Notes:** ⊕ FREE HOUSE ⑂ ⌁ ♟ 8

This 200-year-old establishment, with beamed ceilings and stone-flagged floors, stands in Pickhill
(mentioned in the Domesday Book) and a perfect spot for exploring 'Herriot Country'. Under the same
ownership for over 35 years, the inn offers superb hospitality and a relaxed atmosphere. The same
wide ranging menu, with hand picked wines, is available throughout – in the restaurant, lounge bar or
tap room. There are modern, well equipped bedrooms and a two-bedroom cottage available.
Recommended in the area
Yorkshire Dales; Lightwater Valley Theme Park; Falconry Centre

Roseberry Topping, North York Moors National Park

The Buck Inn

★★★ INN

Address: THORNTON WATLASS, Ripon, HG4 4AH
Tel: 01677 422461
Fax: 01677 422447
Email: innwatlass1@btconnect.com
Website: www.buckwatlass.co.uk
Map ref: 7 SE28
Directions: From A1 at Leeming Bar A684 to Bedale.
B6268 towards Masham. Village 2m **Open:** 8am-
mdnt **Closed:** 25 Dec eve 🄻 **L** Mon-Sat 12-2, Sun
11-3 **D** 6.30-9.30 🍽 **L** Mon-Sat 12-2, Sun 11-3 **D** 6.30-9.30 **Rooms:** 7 (5 en suite) (1 GF)
S £65 **D** £80-£90 **Facilities:** Parking Garden **Notes:** ⊕ FREE HOUSE ♦♦ 🐾 🍷 7

Margaret and Michael Fox have to refit the occasional tile on the inn, but this is a small price to pay for
its idyllic situation on the boundary of the village cricket pitch. Five real ales are served, most from local
independent breweries, and the bar menu offers such specialities as Masham rarebit (Wensleydale
cheese with local ale on toast, topped with bacon); and classics such as fish and chips and lasagne.
Recommended in the area

Lightwater Valley Theme Park; Theakson Brewery Visitor Centre; Yorkshire Dales National Park

Wombwell Arms

Address: WASS, York, YO61 4BE
Tel: 01347 868280
Email: wombwellarms@btconnect.com
Website: www.wombwellarms.co.uk
Map ref: 6 SE57
Directions: From A1 take A168 to A19 junct.
Take York exit, then left after 2.5m, left at Coxwold
to Ampleforth. Wass 2m **Open:** all week noon-3 6-11
(Sat noon-11 Sun noon-4) ⏴ **L** Mon-Thu 12-2, Fri-
Sat 12-2.30, Sun 12-3 **D** Mon-Thu 6.30-9, Fri-Sat

6.30-9.30 ⏶ **L** Mon-Thu 12-2, Fri-Sat 12-2.30, Sun 12-3 **D** Mon-Thu 6.30-9, Fri-Sat 6.30-9.30
Facilities: Parking Garden **Notes:** ⏶ FREE HOUSE ⏶ ⏶ ⏶ 9

The pub was built as a granary around 1620, probably using stone from nearby Byland Abbey, before
becoming an alehouse not long after. Original features include a large inglenook fireplace, oak beams,
and flagstones that continue to stand up well to the diverse footwear of locals, walkers, cyclists and
parents of pupils from nearby Ampleforth College, as well as the paws and claws of their canine
companions. Three cask ales, including Timothy Taylor Landlord and Theakstons Old Peculier, nine
wines by the glass, and twelve malt whiskies are always available in the bars. Freshly prepared meals,
made using locally sourced produce wherever possible, are also available in Poachers Bar and in both
restaurants. Starters include pigeon bruschetta with mushrooms, and trio of smoked fish and twice-
baked cheese soufflé. For a main course you might plump for chicken in creamy leek and Stilton sauce;
roast Barnsley chop with mint and red wine jus; or king prawn risotto with pan-fried scallops. There's
also the classic haddock in real ale batter with home-made chips and mushy peas; Masham pork and
apple sausages with mash and gravy; or the pub's signature steak, Guinness and mushroom pie.
Recommended in the area
North Yorks Moors National Park; Byland Abbey, Mouseman Museum, Kilburn

Bolton Abbey

The Star Country Inn

Address: WEAVERTHORPE, Malton, YO17 8EY
Tel: 01944 738273
Email: starinn.malton@btconnect.com
Website: www.starinnweaverthorpe.co.uk
Map ref: 8 SE97
Directions: From Malton take A64 towards Scarborough. 12m, at Sherburn right at lights. Weaverthorpe 4m, inn opposite junct
Open: all wk 6-mdnt, plus Fri-Sun 12-2
Closed: lunch Mon-Thu
📠 🍽 **L** 12-2 Fri-Sun **D** 6-9 all wk
Facilities: Parking Garden **Notes:** 🍺 FREE HOUSE ♦♦

This traditional 18th-century country inn has expanded over the years to incorporate adjoining cottages, which now house overnight accommodation. Its location makes it a handy base for exploring the Yorkshire Wolds, or a day out in Bridlington. The rustic nature of the two bar areas and dining room, where large fires blaze away in winter, creates a welcoming, convivial atmosphere. The food is cooked to traditional recipes using fresh local produce. Bar meals may include chicken breast wrapped in bacon with mozzarella; and king prawn balti served with rice, poppadoms, and home-made mango chutney. Typical dishes from either the main menu or the specials board include pigeon in horseradish sauce; pheasant in red wine sauce, while there's also a good number of fresh fish dishes, ranging from fish pie, trout in lemon butter, and trio of fish in white wine, through to more exotic offerings. To finish, home-made desserts, such as apple and blackberry crumble, spiced roast rhubarb with creamy rice pudding, and rich chocolate tart ensure that no-one should leave wanting more. There is a beer garden and a large car park.

Recommended in the area

Nunnington Hall; Sledmere House; Castle Howard

The Dove Valley Trail

Cadeby Inn

Address: Main Street, CADEBY,
Doncaster, DN5 7SW
Tel: 01709 864009
Email: info@cadeby-inn.co.uk
Website: www.cadeby-inn.co.uk
Map ref: 8 SE50
Open: noon-11 ⓫ L all wk 12-5.30 🍽 L all wk
12-9.30 D Mon-Sat 12-9.30, Sun 12-8 **Facilities:**
Parking Garden **Notes:** ⊕ FREE HOUSE ⭥ ♟ 6

Written large on the frontage of this handsome free house is 1751, the year it was built as a farmhouse, whose original stone walls still enclose the spacious front garden. Food can be enjoyed in the stone-walled traditional bar or the more contemporary restaurant. Local supplier-sourced seasonal menus offer freshly prepared dishes of oven-roasted halibut with prawn and Champagne sauce; chicken breast stuffed with sun-dried tomatoes and Brie; or a selection of steaks. Game may appear on the specials blackboard. End with warm rice pudding, spiced plums and nutmeg. At the rear is a patio and garden, ideal for alfresco dining or drinking.

Recommended in the area

Peak District National Park; Yorkshire Sculpture Park; National Coal Mining Museum

---

Cubley Hall

Address: Mortimer Road, Cubley,
PENISTONE, S36 9DF
Tel: 01226 766086
Fax: 01226 767335
Email: info@cubleyhall.co.uk
Website: www.cubleyhall.co.uk
Map ref: 7 SE20
Directions: M1 junct 37, A628 towards Manchester.
Hall just S of Penistone **Open:** all week **D** Mon-Fri
until 9.30, Sat-Sun until 10 🍽 **L** Sun 12.30-3.30
D Sun, last orders at 5.45 **Facilities:** Parking Garden **Notes:** ⊕ FREE HOUSE ⭥ ♟ 7

Steeped in history, Cubley Hall started out in the 1700s as a farm on a Pennine packhorse route, was later transformed into a gentleman's residence, and then became a children's home. Many original features survive, including the oak-beamed restaurant that was tastefully converted from a barn. The menu offers a choice of pizzas, pastas, chargrills and blackboard specials. Favourites include 'posh fish and chips' and English brisket beef with fondant mash, tarragon carrots and caramelised shallots.

Recommended in the area

Yorkshire Sculpture Park; Millennium Galleries; Peak District National Park

Langsett

The Fat Cat

Address: 23 Alma Street, SHEFFIELD, S3 8SA
Tel: 0114 249 4801
Fax: 0114 249 4803
Email: info@thefatcat.co.uk
Website: www.thefatcat.co.uk
Map ref: 8 SK38
Open: all week noon-11 (Sat-Sun noon-mdnt)
Closed: 25 Dec ≥ L all wk 12-2.30 D Mon-Sat 6-8
Facilities: Parking Garden
Notes: ⊕ FREE HOUSE ⋔ ⋔

A smart Grade II listed, back street city pub, the Fat Cat dates from 1852 and is reputed to be haunted. Ale afficionados will delight in the constantly changing list of guest beers, especially from micro-breweries. Traditional scrumpy and unusual bottled beers are also sold, while the Kelham Island Brewery, owned by the pub, accounts for at least four of the ten traditional draught real ales. There are open fires inside, and an attractive walled garden outside. Home-cooked food — steak pie; spinach and red bean casserole — includes vegetarian and vegan options.

Recommended in the area

Kelham Island Museum; Winter Gardens; Millennium Galleries

Hetchell Crags

Kaye Arms Inn & Brasserie

Address: 29 Wakefield Road, Grange Moor,
WAKEFIELD, WF4 4BG
Tel: 01924 848385
Fax: 01924 848977
Email: kayearms@hotmail.co.uk
Website: www.thekayearms.com
Map ref: 8 SE32
Directions: On A642 between Huddersfield & Wakefield
Open: noon-2.30 5.30-11 (Sat-Sun noon-11)
Closed: 25 Dec-2 Jan, Mon ⮐ L all week 12-2.30
D all week 5.30-9.30 **Facilities:** Parking
Notes: ⊕ FREE HOUSE ☙ 15

The Kayes has stood overlooking the landscape of Grange Moor for over 500 years and has, over the last 40, become a popular dining destination. As a pub it provides the comfort of the old world and mixes it with the tradition of the area, and serves quality local produce dishes. The mixture of the old and the new, from pickled herrings to pressed game terrine with handmade bread and chutney to the famous signature dish of twice baked farmhouse cheese soufflé, the choice makes deciding a rather difficult affair. Main course range from hand-reared venison to beer battered scampi, Anglaise chicken to 4-hour roasted belly pork, and are priced for all pockets. Owners Paul and Helen Andrews Garth have brought years of experience in catering back to their roots in Yorkshire and strive to give all their customers an experience of hospitality and welcome. Families are encouraged and children's meals are taken from the main menu. There is also an extensive wine by the glass list and wine menu.

Recommended in the area

National Coal Mining Museum; Temple Newsam; Yorkshire Sculpture Park

SCOTLAND

Urquhart Castle, Loch Ness

The Lairhillock Inn

Address: NETHERLEY, By Stonehaven,
Aberdeenshire, AB39 3QS
Tel: 01569 730001
Fax: 01569 731175
Email: info@lairhillock.co.uk
Website: www.lairhillock.co.uk
Map ref: 10 NO89 **Directions:** From Aberdeen
take A90. Right towards Durris on B9077 then left
onto B979 to Netherley **Open:** all week 11am-mdnt
Closed: 25-26 Dec, 1-2 Jan **L** all wk 12-2 **D** all

wk 6-9.30 **D** Tue-Sat 7-9.30 **Facilities:** Parking Garden **Notes:** FREE HOUSE 7

Set in beautiful rural Deeside yet only 15 minutes from Aberdeen, this 200-year-old former coaching inn offers real ales like Cairngorm Trade Winds in the bar and real fires in the comfortable lounge. Traditional and gastro-pub cuisine is available in the bar while there's fine dining in the Crynoch Restaurant; the menus offer robust dishes, using fresh, quality local produce. Try their own home smoked salmon or smoked scallops followed by spring lamb loin in a herb crust and vegetable stack.
Recommended in the area
Dunnottar Castle; Crathes Castle and Garden; Storybook Glen

Tigh an Truish Inn

Address: CLACHAN-SEIL, Oban,
Argyll & Bute, PA34 4QZ
Tel: 01852 300242
Website: www.tighantruish.co.uk
Map ref: 9 NM71 **Directions:** 14m S of Oban take
A816. 12m, onto B844 towards Atlantic Bridge
Open: all week 11-11 (Mon-Fri 11-2.30 5-11
Oct-Mar) **Closed:** 25 Dec & 1 Jan **L** all wk 12-2
D all wk 6-8.30 (Apr-Oct) **Facilities:** Parking Garden
Notes: FREE HOUSE

The 18th-century Tigh an Truish (meaning 'House of the Trousers' – you'll need to ask why) stands next to the famous Bridge over the Atlantic, on the beautiful island of Seil. The main bar offers a selection of single malts, ales from local brewers and occasional guests from further afield. Light bar meals appear on the lunchtime menu, while for dinner expect prawns and lobster caught by Firth of Lorne fishermen; salmon and mussels from Argyll; and perhaps venison in pepper cream and Drambuie sauce. Families are welcome to use the separate lounge bar, stocked with children's books and a highchair.
Recommended in the area
Caithness Glass; Dunstaffnage Chapel; Kilmodan Sculptured Stones

The Inn at Inverbeg

★★★★ 🛏 INN

Address: LUSS, Argyll & Bute G83 8PD
Tel: 01436 860678
Fax: 01436 860203
Email: inverbeg.reception@loch-lomond.co.uk
Website: www.innatinverbeg.co.uk
Map ref: 9 NS39
Directions: 12m N of Balloch
Open: all day all week 11-11 **Rooms:** 20 en suite
(5 GF) **S** £59-£149 **D** £69-£159 **Facilities:** Parking
Notes: ⊞ ♦♦ ♉ 30

Set back from the road that skirts Loch Lomond's western shore, this completely modernised old inn is close enough to Glasgow to make a day's visit there as practicable as a Highlands tour. A great deal of thought has gone into the leather-furnished interior, which sports an impressive hand-crafted elm bar. Mr C's Fish and Whisky Restaurant offers all manner of fish dishes, over 200 whiskies, 30 wines available by the glass, and real ales, including some from the Loch Fyne and Houston breweries. The fish and seafood, locally caught, of course, includes haddock, cod and coley; West Coast oysters, squid, langoustines and steamed mussels; and the thick Scottish fish soup called cullen skink. Try the West Coast Fish Tea - fish and hand-cut chips, mushy peas, bread and butter. But it's not all about fish: meat dishes include Buccleuch Estate steak burgers and sirloin steaks; grilled game sausages; and Cajun chicken, while vegetarians might go for penne pomodoro. There's one more thing – deep-fried mini Mars bars. As the menu says "Yes, you read it right but you'll be surprised." Listen to traditional live folk music every Friday and Saturday from March through until November.
AA Pub of the Year for Scotland 2009-2010.

Recommended in the area

Luss (conservation village); Burrell Collection, Glasgow; The Hill House, Helensburgh

Glasgow Science Centre

Edinburgh Castle

The Steam Packet Inn

Address: Harbour Row, ISLE OF WHITHORN, Newton
Stewart, Dumfries & Galloway, DG8 8LL
Tel: 01988 500334
Fax: 01988 500627
Email: steampacketinn@btconnect.com
Website: www.steampacketinn.com
Map ref: 5 NX43
Directions: From Newton Stewart take A714, then
A746 to Whithorn, then Isle of Whithorn
Open: all week 11-11 (Sun noon-11) **Closed:** 25

Dec, winter Tue-Thu 2.30-6 ⓑ **L** all wk 12-2 **D** all wk 6.30-9 **Facilities:** Parking Garden
Notes: ⊕ FREE HOUSE ⁙ ⼞ 🍷 9

The Steam Packet is a family-run, quayside pub with a picturesque village setting at the southern tip
of the Machars peninsula. The inn offers a window on the local fishermen at work, while the menu
features the fruits of their labours. Food is served in the two bars, the dining room and conservatory.
Seven en suite bedrooms, including deluxe rooms, are available.

Recommended in the area

Whithorn Story Visitor Centre; Creetown Gem and Rock Museum; The Tollbooth Arts Centre

The Jigger Inn

Address: The Old Course Hotel,
ST ANDREWS, Fife, KY16 9SP
Tel: 01334 474371
Fax: 01334 477688
Website: www.oldcoursehotel.co.uk
Map ref: 10 NO51
Directions: Please telephone for directions
Open: all day all week 11-11 (Sun noon-11)
Closed: 25 Dec ▨ **L** all wk 12-9.30 **D** all wk
12-9.30 **Facilities:** Parking Garden
Notes: ⊕ FREE HOUSE ♦♦ ♚ 8

This whitewashed, former stationmaster's lodge on a long-dismantled railway line stands now as the unique 19th hole in the grounds of the most famous golf course – The Old Course. St Andrew's is renowned, of course, throughout the world as the Home of Golf. Therefore, don't be surprised by the abundant golfing memorabilia, and golfers comparing their scorecards as they warm themselves in front of a crackling, open-hearth fire cradling a pint of something Scottish – St Andrew's Ale from Belhaven Brewery maybe. This traditional Scottish pub is always busy and offers warm hospitality at its very best. Tiger Woods, Justin Timberlake and Prince William have all been spotted here. All-day availability is one advantage of the short, simple menu that lists soups and salads such as minestrone soup with cannellini beans and parmesan crostini and Caesar salad, or triple-decker sandwiches, wraps and ciabatta. For something more substantial, there is St Andrew's beer-battered fish with chunky chips, grilled Speyside rib eye steak, Jigger cheese and bacon burger, sausage and mash with onion gravy or warm sun-blushed tomato, goat's cheese and rocket tart with gremolata dressing.

Recommended in the area

St Andrews Cathedral; West Sands Beach; Fife Folk Museum

Loch Ard in the Trossachs region

Cawdor Tavern

Address: The Lane, CAWDOR, Nairn,
Highland, IV12 5XP
Tel/Fax: 01667 404777
Email: enquiries@cawdortavern.info
Map ref: 12 NH85
Directions: From A96 (Inverness-Aberdeen) take
B9006 & follow Cawdor Castle signs. Tavern in
village centre **Open:** all week 11-3 5-11 (Sat 11am-
mdnt Sun 12.30-11) **Closed:** 25 Dec, 1 Jan
L Mon-Sat 12-2, Sun 12.30-3 **D** all wk 5.30-9

D all wk 5.30-9 **Facilities:** Parking Garden **Notes:** ⊕ FREE HOUSE ♦♦ ♠ ♀ 8

The Tavern is at the heart of a beautiful conservation village, close to the famous castle, and was
formerly a joinery workshop for the Cawdor Estate. The handsome oak panelling in the lounge bar
came from the castle and was a gift from the former laird. Roaring log fires keep the place cosy on long
winter nights, while in the summer guests can sit on the patio. The menu options include prime meats,
fresh local seafood, game and vegetarian dishes, complemented by a hand-picked wine list.
Recommended in the area
Cawdor Castle; Fort George; Culloden Battlefield

The Plockton Hotel

★★★ 75% SMALL HOTEL

Address: Harbour Street, PLOCKTON,
Highland, IV52 8TN
Tel: 01599 544274
Fax: 01599 544475
Email: info@plocktonhotel.co.uk
Website: www.plocktonhotel.co.uk
Map ref: 11 NG83
Directions: On A87 to Kyle of Lochalsh take turn at
Balmacara. Plockton 7m N **Open:** all day all week

11am-mdnt (Sun 12.30pm-11pm) ⊯ **L** all wk 12-2.15 **D** all wk 6-10 ⊠ **L** all wk 12-2.15 **D** all wk 6-10
Rooms: 15 en suite (1 GF) **S** £62.50-£90 **D** £125 **Facilities:** Garden **Notes:** ⊞ FREE HOUSE ⦁⦁ ☖ 6

The award-winning Plockton Hotel sits right next to the gently lapping waters of Loch Carron, a
sheltered sea loch warmed by the Gulf Stream and fringed with palm trees. It is the only waterfront
hostelry in this lovely National Trust village, the location for the cult film *The Wicker Man*. The
breathtaking view, across the bay to the Applecross Hills, is enjoyed by many of the hotel's comfortable
en suite bedrooms. Converted from a ship's chandlery in 1913, this establishment has been run by
the Pearson family and their staff for nearly 20 years. Menus are based on the very best of Highland
produce, with seafood a major strength: expect to find locally caught langoustines, shellfish from Skye,
fresh fish landed at Gairloch and Kinlochbervie, and smoked fish from Aultbea. Products from the
smokehouse feature in one of the hotel's specialities – cream of smoked fish soup. Other starters may
include Talisker whisky pâté and fresh Plockton prawns. Top quality Highland beef appears in flamed
peppered whisky steaks from the charcoal grill. Other main courses include casserole of Highland
venison, Argyle chicken, and wild boar burger with salad and fries. A fine range of malts is offered.

Recommended in the area

Isle of Skye; Eilean Donan Castle; Applecross Peninsula

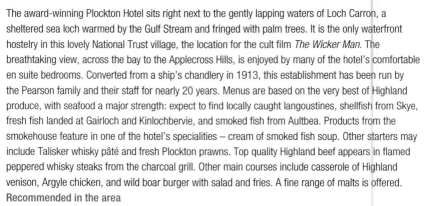

Plockton Inn & Seafood Restaurant

Address: Innes Street, PLOCKTON,
Highland, IV52 8TW
Tel: 01599 544222
Fax: 01599 544487
Email: info@plocktoninn.co.uk
Website: www.plocktoninn.co.uk
Map ref: 11 NG83
Directions: On A87 to Kyle of Lochalsh take turn at
Balmacara. Plockton 7m N
Open: all day all week ⓑ **L** all wk 12-2.30 **D** all wk
6-9 **D** all wk 6-9 **Facilities:** Parking Garden **Notes:** ⊕ FREE HOUSE ⁑ ⌁

Situated in one of Scotland's most beautiful fishing villages, near the harbour, this inn is a great base to explore the Isle of Skye and the Torridon Mountains. The inn has regular music nights in the bar, making for a lively atmosphere. A good choice of real ales is offered, plus more than 50 malt whiskies. There are two eating areas inside, the Dining Room and Lounge Bar, plus an area laid with decking outside. Fresh West Coast fish and shellfish are a speciality, plus West Highland beef, game and lamb.
Recommended in the area
Eilean Donan Castle; Lochalsh Woodlands (NTS); Strome Castle (NTS)

Moulin Hotel

★★★ 73% HOTEL
Address: 11-13 Kirkmichael Road, Moulin,
PITLOCHRY, Perth & Kinross, PH16 5EH
Tel: 01796 472196
Fax: 01796 474098
Email: enquiries@moulinhotel.co.uk
Website: www.moulinhotel.co.uk
Map ref: 10 NN95
Directions: From A924 at Pitlochry take A923.
Moulin 0.75m **Open:** all day all week 11-11 (Fri-Sat
11am-11.45pm Sun noon-11) ⓑ **L** all wk 12-9.30 **D** all wk 12-9.30 ⓞ **D** all wk 6-9 **Rooms:** 15 en
suite **S** £50-£75 **D** £65-£90 **Facilities:** Wi-fi, Parking Garden **Notes:** ⊕ FREE HOUSE ⊗ ⁑ ♣ 20

Built in 1695 and situated on an old drovers' road near to Pitlochry, this inn is popular as a walking and touring base, and offers comfortable accommodation. Locals and visitors enjoy the home-brewed beers and menus that reflect the inn's location. Try haggis, neeps and tatties, or venison Braveheart. The courtyard garden is a delight in summer while winter log fires warm the interior's nooks and crannies.
Recommended in the area
Edradour Distillery; Scottish Hydro Electric Visitor Centre, Dam & Fish Pass; Blair Castle, Blair Atholl

The Black Bull

★★★★ INN

Address: Market Place, LAUDER,
Scottish Borders, TD2 6SR
Tel: 01578 722208
Fax: 01578 722419
Email: enquiries@blackbull-lauder.com
Website: www.blackbull-lauder.com
Map ref: 10 NT54
Directions: In centre of Lauder on A68
Open: 12-11 all week ▪ ▼◎▪ **L** 12-2.30 **D** 5-9
Rooms: 8 en suite **S** £80-£110 **D** £120-£150
Facilities: Parking
Notes: ⊕ PERTHSHIRE TAVERNS LTD ▪♦ ♟ 16

A handsome white-painted former coaching inn, the Black Bull stands three storeys high and dates from 1750. The building has been restored to create a cosy haven in the heart of the Borders, just 20 minutes' drive from Edinburgh. The interior is full of character with lots of interesting pictures and artefacts. The large dining room used to be a chapel and the church spire remains in the roof. Food is also served in the Harness Room Bar or the cosy lounge. The same seasonal menu is served throughout, specialising in quality country fare prepared from locally grown produce where possible. Aberdeen Angus beef and Texel lamb from Wedderlie Farm features regularly. Additional dishes are also offered from the specials board, and there's an interesting choice of wines and ales. The accommodation is beautiful, and includes three bedrooms that are suitable for family occupation. All have hairdryers, TV, telephone, internet access, luxurious toiletries, and tea- and coffee-making facilities. Decorated in period style, the rooms have modern baths and/or showers.

Recommended in the area

Thirlstone Castle; Mellerstain House; Melrose Abbey

Loch Scavaig from Elgol, Isle of Skye

Inn at Kippen

Address: Fore Rd, KIPPEN, Stirling, FK8 3DT
Tel: 01786 870500
Email: info@theinnatkippen.co.uk
Website: www.theinnatkippen.co.uk
Map ref: 9 NS69
Directions: Off A811, 10m W of Stirling
Open: all week ⛾ ⏲ noon-9

Relax in front of the wood-burning stove in this old village inn at the foot of the Campsie Hills. While enjoying a bar snack take a look round at the enlarged photographs of old Kippen. The restaurant menu changes frequently, reflecting the best produce that the locality can provide. Examples are pork chop with black pudding, apple purée, shallots and jus; roast breast and confit leg of pheasant with mushroom and bacon; and pan-fried rainbow trout with smoked haddock mash, fennel, salsify and sauce vièrge. With your well-behaved dog at your feet, enjoy the sun out on the patio.

Recommended in the area

Stirling Castle; Queen Elizabeth Forest Park; Loch Lomond

WALES

Little Haven and Broad Haven beach

Caesars Arms

Address: Cardiff Road, CREIGIAU,
Cardiff, CF15 9NN
Tel: 029 2089 0486
Fax: 029 2089 2176
Email: caesarsarms@btconnect.com
Website: www.caesarsarms.co.uk
Map ref: 2 ST08
Directions: 1m from M4 junct 34
Open: all week noon-2.30 6-10 (Sun noon-4)
Closed: 25 Dec, 1 Jan, Sun eve
Facilities: Parking Garden **Notes:** 🛢 FREE HOUSE ♦♦ ⌐ ♟ 8

Just ten miles outside Cardiff, Caesars Arms sits tucked away down winding lanes. With fine views of the surrounding countryside from its heated patio and terrace, it attracts a well-heeled clientele. And it is little wonder, as its restaurant has a vast selection of fresh fish, seafood, meat and game taking pride of place. The emphasis here is on locally sourced food, displayed on shaven ice. Starters might include imaginative choices such as Bajan fishcakes, scallops with leek julienne or cherry-smoked duck breast with organic beetroot. Main courses take in hake, halibut, Dover sole and lobster, as well as a show-stopping Pembrokeshire sea bass baked in rock salt, which is cracked open and filleted at your table. But it's not all about fish – other choices include steak from slow-reared, dry-aged pedigree Welsh Blacks plus lamb and venison from the Brecon Beacons and free-range chickens from the Vale of Glamorgan. Home-grown organic herbs, salads and vegetables are all used as much as possible, and the inn has its own smokery. Another attraction is the farm shop, which provides a range of home-produced honey, free-range eggs, Welsh cheeses, home-baked bread and chef's ready-prepared meals to take away.

Recommended in the area

Castell Coch; Llandaff Cathedral; St Fagans: National History Museum

Ty Gwyn Inn

★ ★ ★ INN

Address: BETWYS-Y-COED, Conwy, LL24 0SG
Tel: 01690 710383 & 710787
Fax: 01690 710383
Email: mratcl1050@aol.com
Website: www.tygwynhotel.co.uk
Map ref: 5 SH75
Directions: At junct of A5 & A470, 100yds S of
Waterloo Bridge **Open:** all week 12-2 6.30-11
Closed: 1wk Jan ⚏ **L** all wk 12-2 **D** all wk 6.30-9
🍽 **L** all wk 12-2 **D** all wk 6.30-9 **Rooms:** 13 (10 en suite) (1 GF) **S** £40-£70 **D** £54-£120
Facilities: Parking **Notes:** ⊕ FREE HOUSE ♦♦

Judging from the many comments on the website, everybody who has drunk, eaten or stayed at this atmospheric old coaching inn, a few miles inside Snowdonia National Park, has thoroughly enjoyed their experience. In 1815 Thomas Telford built the impressive cast iron bridge opposite. Owned and run for the past 28 years by the Ratcliffes, Martin (chef since day one) and his wife Nicola are now in charge. Within, it's all beamed ceilings and white walls, and crammed with antiques, pictures and china. Locally well-regarded international cuisine is typified by starters of spicy Thai salad, sesame, soya and sweet chilli; and natural smoked cod and Mediterranean prawn gratin, with oven-baked rich creamy cheese and mustard sauce. The theme continues with fresh fillet of line-caught wild sea bass, king prawns, saffron and garlic; roast rack of venison loin, wild mushroom risotto and port reduction; and rosemary-scented roast rack of Snowdon lamb with roast onion and peppercorn marmalade. There is also a specials board. Sound out the next themed dinner evening. As well as some rooms having four-poster beds, two of the recently refurbished bedrooms now have relaxing spa tubs.

Recommended in the area

Conwy Castle; Llechwedd Slate Caverns; Mt Snowdon

Worm's Head

The Groes Inn

★★★★★ ❀ INN
Address: CONWY, Conwy, LL32 8TN
Tel: 01492 650545
Fax: 01492 650855
Email: reception@groesinn.com
Website: www.groesinn.com
Map ref: 5 SH77
Directions: Exit A55 to Conwy, left at mini rdbt by
Conwy Castle onto B5106, 2.5m inn on right **Open:**
all week 12-3 6-11 (Sun 12-11) **Rooms:** 14 en suite
(6 GF) **S** £85-£120 **D** £105-£200 **Facilities:** Parking Garden **Notes:** ⊕ FREE HOUSE ⋔ ⋔ ☗ 10

Dating back to the 15th century, The Groes successfully blends the old world charm of beams and open fires with the contemporary style of its luxury bedrooms. Together with an award-winning restaurant and excellent service, the inn even has its own brew, Groes Ale. Fresh local ingredients are at the heart of the impressive traditional British and Welsh dishes. Set in beautiful countryside just minutes from Conwy and the North Wales coastline, it is a world away from the hustle and bustle of everyday life.
Recommended in the area
Snowdonia; Bodnant Gardens; Conwy Castle

The Queens Head

Address: Glanwydden, LLANDUDNO JUNCTION,
Conwy, LL31 9JP
Tel: 01492 546570
Fax: 01492 546487
Email: enquiries@queensheadglanwydden.co.uk
Website: www.queensheadglanwydden.co.uk
Map ref: 5 SH77
Directions: From A55 take A470 towards Llandudno.
At 3rd rdbt right towards Penrhyn Bay, then 2nd right
into Glanwydden **Open:** 11.30-3 6-10.30 (Sat-Sun

11.30-10.30) **L** Mon-Fri 12-2, Sat-Sun 12-9 **D** Mon-Fri 6-9, Sat-Sun 12-9 **L** Mon-Fri 12-2,
Sat-Sun 12-9 **D** Mon-Fri 6-9, Sat-Sun 12-9 **Facilities:** Parking Garden **Notes:** ⊕ FREE HOUSE ♥ 7

The village of Glanwydden is just five minutes' drive from the Victorian seaside resort of Llandudno, its
shops and grand, curving beach. In the other direction lie the countryside and the mountains, making
this 18th-century country pub and restaurant, once the wheelwright's cottage, well placed for both.
Last September, it became the AA's Pub of the Year for Wales 2009-2010, an award proprietor Robert
Cureton was delighted to receive at a ceremony in London from TV news presenter, Natasha Kaplinsky.
In winter the bar's log fire will be blazing, while in summer you can take your drinks out on to the pretty
terrace. At any time of the year your fellow evening imbibers might, following their pre-theatre dinner,
be heading for the town's Venue Cymru. Typically, a meal could be smoked salmon and trout mousse;
chargrilled Welsh rump steak; and raspberry and amaretto trifle. Lighter dishes include salmon and
coriander fishcakes; and fresh asparagus risotto, while more hearty are Jamaican chicken curry; and
sautéed lamb's liver and crispy bacon. There's more of the same, as well as roasts, on Sundays, while
the wine list offers plenty of choice too.
Recommended in the area
Conwy Castle; Great Orme Heritage Coast; Bodelwyddan

Harlech castle

The Wynnstay Arms

★★★★ ◎◎ RESTAURANT WITH ROOMS

Address: Well Street, RUTHIN, Denbighshire, LL15 1AN
Tel: 01824 703147
Fax: 01824 705428
Email: reservations@wynnstayarms.com
Website: www.wynnstayarms.com
Map ref: 5 SJ15 **Open:** all day all week 🍴 L all wk 12-2
D Mon-Sat 5.30-9.30, Sun 12-7 🍽 L Sun D Tue-Sat
Rooms: 7 en suite S £45-£60 D £65-£110 **Facilities:** Parking
Notes: 🛢 FREE HOUSE 🐕 🚭 🍷 8

This 460-year-old, black and white timber-framed inn once
hosted meetings of the Jacobites. Food is still important in this
comfortable and contemporary town centre gastro-pub. The single menu, available in both Bar W, the
place for a casual drink and a meal, and in the more formal Fusions Brasserie, offers a good choice.
Typical are Welsh steaks with various sauces; pan-roasted pork tenderloin with bacon mash; chicken
curry; Italian meatballs; and pan-roasted sea bass. There are seven well-appointed en suite bedrooms.
Recommended in the area
Chester Roman City; Snowdonia National Park; Offa's Dyke Path

Penhelig Arms Hotel & Restaurant

Address: Terrace Road, ABERDYFI,
Gwynedd, LL35 0LT
Tel: 01654 767215 **Fax:** 01654 767690
Email: info@penheligarms.com
Website: www.penheligarms.com
Map ref: 2 SN69 **Directions:** On A493 W of
Machynlleth **Open:** 11-11 **Closed:** 25-26 Dec
🍴 L 12-2 D 6-9 🍽 L 12-2 D 7-9
Facilities: Parking Garden
Notes: 🛢 S A BRAIN & CO LTD 🐕 🚭 🍷 22

The Penhelig Arms has been in business since 1870 and offers spectacular views over the tidal Dyfi
estuary, plus real ales, 13 malt whiskies and a wine list comprising about 80 wines. Food is served
in the bar or waterfront restaurant. The brasserie-style menu is strong on fresh fish; crab and lobster
arriving straight from the quay, backed up by Welsh beef and lamb, and dishes might include plaice
grilled with a parmesan crust. In winter a real log fire welcomes all to the wood-panelled Fisherman's
Bar. In the summer months, the Penhelig's own seating area opposite is the place to enjoy fine views.
Recommended in the area
Centre for Alternative Technology; Tal-y-Llyn Railway; Celtica

Cefn Cyff ridge, Brecon Beacons

Clytha Arms

Address: Clytha, ABERGAVENNY, Monmouthshire, NP7 9BW
Tel/Fax: 01873 840209
Email: theclythaarms@tiscali.co.uk
Website: www.clytha-arms.com
Map ref: 2 SO21 **Directions:** From A449/A40 junction (E of Abergavenny) follow signs for 'Old Road Abergavenny/Clytha' **Open:** noon-3 6-mdnt (Fri-Sun noon-mdnt) **Closed:** 25 Dec, Mon L 🍴 L Tue-Sun 12.30-2.30 **D** Mon-Sat 7-9.30 🍽 L Tue-Sun

12.30-2.30 **D** Mon-Sat 7-9.30 **Facilities:** Parking Garden **Notes:** ⊕ FREE HOUSE ⁛ 🐾 🍷 10

Andrew and Beverley Canning have been running this free house for 17 years. Once a dower house, it is surrounded by lawns and interesting gardens, and is not far from the River Usk. Happily informal in character, it offers six different real ales a week (that's 300-plus a year), a good choice of wines by the glass, and snacks and tapas. In the restaurant, try leek and laver rissoles with beetroot chutney, fillet of Hereford beef with pink peppercorns, or faggots and peas with Rhymney gravy.

Recommended in the area

Brecon Beacons National Park; Blaenafon World Heritage Site; Castell Dinas

The White Hart Village Inn

Address: LLANGYBI, Usk,
Monmouthshire, NP15 1NP
Tel: 01633 450258
Email: info@whitehartvillageinn.com
Website: www.whitehartvillageinn.com
Map ref: 2 ST39
Directions: M4 junct 25 onto B4596 (Caerleon road) through town centre on High St, straight over rdbt onto Usk Rd, continue to Llangybi
Closed: Mon & Tue
Facilities: Parking Garden

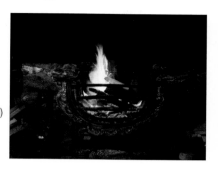

Located in the beautiful Usk Vale, this historic, award-winning inn was originally built in the 12th century for Cistercian monks. In the early 1500s it became the property of Henry VIII as part of Jane Seymour's wedding dowry, and a century later Oliver Cromwell is reputed to have used it as his Gwent headquarters. The interior still retains original 12th-century fireplaces, eleven more fireplaces from the 1600s, a wealth of exposed beams, original Tudor plasterwork and even a priest hole. Rooms are in The Hay Loft, which were built as stables in Victorian times, and are thus rich in character. With fresh local meat and seafood delivered daily, the chefs here have been consistently creating wonderful dishes to whet your appetite for the last three years. A modern European style now dominates, heavily influenced by the rich flavours and aromas of Italian cooking. A daily specials board adds yet further choice, with enticing dishes prepared from the finest seasonal produce. For the finale, there are home -made gourmet puddings and fresh coffees. Tapas and seafood evenings are held from time to time and occasional barbecues, hog roasts and live jazz take place on the extensive flagstone seating area to the rear, from which there are far-reaching views to the Wentwood Hills.

Recommended in the area

Gwent Rural Life Museum; Tintern Abbey; Brecon Beacons National Park

The Greyhound Inn/Hotel

Address: LLANTRISANT, Usk,
Monmouthshire, NP15 1LE
Tel: 01291 672505 & 673447
Fax: 01291 673255
Email: enquiry@greyhound-inn.com
Website: www.greyhound-inn.com
Map ref: 2 ST39 **Directions:** M4 junct 24, A449
towards Monmouth, exit at 1st junct for Usk. 2nd left
for Llantrisant. Or from Monmouth A40, A449 exit
Usk. Left into Twyn Sq follow Llantrisant signs. 2.5m

under A449 bridge. Inn on right **Open:** 11-11 **Closed:** 25 & 31 Dec, 1 Jan, Sun eve ♿ **L** 12-2.15
D Mon-Sat 6-10 🍽 **L** 12-2.15 **D** Mon-Sat 6-10 **Rooms:** 10 en suite (5 GF) **S** £56-£60 **D** £72-£80
Facilities: Parking Garden **Notes:** 🍺 FREE HOUSE ♦♦ 🐾 🍷 10

The Greyhound has log fires for winter and lovely gardens for summer, with a selection of real ales,
10 house wines and excellent home cooking to enjoy. The menu and specials board include seasonal
dishes, fresh fish and old pub favourites. Stay overnight to relax and soak up the great atmosphere.
Recommended in the area
Welsh Folk Museum; Big Pit, Blaenavon; Greenmeadow Community Farm

The Woodlands Tavern Country Pub & Dining

Address: LLANVAIR DISCOED,
Monmouthshire, NP16 6LX
Tel/Fax: 01633 400313
Email: info@thewoodlandstavern.co.uk
Website: www.thewoodlandstavern.co.uk
Map ref: 2 ST49 **Directions:** 5m from Caldicot &
Magor **Closed:** Mon, Sun eve ♿ 🍽 **L** Tue-Sat 12-2,
Sun 12-3 **D** Tue-Fri 6-9, Sat 6-9.30 **Facilities:** Parking **Notes:** 🍺 FREE HOUSE ♦♦ 🐾 🍷 8

Situated in the heart of Llanvair Discoed, this pub is close to the Roman town of Caerwent and at the
foot of Gray Hill, Wentwood forest and reservoir; known for its historical interest and natural beauty.
Chef Keith, wife Sue and their team provide a warm welcome and offer a varied menu of freshly
prepared and locally sourced quality food with a regularly changing specials board, where fish is
highlighted. Enjoy meals in the informal restaurant, or the comfortable bar for a bar meal or drink.
Recommended in the area
Caerwent Roman Town; Wye Valley Forest Park; Chepstow Castle

The Lion Inn

Address: TRELLECH, Monmouth,
Monmouthshire, NP25 4PA
Tel: 01600 860322
Fax: 01600 860060
Email: debs@globalnet.co.uk
Website: www.lioninn.co.uk
Map ref: 2 SO50
Directions: From A40 take B4293, for Trellech.
M8 junct 2, 2nd left at 2nd rdbt, B4293
Open: 12-3 6-11 (Fri-Sat noon-mdnt Sun 12-4.30

Mon eve 7-11pm Thu eve 6-mdnt) **Closed:** Sun eve 🅱 ⅼ◎ⅼ **L** Mon-Fri 12-2, Sat-Sun 12-2.30 **D** Mon
7-9.30, Tue-Sat 6-9.30 **Facilities:** Parking Garden **Notes:** ⊕ FREE HOUSE ♦♦ 🐾

This popular and well-established free house is opposite St Nicholas's Church. Guests are greeted by
welcoming real fires in the winter months, while in the summer drinks and meals can be served in the
garden, which overlooks fields and features a stream and large aviary. The former brew house has won
many accolades for its food and hospitality over the years, and its reputation is growing. Visitors aiming
to explore the nearby walking trails and notable historic buildings, or visit Trellech's own archaeological
dig, will find it a useful staging post. The extensive pub menu caters for all tastes, from bar snacks
and basket meals to blackboard specials, including fresh fish dishes. There is also an adventurous
menu featuring wild and hedgerow ingredients, such as nettles and wild mushrooms. Real ales include
Bath Ales, Wye Valley Butty Bach, Rhymney Best, Cottage Brewery and many more regularly changing
brews. Anyone who wants to extend their visit to the Lion can stay overnight in the pub's one-bedroom
cottage, which is suitable for up to three guests. It features an en suite bathroom and kitchenette. Dogs
are allowed at the pub, and water and biscuits are provided for them.

Recommended in the area

Tintern Abbey; Chepstow Castle; Wye Valley Forest Park

St Govans Chapel, Pembrokeshire Coast National Park

The Swan Inn

Address: Point Road, LITTLE HAVEN,
Haverfordwest, Pembrokeshire, SA62 3UL
Tel: 01437 781880
Fax: 04137 781880
Email: enquiries@theswanlittlehaven.co.uk
Website: www.theswanlittlehaven.co.uk
Map ref: 1 SM81
Directions: From Haverfordwest take B4341 (Broad Haven road). In Broad Haven follow signs for seafront & Little Haven, 0.75m

Open: 11-3 5.30-mdnt (Sat-Sun 11am-mdnt) **Closed:** Mon (Jan) ⓔ **L** all wk 12-2 **D** Mon-Sat 6-9
⦿ **L** all wk 12-2 **D** Mon-Sat 6-9 **Facilities:** Garden **Notes:** ⊕ FREE HOUSE ♦ ✈ ♛ 8

This historic seaside inn has been impeccably renovated but retains its rustic charm thanks to the beams, blazing log fires, old settles and exposed stone walls. It was built by a fisherman and is literally just a stone's throw from the beach, offering great Pembrokeshire views from some tables. Cooking, with the emphasis on seasonal, local produce, is modern British in style, and is very accomplished, though informal. Diners can eat in the elegant contemporary upstairs dining room, or in the intimate restaurant below. The menu might include honey and parsnip soup; local diver-caught scallops; corn-fed chicken and foie gras terrine; dressed St Brides Bay crab; roast belly pork with black pudding and cider sauce; or Welsh rib-eye steak with béarnaise sauce, red onion confit and chips. There are also vegetarian options, such as wild mushroom and butternut squash risotto. To follow, you may be offered vanilla pannacotta with Kirsch-soaked cherries, Welsh cheeses or locally made ice cream. The busy bar serves a range of bar snacks and well-kept real ales, and there are many wines available by the glass, all to be enjoyed in one of the leather armchairs.

Recommended in the area

Pembrokeshire Coast National Park; West Wales Divers; Skomer Island

The Stackpole Inn

Address: STACKPOLE, nr Pembroke, Pembrokeshire, SA71 5DF
Tel: 01646 672324
Fax: 01646 672716
Email: info@stackpoleinn.co.uk
Website: www.stackpoleinn.co.uk
Map ref: 1 SR99
Directions: From Pembroke take B4319 & follow signs
for Stackpole, approx 4m **Closed:** Sun eve (winter)
Facilities: Parking Garden **Notes:** ⊕ FREE HOUSE ♦♦ ☛ ♟ 12

Location, location, location. The meaning of the phrase becomes
crystal clear in the context of this 17th-century inn, standing in
beautiful gardens within the Pembrokeshire Coast National Park.
Nearby are stunning cliffs, bays and beaches, and the huge natural arch known as the Green Bridge
of Wales. It's a freehouse, and there's always a guest from elsewhere to accompany three Welsh ales.
The bar surface is made from slate, while the wood for the ceiling beams came from ash trees grown
on the estate. Warmth is provided by a wood-burning stove set within the stone fireplace. Produce
from the local countryside and coastal waters plays a major part in the home-cooked repertoire. At
lunchtime, for instance, Thai style fish cakes on sticky vegetable rice with soy reduction; and steamed
Bantry Bay mussels in garlic and Parmesan cream; and a vegetarian dish of the day. Evening starters
include Perl Las (organic Welsh blue cheese), bitter leaf salad, pickled walnuts and grapes poached
in Sauternes; and chicken liver, toasted hazelnut and roast garlic parfait. Typical mains are slow-roast
shoulder of Welsh lamb on fennel confit with light rosemary jus; and baked field mushroom, spinach
and red lentil gâteau with rich wild mushroom gravy. Mackerel, fresh lobster and sea bass tend to
feature as specials. Wines come from around the world, including Wales.

Recommended in the area

Pembrokeshire Coastal Path; Caldey Island; Gower Peninsula

Rhossili beach

The White Swan Inn

Address: Llanfrynach, BRECON, Powys, LD3 7BZ
Tel:　　01874 665276
Fax:　　01874 665362
Website: www.the-white-swan.com
Map ref: 2 SO02
Directions: 3m E of Brecon off A40, take B4558,
follow Llanfrynach signs
Closed: 25-26 Dec, 1 Jan, Mon
(ex summer, Dec & BH) **Facilities:** Parking Garden
Notes: ⊕ FREE HOUSE ♦♦ ♟ 8

A 17th-century coaching inn, completely restored, The White Swan is set in the village of Llanfrynach, by the foothills of the Brecon Beacons, an outstandingly beautiful area. The bar has oak flooring, old beams and leather sofas by an open fire, providing the perfect setting for traditional local ales. There is also a spacious restaurant with a coal burner, flagstone floors and beams; in summer you can sit outside. A seasonal menu of innovative dishes is based on produce sourced from local farms.

Recommended in the area

Brecon Beacons National Park; South Wales Borderers Museum; Hay-on-Wye book shops

The Castle Coaching Inn

Address: TRECASTLE, nr Brecon, Powys, LD3 8UH
Tel: 01874 636354
Fax: 01874 636457
Email: enquiries@castle-coaching-inn.co.uk
Website: www.castle-coaching-inn.co.uk
Map ref: 2 SN82
Directions: On A40 W of Brecon
Open: all week noon-3 6-11 (Sun 7-10.30)
 L Sat-Sun 12-2 D Mon-Sat 6.30-9, Sun 7-9
Facilities: Parking Garden **Notes:** ⊕ FREE HOUSE

Once a Georgian coaching inn on the old London to Carmarthen coaching route, The Castle sits right on the northern edge of the Brecon Beacons/Black Mountain area, with myriad streams flowing down to join the River Usk nearby. The inn has been carefully restored in recent years, and retains lovely old fireplaces, a remarkable bow-fronted bar window and has a peaceful terrace and garden. A good selection of real ales is on offer, including Fuller's London Pride, Breconshire Brewery Red Dragon and Timothy Taylor Landlord. Food can be eaten in the bar or more formally in the restaurant, and bar lunches feature tasty, freshly-cut sandwiches (maybe roast beef, turkey or Stilton), a ploughman's with cheese or perhaps duck and port pâté, and hot crusty baguettes with fillings such as steak with melted Stilton or bacon with mushrooms and melted mature cheddar. Of the more substantial offerings, specialities include mature Welsh 12oz sirloin steak served with mushrooms and onion rings; home-made lasagne with parmesan cheese; and supreme of chicken with a Marsala and mascarpone sauce. The tasty desserts are worth saving room for, and might include strawberry crush cake, hot jaffa puddle pudding; and Dutch chunky apple flan. Or perhaps sample the fine selection of Welsh farmhouse cheeses. There is a separate children's menu with the usual favourites.

Recommended in the area

Dan-yr-Ogof The National Showcaves Centre; Brecon Beacons National Park; Usk Reservoir

Llynau Mymbyr lake near Capel Curig, Snowdonia National Park

The Hand at Llanarmon

★★★★ ❀ INN

Address: LLANARMON DYFFRYN CEIRIOG,
Ceiriog Valley, Wrexham, LL20 7LD
Tel: 01691 600666
Fax: 01691 600262
Email: reception@thehandhotel.co.uk
Website: www.thehandhotel.co.uk
Map ref: 5 SJ13
Directions: Exit A5 at Chirk follow B4500 for 11m.
Through Ceiriog Valley to Llanarmon D. C.

Open: all week 🐾 🍴 L Mon-Sat 12-2.20, Sun 12.30-2.45 D 6.30-8.45 **Rooms:** 13 en suite (4 GF)
S £52.50-£70 **D** £90-£125 **Facilities:** Parking Garden **Notes:** ⊞ FREE HOUSE ⭒ 🐎 ♟ 7

Built beside the old drovers' road from London to Anglesey, this 16th-century farmhouse was a stopping place for drovers and their flocks. Yet The Hand only became a fully-fledged inn in the 1950s, and it still retains its original oak beams and large fireplaces. This classic country inn has a unique dining room and comfortable bedrooms. Chef Grant Mulholland has built a strong reputation for superb cuisine.
Recommended in the area
Chirk Castle; Llangollen Railway; Horse Drawn Boat Centre, Llangollen

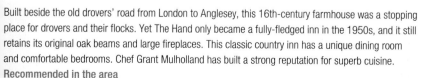

Roman Steps or Bwlch Tyddiad towards Cwm Bychan in the Rhinogs, Snowdonia National Park

MAPS

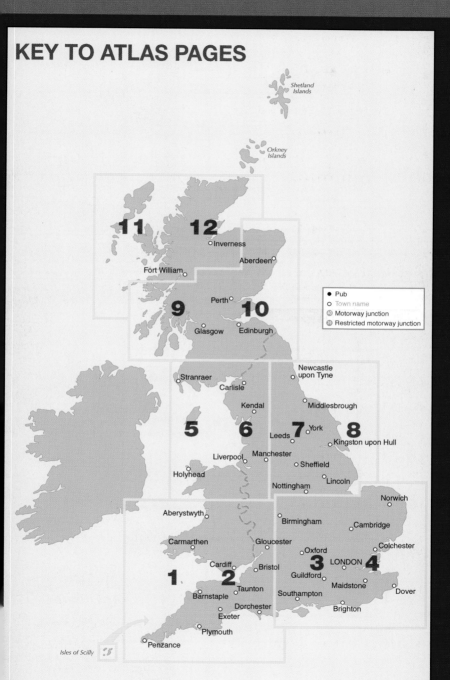

KEY TO ATLAS PAGES

Shetland Islands

Orkney Islands

11 12
Inverness
Aberdeen
Fort William

- ● Pub
- ○ Town name
- Motorway junction
- Restricted motorway junction

9   Perth   10
Glasgow   Edinburgh

Stranraer
Carlisle
Kendal
Newcastle upon Tyne
Middlesbrough
5   6   7 York   8
Leeds
Kingston upon Hull
Liverpool   Manchester
Sheffield
Holyhead
Nottingham   Lincoln

Norwich
Aberystwyth
Birmingham   Cambridge
Carmarthen   Gloucester   Colchester
Cardiff   Bristol   Oxford   LONDON
1   2   3   4
Guildford
Barnstaple   Taunton   Southampton   Maidstone   Dover
Dorchester   Brighton
Exeter
Plymouth
Isles of Scilly   Penzance

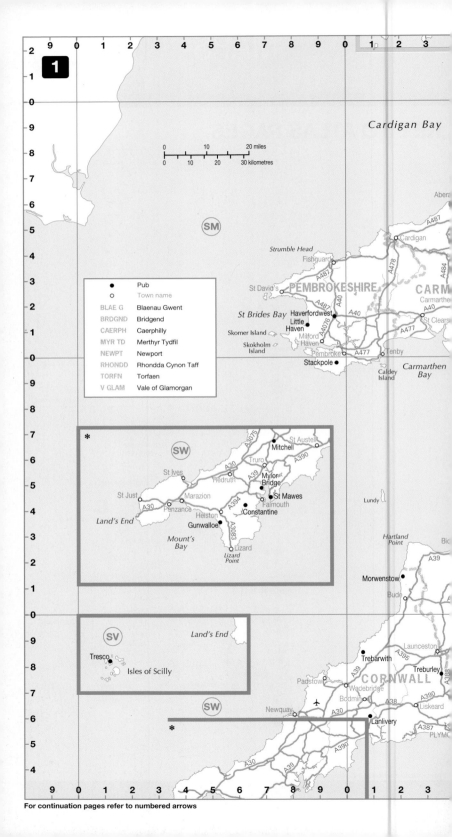

1

Cardigan Bay

| 0 | 10 | 20 miles |
| 0 | 10 | 20 | 30 kilometres |

(SM)

Strumble Head
Fishguard
Cardigan

St David's PEMBROKESHIRE CARM

St Brides Bay Haverfordwest
Little
Haven

Skomer Island
Skokholm
Island Milford
Haven
Pembroke
Stackpole ●
Caldey
Island

Carmarthe
St Clears
Tenby

Carmarthen
Bay

●	Pub
○	Town name
BLAE G	Blaenau Gwent
BRDGND	Bridgend
CAERPH	Caerphilly
MYR TD	Merthyr Tydfil
NEWPT	Newport
RHONDD	Rhondda Cynon Taff
TORFN	Torfen
V GLAM	Vale of Glamorgan

*

(SW)

St Austell
Mitchell

St Ives
Truro
Redruth
Mylor
Bridge
St Mawes

St Just
Marazion
Penzance
Helston
Falmouth
Constantine
Gunwalloe

Land's End

Mount's
Bay
Lizard
Lizard
Point

Lundy

Hartland
Point
Bid
A39

Morwenstow ●
Bude

*

(SV) Land's End
Tresco
Isles of Scilly

Trebarwith ●
Treburley ●

Padstow
CORNWALL

(SW)
Newquay
Wadebridge
Bodmin
Liskeard
Lanlivery
PLYM

Abera

A487
A484

Carmarthe
A40

A477

A487
A40
A477
A476

A30
A3075
A390
A39
A394
A3083

A39
A395
A388
A39
A30
A38
A390
A387

For continuation pages refer to numbered arrows

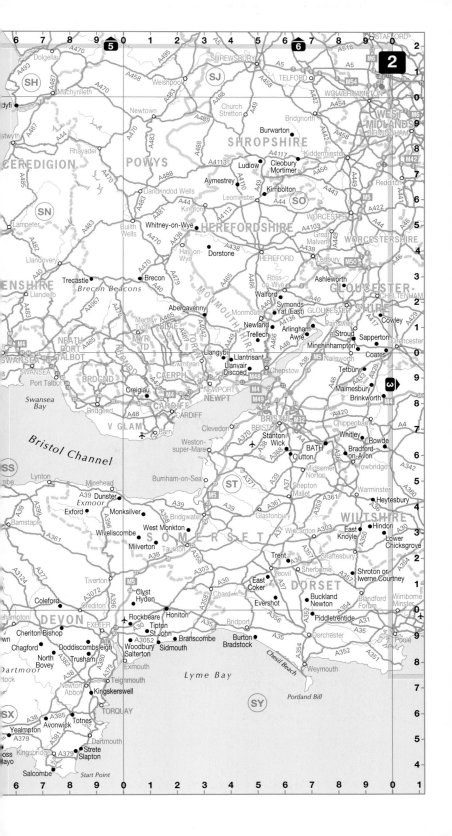

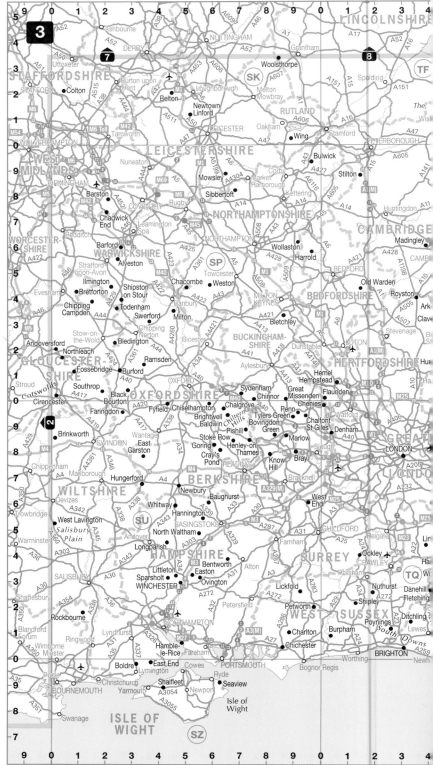

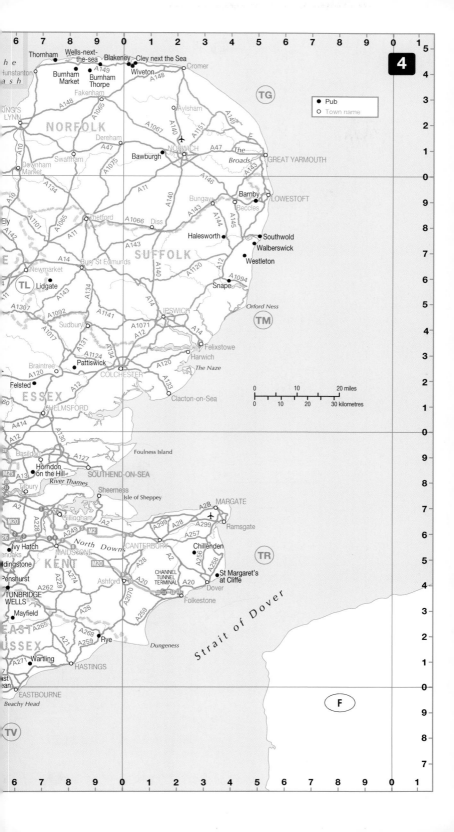

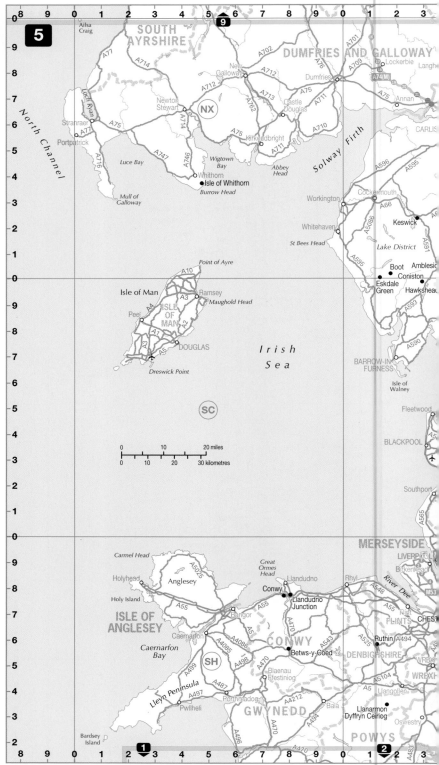

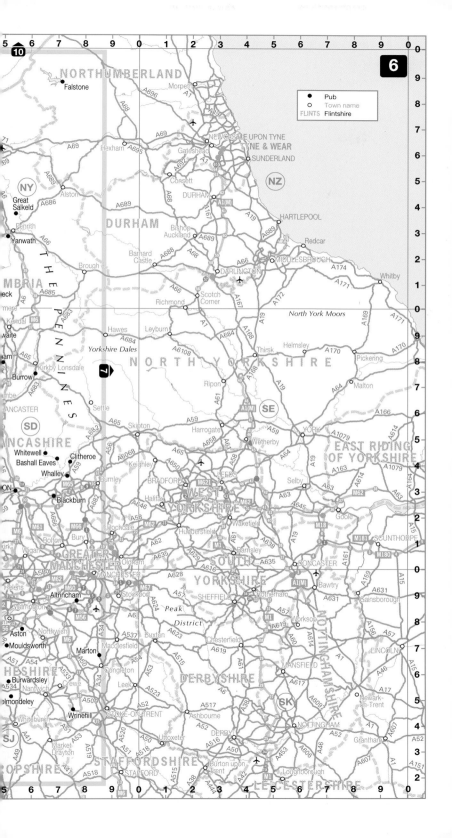

8

Pub
Town name
FLINTS Flintshire

0 10 20 miles
0 10 20 30 kilometres

TYNE & WEAR

SUNDERLAND
...ington

NZ

HARTLEPOOL

Redcar

MIDDLESBROUGH A174

Whitby

A19 A172 A171 A171

Osmotherley

...allerton *North York Moors*

...hill Thirsk Fadmoor

...KSHIRE A170 Pickering SCARBOROUGH

A168 Wass A170 *Flamborough Head*

Boroughbridge A19 Crayke A64 Weaverthorpe

A1(M) Malton A165

...ton A59 A614

...resborough Bridlington

Wetherby A166 A614 Driffield

A64 A19 YORK A1079 A164

A162 A163 EAST RIDING A164

SE OF YORKSHIRE A165

Selby A614 A1079 Beverley

A63 A164

M62 A63 KINGSTON UPON HULL

...kefield A645 Goole A15 *River Humber* A1033

...rnsley A635 A19 M18 A1077 A160 TA

Cadeby DONCASTER M181 SCUNTHORPE Immingham *Spurn Head*

A1(M) A161 M180 GRIMSBY

Bawtry A159 A18 Cleethorpes

...d Rotherham Gainsborough A46

EFFIELD A631 A631 Market A16 A1031

A57 Rasen *The Wolds* Louth Mablethorpe

A619 A156 A46 A157 A153 A16 A52

...terfield Worksop A57 A158 A16

SK A614 A1 LINCOLN Horncastle A158 Skegness

...REM MANSFIELD A616 A46 A15 LINCOLNSHIRE A52 TF

A617 Newark- A153 *The* A149 **4**

A60 A6097 on-Trent Sleaford Boston *Wash* Hunstanton

Farndon A17 A52 A16

...ERBY NOTTINGHAM A1 A607 A52 NORFOLK

A453 Colston A52 Grantham A151 A17 A148

...Loughborough A6 Bassett A607 Spalding A151 KING'S

A46 A606 LYNN

LE...CESTERSHIRE A1 A47

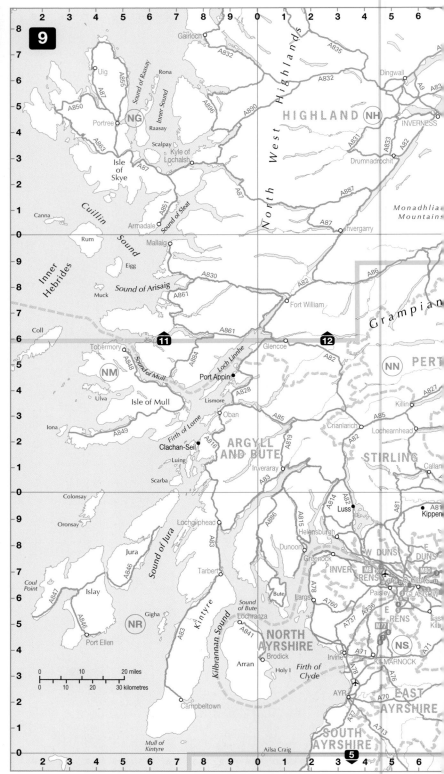

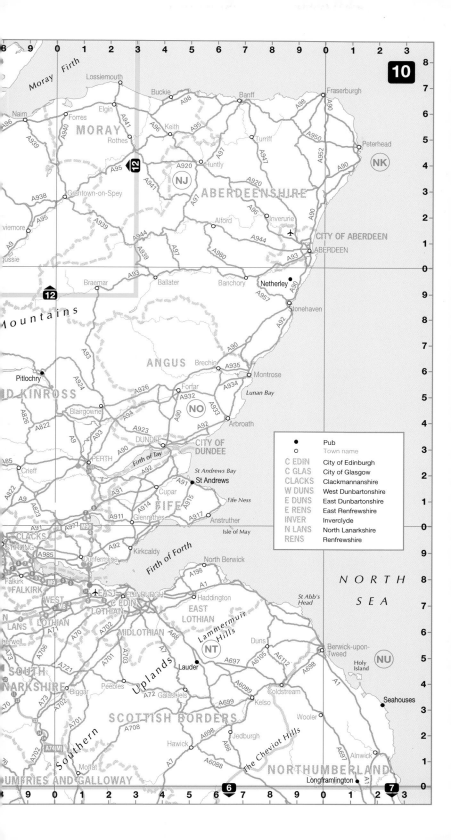

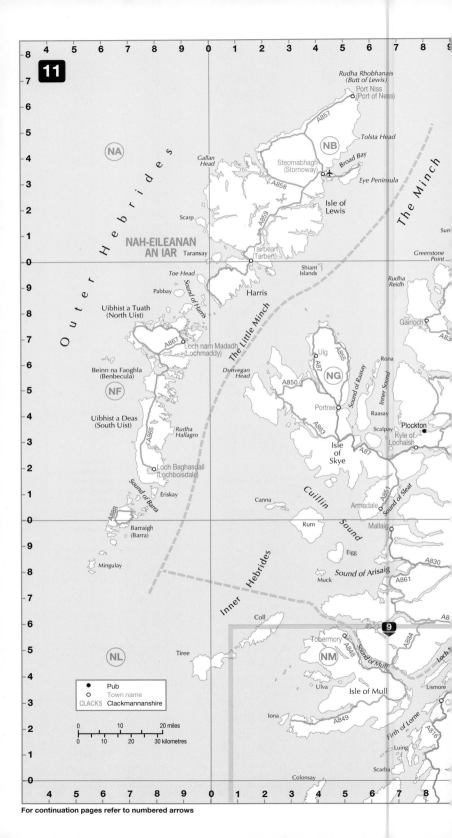

Rudha Rhobhanais
(Butt of Lewis)
Port Niss
(Port of Ness)

A857

Tolsta Head

NA

Gallan
Head

Steornabhagh
(Stornoway)

Broad Bay

NB

Eye Peninsula

Outer Hebrides

A858

Isle of
Lewis

The Minch

Scarp

NAH-EILEANAN
AN IAR   Taransay

Tairbeart
(Tarbert)

A859

Greenstone
Point

Shiant
Islands

Sum

Toe Head

Harris

Rudha
Reidh

Pabbay

Sound of Harris

Uibhist a Tuath
(North Uist)

Gairloch

A83

A867

Loch nam Madadh
(Lochmaddy)

The Little Minch

Uig

A865

Rona

Beinn na Faoghla
(Benbecula)

A87

NF

Dunvegan
Head

A850

NG

Sound of Raasay

Inner Sound

Uibhist a Deas
(South Uist)

Portree

Raasay

Plockton

A865

Rudha
Hallagro

A863

Scalpay

Kyle of
Lochalsh

Loch Baghasdail
(Lochboisdale)

Isle of
Skye

A87

Eriskay

Canna

Cuillin
Sound

Armadale

A851

Sound of Sleat

A888

Barraigh
(Barra)

Rum

Mallaig

Mingulay

Eigg

A830

Inner Hebrides

Sound of Arisaig

A861

Muck

NL

Coll

9

A8

Tobermory

A848

Sound of Mull

Loch

Tiree

NM

Lismore

Ulva

Isle of Mull

● Pub
○ Town name
CLACKS Clackmannanshire

Iona

A849

Firth of Lorne

A816

0   10   20 miles

0   10   20   30 kilometres

Luing

Scarba

C

Colonsay

For continuation pages refer to numbered arrows

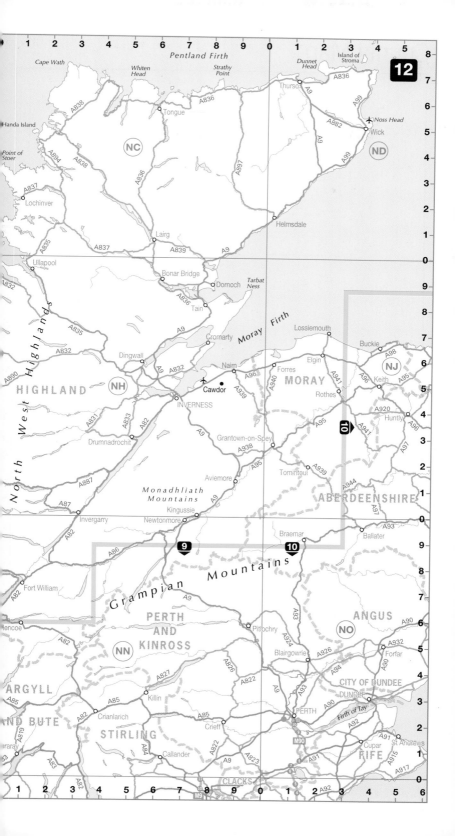

County Map

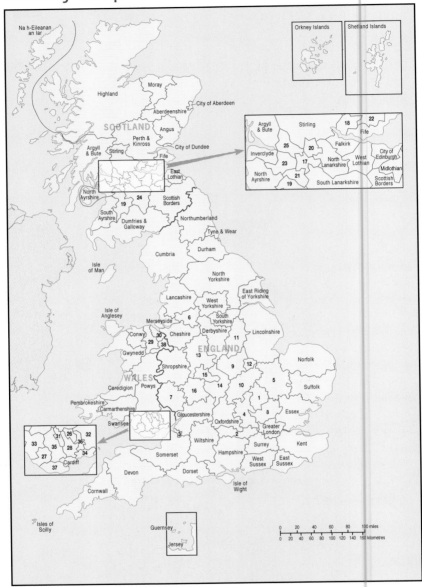

England

1	Bedfordshire
2	Berkshire
3	Bristol
4	Buckinghamshire
5	Cambridgeshire
6	Greater Manchester
7	Herefordshire
8	Hertfordshire
9	Leicestershire
10	Northamptonshire
11	Nottinghamshire
12	Rutland
13	Staffordshire
14	Warwickshire
15	West Midlands
16	Worcestershire

Scotland

17	City of Glasgow
18	Clackmannanshire
19	East Ayrshire
20	East Dunbartonshire
21	East Renfrewshire
22	Perth & Kinross
23	Renfrewshire
24	South Lanarkshire
25	West Dunbartonshire

Wales

26	Blaenau Gwent
27	Bridgend
28	Caerphilly
29	Denbighshire
30	Flintshire
31	Merthyr Tydfil
32	Monmouthshire
33	Neath Port Talbot
34	Newport
35	Rhondda Cynon Taff
36	Torfaen
37	Vale of Glamorgan
38	Wrexham

Location Index

Location Index

Location Index

Location Index

Location Index

Location Index

Location Index

Pub Index

Pub Index

Pub Index

Pub Index

Pub Index

Pub Index

Pub Index

Pub Index

Credits